KNOWLEDGE IN POLICY
Embodied, inscribed, enacted

Richard Freeman and Steve Sturdy

First published in Great Britain in 2015 by

Policy Press
University of Bristol
1-9 Old Park Hill
Bristol BS2 8BB
UK
+44 (0)117 954 5940
pp-info@bristol.ac.uk
www.policypress.co.uk

North America office:
Policy Press
c/o The University of Chicago Press
1427 East 60th Street
Chicago, IL 60637, USA
t: +1 773 702 7700
f: +1 773 702 9756
sales@press.uchicago.edu
www.press.uchicago.edu

British Library Cataloguing in Publication Data
A catalogue record for this book is available from the British Library

Library of Congress Cataloging-in-Publication Data
A catalog record for this book has been requested

ISBN 978-1-4473-0999-4 paperback

Cover design by Policy Press
Front cover image: istock
Printed and bound in Great Britain by CMP, Poole
Policy Press uses environmentally responsible print partners

Contents

List of tables and figures

Tables

Figures

Notes on contributors

Natércio Afonso is a former secondary teacher and school inspector, and was Head of the Education Inspectorate at the Portuguese Ministry of Education. He became Associate Professor at the Institute of Education, University of Lisbon, in 1998, where he taught courses in public policy and educational administration. He worked on REGULEDUC, a major European study of regulation and inequality in education systems (SERD-2000-00069), as well as on the consortium project KNOWandPOL. His publications have focused on education policy, school management and school evaluation.

Gaëtan Cerfontaine is a PhD student in social and political science and associate researcher at the Centre de Recherche et d'Interventions Sociologiques, University of Liège, Belgium. He is also a lecturer at the Haute Ecole Charlemagne and visiting scholar in social sciences at the Haute Ecole de la Province de Liège. His principal research interests are in: organisational studies; science, technology and society (STS); mental health policy; and tourism; and his publications include 'La santé mentale à l'épreuve de la qualité', *Observatoire: Revue d'Action Sociale et Médico-Sociale* (2012) and, with Frédéric Schoenaers and Sophie Thunus, 'La santé mentale en Belgique: l'hôpital renégocié', *Sociologie Santé* (2011).

Estela Costa is Assistant Professor at the Institute of Education, University of Lisbon, where she also completed her PhD and worked on the KNOWandPOL project. Her work is concerned with the evaluation of educational organisations and the transnationalisation of education policies, and her publications include: 'The role of network-based knowledge in legitimating education policy options and policy debate in Portugal', *Journal of US–China Public Administration* (2011); 'Dealing with opposition: uncomfortable moments in research', *European Education Research Journal* (2011); and, with Luis-Miguel Carvalho and Natércio Afonso, 'Espaces, acteurs et modalités de l'hybridité politique', *Spirale* (2013).

Alma Demszky studied sociology and psychology in Budapest, Basel and Munich and completed her PhD at the Technical University of Chemnitz, Germany. She was responsible for the German contribution to the KNOWandPOL project and is now a lecturer at the University of Munich. Her research interests are in the sociology of education, social inequalities, political decision-making and modes of socialisation in everyday life. Her publications include: *Alltägliche Gesellschaft: Netzwerke alltäglicher Lebensführung in einer großstädtischen Wohnsiedlung* (Mehring, 2006); with Katherina Mayr and Elias Sanaa, 'Wissen und Wollen: Die Produktion von Wissen im politischen Gestaltungsprozess', *Soziale Welt* (2009); and, with Armin Nassehi, 'Perpetual loss and gain: translation, estrangement and cyclical recurrence of experience-based knowledges in public action', *Policy and Society* (2012).

Gábor Eröss is a sociologist and Head of Social Policy at the Institute for Sociology, Centre for Social Sciences of the Hungarian Academy of Sciences. He is a former Andrew W. Mellon Fellow (Paris, 2003–04) and Humboldt Fellow (Berlin, 2008–09), and was leader of a Hungarian team in the KNOWandPOL project. Among his main research interests are cultural sociology, education and health policy, and the social anthropology of education. He is co-author or co-editor of four books and numerous papers on identity, educational inequality and health and education policy.

Bori Fernezelyi is a PhD student in sociology and social anthropology at Central European University, Budapest, where she is working on informal payments in the Hungarian health care system. She spent time as an academic visitor at the University of California, Los Angeles (UCLA), and worked on the KNOWandPOL project as a researcher at the Institute for Sociology, Centre for Social Sciences of the Hungarian Academy of Sciences. Her MA dissertation, an ethnographic study of a mental hospital, was published as *Depression debate* (VDM Verlag, 2007).

Richard Freeman teaches theory and method in the Graduate School of Social and Political Science, University of Edinburgh. He is a former Fulbright Scholar and Jean Monnet Fellow, and has held visiting positions at the Hanse-Wissenschaftskolleg, Bremen; the Institut d'Études Politiques ('Sciences Po'), Paris; and Yale University, New Haven. He is author of *The politics of health in Europe* (Manchester UP, 2000), and co-editor of *Comparative studies and the politics of modern medical care* (Yale UP, 2009), *Social policy in Germany* (Harvester Wheatsheaf, 1994) and *Welfare and culture in Europe* (Jessica Kingsley, 1999), as well as author of more than 50 other journal articles and chapters in books.

Maria José Freitas is a researcher and lecturer in the Faculty of Social Studies at Zuyd University in Maastricht in the Netherlands, where she teaches comparative social research on an MA programme in European Studies. Based at Zuyd's Research Centre on Social Integration (CESRT), her current research is concerned with collective knowledge generation in EU projects. Her other research interests include social research methodology, European social work education, local and regional social policy development, and 'shrinking' cities.

Sotiria Grek is Lecturer in Social Policy in the School of Social and Political Science, University of Edinburgh. Her principal research interest is in the Europeanisation of education governance: she is currently funded by the UK's Economic and Social Research Council to work on transnational policy learning (RES-000-22-3429) and governing by inspection (RES-062-23-2241). She recently published, with Martin Lawn, *Europeanising education: governing a new policy space* (Symposium, 2012).

Jo Maybin is interested in the practices involved in making and implementing health policy. She is a Fellow at The King's Fund, a London-based think-tank working to improve health and health services in England. She completed her PhD in Politics at the University of Edinburgh in 2012, exploring how policymakers in England's Department of Health use knowledge in their work. Her current research focuses on the theory and practice of governance processes in the National Health Service and, in particular, on how managers and policymakers can understand both staff and patient experiences of care. She is author, with Richard Freeman, of 'Documents, practices and policy', *Evidence and Policy* (2011).

Frédéric Schoenaers is Professor of Sociology at the Institute of Human and Social Sciences, University of Liège and Visiting Professor at the University of Lille 1. His main interest lies in the transformation and modernisation of the state and the introduction of New Public Management in the public sector. His recent publications include, with Bernard Delvaux, 'Knowledge, local actors and public action', *Policy and Society* (2012) and, with François Pichault, 'Le middle management sous pression: la difficile intégration du référentiel managérial du NPM dans les organisations au service de l'intérêt général', *Revue internationale de psychosociologie et de gestion des comportements organisationnels* (2012).

Jen Smith-Merry is Senior Lecturer in Qualitative Health Research in the Faculty of Health Sciences, University of Sydney, Australia. Her work focuses on problems of knowledge and practice in mental health and patient safety. She has a particular interest in the use of embodied or tacit knowledge in policymaking, including the experiential knowledge of practitioners and health service users. Her recent work has been published in *Society and Mental Health*, the *International Journal of Mental Health Systems* and *Policy and Society*.

Steve Sturdy is Head of Science, Technology and Innovation Studies at the University of Edinburgh. His research focuses on the relationship between medical science, medical policy and medical practice from the mid-19th century to the present. He currently holds a Wellcome Trust Senior Investigator Award in Medical Humanities to investigate the socio-technical trajectories that have led, since the 1960s, to the current ferment of activity around genomic medicine. Previous publications include the edited volumes *Medicine, health and the public sphere in Britain 1600–2000* (Routledge, 2002) and, with Roger Cooter and Mark Harrison, *War, medicine and modernity* (Sutton, 1998) and *Medicine and modern warfare* (Rodopi, 1999), as well as the 2013 special issue of *Sociology* on *Genetics and the Sociology of Identity*, co-edited with Christine Hauskeller and Richard Tutton.

Sophie Thunus is Research Fellow at the Centre de Recherche et d'Interventions Sociologiques, Institute of Human and Social Sciences, University of Liège, where she is also Lecturer in the Sociology of Organisation. Her main research interests are in organisational studies, mental health policy and the sociology of knowledge; her PhD is on mental health policy in Belgium in recent decades. Her publications include 'Enjeux, obstacles et atouts d'un modèle de soins aux contours indéterminés', *Observatoire: Revue d'Action Sociale et Médico-Sociale* (2012) and, with Frédéric Schoenaers, 'When policy makers consult professional groups in public policy formation: transversal consultation in the Belgian mental health sector', *Policy and Society* (2012).

Preface and acknowledgements

The origins of this book lie in a joint research project, which brought together all but two of its contributors. The KNOWandPOL consortium was funded by the European Commission under its Sixth Framework Programme between 2006 and 2011, and involved 12 teams from eight European countries. We set out to investigate the ways in which knowledge is produced and used in policymaking in different contexts: we focused on the health and education sectors, and were interested in their local, national and international dimensions.

During the project's design and specification phase, we talked much about policy, not least because we knew how to do so. We talked less about knowledge, perhaps precisely because we had no readily available language in which to problematise and discuss it. Nevertheless, although our research questions were undoubtedly ambitious, they did not seem intrinsically or unduly problematic. Like many of our research subjects – and, indeed, like most people most of the time – we took knowledge for granted.

As soon as we began to analyse our data, however, it was clear that we had to know what knowledge was in a much more specific, substantial and coherent way, one that might apply across countries and contexts but still capture the various dynamics of particular settings. To speak in terms of professional, administrative or lay knowledge, or of information, experience and scientific research, was only to reify the nebulous and invariably mixed categories used by our participants. We began instead to think in terms of the form that knowledge takes, whether apparently embodied in human beings, embedded in texts and instruments, or emergent in practice. Our theoretical basis for doing so, and its potential implications and applications, are what is set out in this volume.

The book begins with an introductory chapter that sets out the framework we used for thinking about knowledge in policy. The subsequent, substantive chapters are then ordered in three parts. These present our typology and how it works in different settings, explore its three component elements in detail, and discuss problems in (and the politics of) the relationship between them. Part One shows how our model can be used to map a policy domain, in this case, mental health in Scotland (Chapter Two), as well as chart the inherently labile process of regulation in action, in respect of the evaluation of Portuguese schools (Chapter Three). A case study of the World Health Organization's work on mental health in Europe describes the production and dissemination of knowledge across countries (Chapter Four).

Part Two then focuses on each of our three different phases of knowledge in turn, providing more detailed illustration and discussion of the properties of each. Chapter Five is concerned with the embodied knowledge of professional civil servants in England's Department of Health; Chapter Six with the inscriptions entailed in international standard-setting in schools; and Chapter Seven with the enactment of knowledge in a policy research project.

Part Three addresses problems in the transition between embodied, inscribed and enacted knowledge. New kinds of knowledge may be resisted and transmuted by established interests, as in the case of mental health reform in Hungary (Chapter Eight). Different forms of knowledge may simply conflict, as in debates over the integration of children with learning disabilities in schools in Germany (Chapter Nine). And this propensity for change and conflict means that policymaking will always entail a significant degree of knowledge work, as in the development of mental health care networks in Belgium (Chapter Ten). A concluding chapter (Chapter Eleven) restates and summarises our argument, drawing out some of its implications for further research, as well as for policy and practice.

We gratefully acknowledge the financial support for the KNOWandPOL project provided by the European Commission (contract number 028848-2), and note that the views set out here are those of the editors and contributors only and do not necessarily reflect the official opinion of the European Union. It follows that we owe much to many colleagues in the consortium, and specifically to its Directors, Bernard Delvaux and Eric Mangez of the University of Louvain. We would also like to thank our editors at Policy Press for their judicious support in preparing the volume, to reviewers of an earlier draft for their insight and advice, and to Cera Murtagh for help with preparing the manuscript.

Richard Freeman and Steve Sturdy
Edinburgh, November 2013

ONE

Introduction: knowledge in policy – embodied, inscribed, enacted

Richard Freeman and Steve Sturdy

Introduction

In recent years, both policy scientists and policymakers have taken a growing interest in the role of knowledge in the formulation, implementation and regulation of policy. This burgeoning literature encompasses a striking diversity of ideas about what counts as knowledge, what different types of knowledge there may be and how they are to be observed empirically. Different approaches attend variously to: the source or derivation of knowledge (eg from experience or from scientific investigation); its epistemic content (ideas or information); the characteristics of those who have or hold it (administrative, professional or lay); or its function or purpose (agenda-setting or evaluation). The logic of such categorisations is usually implicit, and many categorisations seem to incorporate different logics within a single scheme. Each seems to be searching for some way of 'capturing' knowledge such that it may be researched and used.

In this chapter, we propose a new phenomenology of knowledge based not on who knows what, how or why, but on the forms that knowledge may take. Drawing a simple analogy with the three phases of matter – solid, liquid and gas – we argue that knowledge too exists in three phases, which we characterise as embodied, inscribed and enacted. Furthermore, just as matter may pass from one phase to another, so too can knowledge be transformed, through various kinds of action, between phases. After reviewing the literature on knowledge and policy, we elaborate this three-phase model in the third section of the chapter. We then conclude by discussing some of the implications of our perspective for future work, both in research and policy.

This model is intended as a prolegomenon to future studies. We do not imagine that it can answer some of the most important questions we might ask about the place of knowledge in policymaking. We say almost nothing about the content or meaning (in the propositional sense) of knowledge or, except in passing, about the way in which it is organised and how this might relate to questions of power and social ordering. By the same token, we set aside normative and prescriptive discussion of the relative status of different kinds of knowledge. Our aim is simply to provide a common observational language for talking about knowledge – for 'knowing knowledge', so to speak – as it is manifested in the world. The value and viability of our schema will depend upon how useful it proves when employed in empirical research and reflection – whether it helps to draw attention to aspects of knowledge in policy that had not hitherto been noticed, for instance, or serves as a lingua franca for communicating between different research perspectives, or even provides policymakers with a useful tool for reflecting upon their own practice. But that is itself an empirical question, and we leave it to other chapters in this volume to put it to the test. For now, our task is to outline our scheme and to indicate what we hope to achieve by it.

Knowledge in policy: the literature

In a much-cited review of 'The role of knowledge in the policy process', Claudio Radaelli (1995) identified an important shift in academic thinking about the knowledge–policy relationship. The dominant image of the workings of knowledge in policymaking in the preceding decades was one of 'speaking truth to power', a Quaker phrase taken up by Aaron Wildavsky (1979). According to that view, knowledge and power are quite different things: while knowledge might impinge on policy, it does so as an 'input', generated from outside the world of policy and power. Radaelli observed that recent work on knowledge and policy challenged that presumed dichotomy. His review ranged over a broad field of largely discrete literatures that looked at how knowledge circulated and functioned within the work of policy itself. These included work on: knowledge utilisation and evaluation; the importance of epistemic communities; the diffusion of economic policy paradigms; the use of frame theory to understand policy conflicts; the role of knowledge in agenda-setting and problem-definition; and analysis of policy change as a learning process. All these literatures identified knowledge as a crucial aspect of the policy process: knowledge, on this view, is endogenous to policy, as well as impacting from outside the world of politics.

However, the very diversity of the literatures surveyed by Radaelli posed something of a challenge. As Radaelli (1995, p 159) put it, 'The variety of concepts and approaches to the study of knowledge seems puzzling'. For Radaelli, the main difficulty lay in reconciling the different understandings of the policy process implicit in the various literatures and theoretical approaches that he surveyed. But he also recognised that different approaches to policy implied different ideas about the nature of knowledge. Radaelli's response was simply to adopt a sufficiently catholic view of knowledge to encompass all the approaches that fell under his purview. Consequently, knowledge should be taken to include information, ideas and arguments, as well as well-tested beliefs, and should encompass lay as well as professional and academic knowledge (Radaelli, 1995, p 161). Since Radaelli's review, the diversity of approaches to knowledge among policy academics has, if anything, increased. Indeed, as academic interest in knowledge has grown, so perspectives have proliferated.

Much work remains concerned with understanding how externally generated knowledge finds its way into policy – effectively perpetuating older ideas about 'two communities' of knowledge producers and knowledge users (Caplan, 1979; Weiss, 1979). Recent work on 'evidence-based policy', for instance, often starts from a desire to understand how academically produced knowledge, in particular, might have a greater impact on policy (Cabinet Office, 1999; Davies et al, 2000; Sanderson, 2002). However, this perspective is balanced by a growing body of policy research that echoes Radaelli's finding that policy is itself a domain of ideas and knowledge, which strongly influences just what new, externally generated knowledge policymakers will incorporate into their work. In a review of recent developments in evidence-based policy, for instance, Angela Packwood points to policymakers' essentially 'ideological' preference for particular kinds of evidence, notably, those based on clinical trial methodologies and rigorously quantitative comparison (Packwood, 2002). This echoes other research, such as that of Paul Sabatier (1987, 1988), which has shown how the acceptance and assimilation of evidence into policy depends upon the existing and developing belief systems of particular advocacy coalitions within policy subsystems. More recently, Bergeron and Kopp have examined how ideas and evidence 'take hold' in French policy on drug use. They point to the significance of socialisation, by which they mean 'the processes by which an idea can make sense, in many different ways, for an actor located in a particular cognitive, normative, and social context' (Bergeron and Kopp, 2002, p 47), and they conclude that the analyst's aim must therefore be to understand:

> the different kinds of reasons an actor has to believe in
> certain ideas – ideas that are of course available in a certain
> social context and at a given time – and at the same moment

> explaining why those ideas make sense for him or her.
> (Bergeron and Kopp, 2002, p 46)

Moreover, other work has shown that even where knowledge appears to be produced externally to the field of policy, policy interests may nonetheless inform the way in which that knowledge is generated. Some of the best work in this vein comes from research into science–policy relations. In the mid-1980s, Collingridge and Reeve (1986) argued that science is incapable of delivering the kind of definitive evidence that policymakers often demand, because science itself is always provisional and open to conflicting interpretations.

Nonetheless, policymakers continue to look to science for policy input, while scientists commonly tout the value of their work for policy. In *States of knowledge*, Sheila Jasanoff (2004) has brought together some of the most sophisticated work to date on the relationship between science and policy. The chapters collected in that volume show persuasively that science is often actively oriented towards policy, and that the work of scientific knowledge production and the work of policy, far from being distinct and separate, often proceed simultaneously and inseparably, in what Jasanoff calls a process of 'co-production' of knowledge and policy. There is no a priori boundary between science and policy; insofar as such a boundary may be drawn, it is constructed and negotiated, and does not reflect any inherent distinction between the two fields of activity (see also Jasanoff, 1987; Hilgartner, 2000). And if that is true of science, it is equally the case with other forms of policy-relevant knowledge. In other words, if we are to understand the role of knowledge in policy, we must also consider the role of policy in knowledge. This view of the co-production of knowledge and policy resonates in turn with the idea that in contrast to the circumscribed business of government, the work of 'governance' is distributed through society, including the extra-governmental institutions of knowledge production (eg Kooiman, 2003).

Turning now to a rather different line of attack, it is worth noting that a number of analysts of knowledge and policy have sought to distinguish different kinds or forms of knowledge, with the aim of understanding how they might impact on or inform policy in different ways. Still within the 'knowledge into policy' frame, for instance, Peter Haas (2004) has sought to define a distinct class of what he calls 'usable knowledge', which he argues is more likely to be taken up by policymakers and incorporated into policy. Meanwhile, from a 'knowledge in policy' perspective, in a useful review of the literature on the role of ideas in politics, John Campbell (2002) distinguishes between cognitive paradigms, world views, norms, frames and policy programmes, and calls for more work to elucidate the specific causal mechanisms by which these different kinds of ideas affect policymaking. Other work, originating especially with the work of Majone on evidence and argumentation (eg Majone, 1989), considers knowledge as mobilised in discursive or communicative practice, giving rise to an entire field of 'argumentative policy analysis' that encompasses discourse analysis, frame analysis, interpretative policy analysis and a variety of other approaches with a common basis in the study of communication and argumentation (Fischer and Gottweis, 2012).

Still other scholars seek to categorise different kinds of knowledge on the basis of where that knowledge is generated. In a review of the types and quality of knowledge in social care, for instance, Pawson and colleagues advocate a source-based typology of organisational, practitioner, user, research and policy community knowledges (Pawson et al, 2003, esp pp 18–19), with the ultimate aim of 'distinguish[ing] good quality knowledge from that which should not be relied upon in policy making and practice' (Pawson et al, 2003, p vi). More pervasively, policy scholars are increasingly interested in the role of lay knowledge, or 'the expertise of experience', in policy. This interest can perhaps be traced back to the reflections of Charles Lindblom (1990; cf Lindblom and Cohen, 1979) on the relationship between social-scientific and lay knowledge as part of his argument for epistemological pluralism in support of social change. Subsequently, a concern with the interaction between lay and expert knowledges has become an increasingly prominent theme in studies of deliberative policy (eg Forester, 1999; Fischer, 2003; Hajer and Wagenaar, 2003).

Another recent development in thinking about knowledge in policy has been a shift from looking at knowledge solely in terms of what can be expressed in words – as a matter of explicit propositional or argumentative content – to thinking about various kinds of tacit or practical knowledge. This is part of a wider shift in how policy is conceived, from a purely cognitive or epistemic process of decision-making, to regarding it also as a form of practice. For instance, Wagenaar and Cook (2003) invoke the Aristotelian concept of phronesis – which they take to mean practical reason rather than intellectual knowledge – as a basis for rethinking policy as practice, drawing especially on frame theory to understand how action and practice are oriented, and on work in argumentative policy analysis that considers discourse as a form of linguistic practice. Sanderson (2003, 2004) adopts a somewhat different view of practical reason to include values and judgement of 'what is appropriate' as well as 'what works', and argues that researchers would be better equipped to communicate with policy if they became more attuned to the normative worlds and practical rationality of policymaking. Also in an Aristotelian vein, Tenbensel (2006) adopts the conceptions of universal, pragmatic and normative knowledge, arguing that policymaking combines and integrates these in different ways. The policymaker's essential skill, therefore, is that of epistemic 'versatility': '[A] central requirement of policy work is the task of stitching together phronetic, epistemic and practical-technical knowledge' (Tenbensel, 2006, p 210). In a similar study of what he terms intellectual or epistemological bricolage, Freeman (2007) shows policymakers operating across and between different ways of knowing. Meanwhile, Stone (2008) looks at global policy as a system of knowledge networks and epistemic communities, but recognises the importance of possessing not just scientific and 'bureaucratic knowledge', but also 'the skills and knowledge to traverse global policy processes' (Stone, 2008, pp 34, 25).

Such studies echo the enduringly influential expositions of the differences between 'know-how' and 'know-that' articulated by Gilbert Ryle (1949), and between tacit and explicit knowledge explored by Michael Polanyi (1958) and subsequently taken up by sociologists of scientific knowledge, notably Harry Collins (1993, 2010). These concepts have been widely adopted in research into the role of knowledge in firms and other organisations (eg Howells, 1996) in ways that would seem readily transferable into policy scholarship. Thus, a number of scholars have conceptualised organisations in terms of the structuration, distribution, circulation, production and transformation of different kinds of knowledge, including tacit knowledge. In a seminal paper, for instance, Ikujiro Nonaka (1994) considers the processes of converting tacit into explicit knowledge, and vice versa, as crucial to the processes of organisational learning. Subsequently, Frank Blackler (1995) and Alice Lam (2000), expanding on the work of Collins (1993), have incorporated tacit knowledge into a larger typology of 'embodied', 'embedded', 'embrained', 'encultured' and 'encoded' knowledge, which they develop with a view to understanding how different kinds of organisation function most effectively with different forms of knowledge. The work of Nonaka, Blackler and Lam, like other research into organisational learning (eg Argyris and Schön, 1978; March, 1991; Weick and Westley, 1996), has been highly influential for thinking about how different kinds of knowledge are incorporated into the formulation and implementation of firm- and organisation-level policy. However, despite Heather Canary's (2010) call for a more expansive recognition of the value of such approaches, they have scarcely been recognised by scholars of government and public policy. (The neglect by policy scholars of Donald Schön's contribution to the theory of organisational learning [Argyris and Schön, 1978], and of his equally celebrated work on tacit knowledge in relation to reflective practice [eg Schön, 1983], is all the more surprising in light of the enthusiasm with which some, at least, have adopted his and Martin Rein's development of frame theory [Schön and Rein, 1994] – an indication, perhaps, of the continuing tendency to think of policy in overwhelmingly epistemic rather than practical terms.)

Before concluding this short review, we should mention one other form of knowledge that has only recently begun to be written about in the literature on policy. Knowledge, as sociologists of scientific knowledge have for some time recognised, is not confined to people and the organisations and institutions they make up. Knowledge may also be captured, inscribed and encoded in material objects, most obviously, documents and other forms of information technology. Indeed, such capture and inscription is a crucial aspect of the constitution of knowledge in the modern world; without it, our world could not exist as we know it (eg Shapin, 1984; Latour, 1987; Collins, 1993). Here, too, students of organisations are ahead of policy scholars in appreciating how attention to material forms of knowledge can advance their thinking, most notably, through research into the ways that 'information infrastructure' may inform the structure and performance of organisations (eg Star and Ruhleder, 1996; Star 1999). At the same time, work in the economics of innovation has begun to pay attention to the role of 'codified knowledge' – Collins' (1993) term for the relatively rarified form of knowledge that is capable of being captured in texts or other technologies – in the creation of value at firm and industry level (eg Lissoni, 2001). It seems to us that, if the role of knowledge in policy is to be understood in any depth, far more attention needs to be given to the material as well as the intellectual and practical forms that knowledge may take. Doing so will entail thinking about the nature and function of policy documents, for example, in new ways (Freeman, 2006b; Freeman and Maybin, 2011). It seems to us that if the role of knowledge in policy is to be understood in any depth, far more attention needs to be given to the material as well as the intellectual and practical forms that knowledge may take.

Phases of knowledge

With this literature in mind, we return to the problem from which we started. Those who wish to understand the place of knowledge in policy are faced not just with a multiplicity of methodological approaches and theoretical perspectives, but also with a confusing diversity of ideas about what knowledge is and how it might be characterised and classified. The field is fragmented and divided, not just methodologically and theoretically, but by a fundamental lack of concurrence about the object to be investigated. In consequence, researchers interested in the role of knowledge in policy commonly end up talking past one another, or failing to find relevance in one another's work, while newcomers to the field may find themselves faced with methodological and theoretical choices that are neither helpful nor necessary.

The present chapter outlines a schema for thinking and talking about knowledge that we hope may provide the beginnings of a solution to this problem. However, in order to head off possible misconceptions or misreadings, we should perhaps first make clear what we are *not* attempting to do in presenting this schema. Crucially, we do not mean to offer or imply any particular account of what knowledge *is*. Everyone interested in the role of knowledge in policy has a strong, if often tacit, understanding of what they mean by 'knowledge', and we have no wish to exclude or privilege any particular point of view; our aims are catholic, inclusive and conciliatory. Nor do we offer any particular theory of how knowledge is made, or of how it shapes or influences social action. Although informed by insights from the sociology of scientific knowledge, our intentions are strictly pre-sociological and pre-theoretical; hopefully, our efforts may be useful to anyone who seeks to develop a sociological or ethnographic understanding of the role of knowledge in policy, but we do not ourselves seek to develop such an understanding in the present chapter. Rather, our aim is, as far as possible, to provide a basic observational language, which will enable those working on different aspects of knowledge and policy, and coming from a range of theoretical perspectives, to communicate with one another. We want to help researchers know where to look in order see knowledge in policy, and we want to equip them with the means of talking with other researchers who may be looking at quite different kinds of knowledge and quite other forms of policy.

Our schema starts from the observation that knowledge may exist in the world in three basic forms or 'phases': embodied, inscribed and enacted. So, let us now describe these three phases.

Embodied

Embodied knowledge is the knowledge held by human actors and employed and expressed by them as they go about their activities in the world. It includes that sort of knowledge most often regarded as embodied, namely, so-called tacit knowledge. This is practical and gestural knowledge, deeply embedded in bodily experience and incapable of expression in verbal form. It includes various forms of embodied skill – how to ride a bicycle, for instance, or how to use a keyboard, or how to make a medical diagnosis by touch and feel. However, embodied knowledge, as we understand it here, also includes the kind of knowledge that sits in the mind and finds expression in words: what is sometimes called 'embrained' knowledge.[1]

Bringing tacit and verbal knowledge together in this way elides a distinction that philosophers, in particular, have often sought to maintain. Some suggest, for example, that tacit knowledge can be thought of as 'know-how' and verbal knowledge, which seems to comprise factual or propositional knowledge, as 'know-that'. For our purposes, however, that distinction is misleading and ultimately unhelpful, for know-how is not simply limited to the kinds of physical skill that are sometimes identified with embodied knowledge. Certain kinds of know-how may be expressed in words as instructions or rules, while following rules still requires knowing – tacitly, through experience – how to interpret and apply them. Similarly, certain kinds of verbal and intellectual skill, such as the ability to recall a procedural requirement or read a budget, might be better regarded as forms of know-how rather than factual or propositional knowledge in their own right. In this way, tacit and verbal knowledge seem to entail one another to such an extent that they are properly indistinct.

Any given field of policymaking comprises an array of embodied knowledges: the experience of poverty or ill-health, for example, or of stigma in different forms; knowing how a particular agency works according to a certain set of social relations; knowing how to read what a potential funder is looking for; or knowing how to respond to the minister. Our point is that it is impossible to draw any hard-and-fast distinction between 'know-how' and 'know-that', that is, between factual or propositional and tacit or processual knowledge. In real-world situations, the mobilisation or expression of verbal knowledge invariably involves an element of tacit knowledge, whatever analytic distinctions philosophers might draw. The embrained is also always embodied.

More than any analytical purpose, however, our intention in bringing together tacit and propositional knowledge – 'know-how' and 'know-that' – under the single category of 'embodied knowledge' is to direct attention to the importance of embodied human beings in the distribution, movement and mobilisation of knowledge. It reminds us that in looking at how knowledge functions in the world of policy, one thing we need to observe is the movement and activities of people. It reminds us, too, that embodiment imposes real constraints on knowledge. Since embodied knowledge is, by definition, coexistent with the body of the person or persons who embody it, embodied knowledge is only mobile to the extent that living human bodies are mobile. By the same token, embodied knowledge is also liable to decay and degeneration, through forgetting, mis-remembering and ultimately death. On the positive side, embodied knowledge is also often capable of being rapidly updated, amended and corrected by new experiences or exposure to new information. In its embodied phase, knowledge thus shares in the limitations, the frailty and the fallibility of the human body itself, but also in the adaptability that is one of the most important characteristics of the human animal.

Inscribed

Knowledge may also be inscribed in artefacts: it may be written down in texts, or represented in pictures and diagrams; or it may be incorporated into instruments, tools and machines, among other things.[2] Knowledge inscribed in texts – the standard mechanism of policymaking is the document, whether manifesto, memorandum, briefing, press statement, plan or White Paper – is self-evidently of the verbal or propositional kind we referred to earlier. It might take the form of information, expressed as description, instruction or visual representation, or it might also take the form of argument. Such inscriptions entail displaying and communicating knowledge according to the rules of language or graphic design. However, knowledge is also inscribed in objects and artefacts whose purpose is to mediate and inform our interactions with the world rather than represent it – in measuring instruments, for example, which serve to standardise our observations and actions, or in machines that perform particular actions on our behalf. This is knowledge too, but more know-how than know-that.

Inscribed knowledge has very different properties from embodied knowledge. First, the artefacts on and in which it is inscribed may be remarkably stable, and it is often precisely this that prompts an act of inscription: think of the simple 'I must write that down'. In this way, inscribed knowledge provides a corrective to the instability and fragility of human bodies and memories. It is perhaps the single most fundamental reason for record-keeping. Second, inscribed knowledge is not only stable, but often easily reproduced and highly mobile. This means that it can be communicated or made available to many different individuals separated in time and/or space. It can both travel and remain inert in ways that human bodies simply cannot. Texts and other instruments can thus be used to augment or transcend the physical and mental limitations of human bodies. The letter reaches much further than the voice, and the email travels even faster, while a book or film can reach many more people than we could ever speak to unaided. In this sense, inscribing augments embodiment.

The knowledge inscribed in texts and tools also entails particular ways of seeing, thinking and knowing; such artefacts can consequently serve to constrain and discipline our interactions with the world and with one another. Instruments of observation, measurement and calculation, in particular, provide a means of standardising how we come to know the world. In the world of science and medicine, for example, the blood pressure monitor and the body scanner are vital in creating a common world of knowledge and experience. Furthermore, in the world of government, tools of mapping, social surveying, auditing and reporting provide perceptual and conceptual schemata that frame how the world comes to be known, and so ensure that different aspects of the world, or different parts of it, are made comparable with one another. We might think of them as the laboratory equipment of public administration, its own 'inscription devices' (Latour and Woolgar, 1979). At the same time, they provide a means for different actors to share the same ways of knowing, so forming distinctive knowledge communities. In this way, instruments of observation and calculation build common perceptual worlds, shared by actors remote from one another in space and time.

Texts and other forms of inscribed knowledge can also help to coordinate other kinds of human action besides just perception and knowledge production. Documents, in particular, can be used to circulate and publicise explicit statements about who should act, how and under what circumstances, and as such are vital in the work of government and policy. This kind of instrument[3] includes laws, administrative and accounting rules, professional codes of conduct, guidelines, and manuals – all forms of know-how, inscribed in texts. Here, the advantages that inscribed knowledge provides over embodied knowledge are particularly apparent. Coordination of perception and action naturally occurs on a day-to-day basis without the intervention of documents or other artefacts, through meetings and interaction between embodied individuals. But such coordination can only occur on a purely local basis, since it requires face-to-face meetings between the individuals involved. By contrast, the stability and mobility of documents and other forms of inscribed knowledge makes coordination possible over a much larger area, and involving far larger numbers of people. Because it has been written down, a strategic plan can be set out in essentially the same format to department heads in different locations, and then by them to their staffs (and, in time, to staff yet to be recruited). It is this combination of stability, reproducibility and rapidity of movement that makes knowledge inscribed in plans, budgets, guidelines and other forms of 'immutable mobile' (Latour, 1987) so significant in – and, in practice, often essential to – the coordination of human action on a large scale, that is, to governance and policy.

Enacted

In seeking to characterise embodied and inscribed knowledge, it has been difficult to avoid talking about what that knowledge does – or, more accurately, what we do with that knowledge. In the absence of action, knowledge remains latent: thoughts unspoken, skills not exercised, texts unread and instruments unused are indistinguishable from ignorance or nonsense. It is only when they are enacted that embodied or inscribed knowledge acquire meaning and significance – that their status as knowledge becomes apparent. By the same token, action in the absence of knowledge can scarcely be thought of as action. Action must be informed if it is to make sense, and embodied and inscribed knowledge provide the means of informing and directing action in ways that make it purposeful and meaningful. In action, embodied and inscribed knowledge are, in effect, sublimated in a third phase of *enacted* knowledge. But, crucially, what is expressed in action is often more than, or at least different from, such embodied or inscribed knowledge as preceded it; enactment may actually give rise to new knowledge beyond what has previously been embodied or inscribed. It is for this reason that we see enacted knowledge not just as a representation of other, more material phases of knowledge, but as a distinct phase and form of knowledge in its own right.

Consider a meeting, perhaps the basic unit of the policy process (Freeman, 2008). When a committee convenes, embodied and inscribed knowledge is brought into the room in the form of what each of its individual members knows, whether through education or experience, and in what has been recorded in the minutes of previous meetings and in the documents prescribing the committee's remit and procedural rules. But the committee's knowledge is not limited to what is brought into the meeting. In the course of discussion, the committee may generate now knowledge: new ideas and insights, new aims, and new rules for how to fulfil them. The committee members may leave the meeting knowing things that none of them knew before; the minutes of the meeting may record findings that were not prefigured by any previous documents. In such cases, this new knowledge appears, first, as enacted knowledge, in the speech acts and interactions that constitute the discursive work of the committee, before becoming materialised as new embodiments and inscriptions. It is this evident possibility that enactment may be a source of epistemic novelty that leads us to view it as a distinct phase of knowledge: not simply an expression of such knowledge as is already embodied or inscribed, but as the very act of *knowing*.

The properties of enacted knowledge also differ significantly from those of both embodied and inscribed knowledge. First, enacted knowledge is essentially transient: it endures only as long as the enactment itself. Of course, there are many ways in which it may result in the production of new embodied or inscribed knowledge that outlives the action that produces it – for instance, in professional training or the writing of a new document. But the knowledge so materialised is, in turn, never entirely identical to the enacted knowledge that gives rise to it, and which ceases to exist when the enactment ends. Enacted knowledge is thus knowledge in its most volatile phase: fleeting, highly variable from one instance to the next and often unpredictable in form and expression.

Second, enacted knowledge is generally under-determined by such embodied and inscribed knowledge as may precede and inform it. No two readings of a book, no two performances of a play, are ever the same. For all our accumulated knowledge and experience, we always have a choice about what to do next. Embodied and inscribed knowledge provide resources for action, and may constrain what action is possible, but they do not determine unequivocally what form that action will take. Enactment always allows room for interpretation and judgement. Even rules and laws – forms of knowledge that are expressly intended as a means of directing action – do not entirely determine such action. That is why, for example, the legal corpus is so swollen, not just with subsections and amendments, but with guidelines on how to interpret them and commentaries on how to interpret the guidelines: we may know the rules by heart and by habit, we may refer to the rule book, and we may strive to be faithful to the rules, but the way we enact a rule may still differ from any previous enactment and may, in turn, come to be known as a precedent for future instances of rule-following.[4] In consequence, enacted knowledge, for all that it draws on embodied and inscribed knowledge, is often innovative, even transformative; it is the phase of knowledge where novelty arises.

Third, the enactment of knowledge is in many cases a collective activity – and it is the collective character of enactment, as much as any antecedent knowledge, that determines the forms that enacted knowledge will take. Despite the degree of interpretive flexibility inherent in any enactment, enacted knowledge exhibits forms of reliability, regularity and constancy that are just as significant as those we attribute to embodied and inscribed knowledge, because action, and in particular meaningful and therefore knowledgeable action, is almost always interaction. As such, it is constantly monitored and regulated through the mutual surveillance and sanctioning of all those involved at any moment. Strong sanctions may be exerted against any actor who is judged to break the bounds of what is deemed normal or appropriate action – and this is particularly the case in formal, organised institutional settings: under such circumstances, the patterns of enactment may be remarkably constant and regular, highly conventionalised and highly routinised. Such regularity is a collective achievement: individuals may know things, and they may be able to draw on other knowledge inscribed in documents and other artefacts, but their enactment of that knowledge is channelled by the communities of knowers to which they belong.

So, what is the value of this new phenomenology of knowledge? We opened this chapter with a discussion of the many different ways in which knowledge is thought about and discussed in the policy literature, and we suggested that our new phenomenology would provide a common language whereby researchers looking at knowledge in policy from different theoretical perspectives could communicate with one another. But, beyond this, understanding that knowledge may be embodied, inscribed or enacted may be of value in helping us to see and think about the role of knowledge in policy.

Knowledge moves

For one thing, our schema provides a heuristic that can help researchers and practitioners to know where to look for relevant knowledge, and especially to observe the movement of knowledge through the world of policy. Some of the most interesting questions about knowledge in policy seem to be connected with questions about its movement. Our schema not only serves to highlight the fact that knowledge moves, but also throws light on the different ways in which it moves.

Thus, drawing our category of embodied knowledge to include both tacit and verbal forms of knowledge serves to direct our attention to the importance of embodied human beings in the distribution, movement and mobilisation of knowledge. It reminds us that in looking at how knowledge works in the world of policy, we need to attend to the movement and activities of people. It reminds us, too, that embodiment imposes real constraints on knowledge. Since embodied knowledge is, by definition, coexistent with the body of the person or persons who embody it, embodied knowledge is only mobile to the extent that living human bodies are mobile; the mobilisation of knowledge in policymaking is necessarily in large part a function of those party to it. By the same token, embodied knowledge is also liable to decay and degeneration, through forgetting and mis-remembering, of course, as well as through the attrition that results from the departure of particular individuals from committees, groups or organisations. In its embodied phase, knowledge thus shares in the fallibility and fragility of the human body itself.

Knowledge also moves through the world of policy in the form of inscriptions. Indeed, inscribed knowledge is generally capable of moving much more widely and rapidly than the knowledge embodied in people. It does so, moreover, while retaining a greater degree of stability and reliability than embodied knowledge. This inscribed knowledge has a particular kind of value in the work of policy since it can serve as a common point of reference, a source of shared knowledge around which distributed communities of policy actors can organise and coordinate their actions. Consequently, insofar as we might think of the work of policy as the work of coordinating action, particular importance attaches to the role of inscriptions – and analysts and practitioners alike may learn much by observing just what knowledge finds its way into inscriptions for policy purposes, and by attending to and following the movement of those inscriptions through the policy world.

By the same token, however, if policy is the work of coordinating action, then policy cannot exist without action – or, more precisely, without enacted knowledge. Here, our schema alerts us to an important difference between enacted knowledge, on the one hand, and embodied and inscribed knowledge, on the other – for where embodied and inscribed knowledge are able to move around the world with a greater or lesser degree of continuity and stability, enacted knowledge is generally highly localised and transient, both in space and time. Moreover, it is characterised by a high level of interpretive flexibility, which means that one instance of enactment may differ very significantly from another, even when both instances draw on the same embodied and inscribed knowledge. This makes enacted knowledge an object of special importance for those interested in understanding the work of policy.

On the one hand, enacted knowledge may be the source of considerable novelty in the making of policy. Analysts of the policy process will therefore need to pay careful attention to key instances of enactment, and the circumstances under which they occur, if they are to understand how policy innovations arise. On the other hand, despite its inherent instability, enacted knowledge commonly displays a considerable degree of regularity across different and diverse instances of enactment. Consequently, anyone interested in understanding how policy works to secure conformity or regularity of action will need to attend not only to individual, local instances of enactment, but also to such processes of surveillance and policing as operate to ensure that different instances of enacted knowledge, remote from one another in place and time, nonetheless resemble one another sufficiently closely to be regarded as instances of the same policy.

Towards a sociology and politics of policy knowledge

This mention of surveillance and policing directs us inevitably to recognise that knowledge is ultimately a collective achievement. Individuals may know things – they are themselves bearers of embodied knowledge, and they may have access to inscriptions of many kinds – but their enactment of that knowledge is policed and disciplined by the communities of knowers of which they are part. Consequently, if we are to understand how knowledge relates to the work of policy, we will inevitably have to look not just at how different kinds of knowledge move, but also at how they are distributed differentially through the relevant policy community. Ultimately, that implies going beyond our three-phase phenomenology of knowledge to ask more overtly theoretical questions about the sociology and politics of that community.

Still, our characterisation of the different phases of knowledge can contribute to such analysis. It can do so, for instance, by directing researchers to examine whether different sections of the policy community or different stages in the policy process are characterised by a greater or lesser emphasis on particular phases of knowledge, and, if so, to ask why that might be the case. It can also do so by highlighting the inherent uncertainty and indeterminacy of enacted knowledge, and by alerting researchers to attend to the social processes by which such indeterminacy is itself policed and regulated (or, alternatively, exploited) by different members of the policy community.

Our typology of embodied, inscribed and enacted knowledge thus does not represent a research programme in its own right. Seeing knowledge in this way does not, in itself, provide a way of answering the many questions that scholars have asked about the role of knowledge in policy. It says nothing about the ways that knowledge can be organised, both intellectually and socially, or about how different groups acquire control of certain bodies of knowledge, or about why some bodies or forms of knowledge may become more prominent in the policy process than others. Rather, we offer our analysis as a prolegomenon to any more searching inquiry into knowledge and policy. It is principally a sensitising device that serves to alert researchers to the sheer ubiquity of knowledge in the policy process – as, indeed, in any other area of social life – and to the multiple forms in which knowledge appears in that process. Its effectiveness in this regard may be judged with reference to the empirical case studies that make up much of the rest of the present volume.

Notes

[1] Our debt at this point to the sociologist of scientific knowledge Harry Collins will be apparent. Our category of embodied knowledge combines Collins's (1993) categories of embodied and embrained knowledge.

[2] Our category of inscribed knowledge owes a great deal to Latour's (1987) category of 'inscriptions', but also includes what Collins (1993) thinks of as 'codified' knowledge, namely, the kind of knowledge as may be incorporated into and serve to actuate machines.

[3] In talking here of 'instruments', we are talking specifically of material artefacts such as documents. Policy academics commonly talk of instruments to mean institutionalised forms of (more or less technical) policy *action*, such as surveys, statutory regulation or forms of taxation (eg Lascoumes and Le Galès, 2007). We will come to this later, when we consider enacted knowledge. For now, we are concerned solely with how knowledge is inscribed in artefacts, and therefore speak of policy 'instruments' just as we customarily speak of scientific instruments – as material objects, rather than the practices associated with those objects.

[4] Our discussion of rule-following draws heavily on the insights of David Bloor (1997) and his elaboration of a 'finitist' theory of meaning.

Part One

Policy knowledge in space and time

TWO

Seeing knowledge in mental health in Scotland

Jennifer Smith-Merry

Introduction

The research I present here uses the embodied–inscribed–enacted framework to interrogate data gathered from a large qualitative research project that has sought to understand the way that knowledge functions in relation to Scottish mental health policy. This formed the first part of the work conducted by the Scottish health team under the KNOWandPOL project, which aimed to understand the different dimensions of knowledge use in relation to policymaking across Europe. My overarching interest in this chapter is on how the new framework might help to answer these questions and add to the analytic toolbox from which policy scholars draw.

In order to assess its utility, I applied the embodied–inscribed–enacted schema retrospectively to data already analysed in order to understand what new perspectives it could offer on the way knowledge functions across this particular policy sphere. The original analysis had been conducted before the framework had been devised and, as we shall see, that initial analysis was productive of further research questions. However, in pursuing that further research, it became apparent that the ideas about knowledge employed for the initial analysis were of limited utility for developing our more detailed case studies. It is therefore interesting to revisit those data to determine what new analytical approaches and insights the embodied–inscribed–enacted schema might open up. In doing so, I ask: how can this framework be applied to an existing set of data? What new insights can it add to previous attempts to understand this field? How might we redescribe the different kinds of knowledge that have come to shape this policy domain?

Scotland, mental health and policy: mapping the field

Previous research on mental health policy in Scotland has characterised it as a knowledge-based community with high levels of interaction between actors and a high degree of consensus over aims and approaches to improving mental health (Smith-Merry et al, 2008). As a policy field, mental health in Scotland underwent a radical reorganisation over a short period of time between 2000 and 2010. Drawing on major reviews of the system, new legislation and new policies for services and population mental health were launched: the Mental Health (Care and Treatment) (Scotland) Act 2003; and the government's *National programme for improving mental health and wellbeing*, which began in 2003, and its policy statement *Delivering for mental health* (2006).[1] This happened in the context of a newly devolved Scottish government, just finding its feet and seeking to distinguish itself from England. The newly devolved government declared a focus on values of openness and inclusion, which aimed to open up government and include a multiplicity of voices in decision-making.

The extent to which a particularly Scottish 'style' of policymaking developed out of these circumstances has been debated in the academic literature (Cairney, 2008, 2011; McGarvey and Cairney, 2008; Keating, 2010); what we have found through the KNOWandPOL research was that much of what Scotland did in mental health appeared to be a function of old rivalries with England, which resulted in innovation aimed, among other things, at asserting Scottish difference (Smith-Merry, 2008; Smith-Merry et al, 2013). However, more generally, our research showed how, in this distinctive setting, the mobilisation and circulation of different kinds of knowledge was central, not just to the making of Scottish mental health policy, but to the way it was implemented through the active and knowledgeable participation of a wide range of actors.

The research for the KNOWandPOL project produced a large body of data derived from an initial 'policy-mapping' task and a series of in-depth case studies. The first 'mapping' phase of the project sought to understand the types of knowledge being used and produced in Scottish mental health policy and it is the data from this phase of the research that is drawn on for the substantive primary analysis in this chapter. The research in this phase drew on data from a set of 16 interviews with a range of key actors across the mental health sector in Scotland. The sampling of respondents was purposive, based on the roles that they filled in the mental health system, with the aim being to interview individuals working in key government and non-government positions throughout the sector. Our project advisory group identified potential respondents, who included representatives of service user groups.[2] All respondents we approached agreed to be interviewed.

Interviews were in-depth, ranged from 25 to 90 minutes in length and were semi-structured. The questions guiding the research focused on the knowledge held and produced by the respondent in their work, and how they interacted with others in terms of this knowledge. We asked:

- What knowledge do you draw on in the work of your organisation?
- What knowledge outputs has your organisation produced, or been involved in the production of, over the past two years?
- What areas of knowledge production does your organisation prioritise?
- Does your organisation have particular relationships with others in terms of knowledge production?
- Does the work of your organisation specifically use knowledge produced by international organisations or bodies?

Interviews were transcribed and the data was entered into NVivo, where it was hand-coded.

In analysing the interview data, I attempted to categorise the data according to function and purpose. The initial analysis used codes that were derived inductively from the data, and that were grouped according to actor, theme and knowledge. I brought the codes for knowledge together and separated them into similar 'types' of knowledge based on their function, behaviour and situation. To these groups of codes, I gave a descriptive category. In writing up this data, the categories were separated into either 'knowledge inputs' or 'knowledge outputs' – knowledge used and created by the mental health system (Smith et al, 2007). The knowledge categories we ended up using for this stage of the analysis were:

- **Official/formal:** knowledge that is from official sources or is formalised in some way. The format of these sources is often bound by codes that dictate how they are devised and what sorts of data they contain. They included training, literature reviews, commissioned research, academic work, primary research, evaluation, official letters and emails, official policies, guidance or legislation, and international work. There were 18 instances of this data included as 'knowledge inputs' in the interviews and 36 as outputs.
- **Processual/oral:** knowledge that is transmitted orally through meetings, consultation, reference groups, events, committee

membership, teaching, theatre performances, seminars, networking roadshows, workshops, speeches, conferences and training. Here, knowledge is created, transformed and transmitted through the process of meeting and talking. There were 10 instances of this knowledge included as 'inputs' in the interview data and 47 as outputs.

- **Regulatory:** knowledge that comes from regulatory tools such as benchmarking, codes of practice and regulatory tool development. There was only one instance of this type of knowledge listed as a knowledge input and four instances of regulatory knowledge as an output.

- **Informal/experiential:** knowledge that could be described as tacit, informal or experiential. It is knowledge that does not come from a codified or formalised source and cannot be tested for objective validity. In this category, I included feedback, expertise, practical experience, personal experience, service user knowledge, institutional knowledge, monitoring, briefings, advice and secondment. There were 20 instances of this type of knowledge discussed as knowledge inputs in the interviews and 15 as knowledge outputs.

- **Public education:** knowledge that was used to promote public mental health within the community. In this category were included media work, magazines, television advertisements, leaflets and websites. There were 11 instances of this type of knowledge included as an output, but none as an input.

As will be apparent from reviewing this list, the knowledge categories that emerged inductively from our initial analysis were somewhat heterogeneous. While I set out to classify knowledge into functional categories, only some of the categories were actually functional in any clear sense, while others were more about the epistemic or social organisation of the knowledge (eg official/formal), and others conflated function with a kind of behaviour (processual/oral). Given the preliminary and exploratory aims of this part of the research, this was not a problem at the time. On the contrary, it was invaluable in helping us to understand the dimensions of the mental health policy field, including what forums and processes were particularly important for the creation and mobilisation of knowledge. Among other things, it alerted us to the importance of user groups and their interpenetration with other policy actors. For example, we were able to identify that much of the knowledge creation in the system took place not through the production of official policy documents or guidelines, but through individuals speaking with one another in meetings: this was a system where the spoken word held more sway than formal documents.

The mapping exercise also enabled us to identify a series of case studies that structured the remainder of the KNOWandPOL project work, and through which we were able to explore further the overarching research aim of understanding knowledge in policy. In particular, the knowledge classification we developed for the preliminary phase of the project alerted us to the importance of consultation in building policy impetus, of a practice- and service-user-led social movement in shaping recovery policy, and of international meetings for sustaining domestic policy. Our first case study accordingly used ethnographic observation, interviews and documentary analysis to examine the consultation processes for a new population mental health strategy; our second and third case studies used interviews and documentary analysis to examine, respectively, the emergence and implementation of recovery as a value guiding policy and practice, and the use of targets, indicators and measurement in mental health policy. A final case study looked to Scotland's relationship with the World Health Organization Europe (WHO Europe) in the field of mental health, to determine the way knowledge was used in this context.

It is notable, however, that the exploration of these case studies did not, on the whole, draw further on the categories used in the initial mapping exercise. In practice, when we came to look more closely at how knowledge works in policy, our original categories proved too static to be useful, and we had to employ other categories or theories of knowledge – usually on an ad hoc basis – to capture the dynamics of the policy processes we studied. This was before the schema of embodied–inscribed–enacted knowledge was properly articulated. Had we had that scheme to hand when we conducted our case studies, would it have helped to facilitate our analysis, or to throw light on aspects of the case studies we previously overlooked? In the next section, I reflect on the new perspectives that a re-categorisation of our data using the embodied–inscribed–enacted framework adds.

Types of knowledge: re-analysing our data

In order to re-categorise our original data using the new framework, I merged inputs and outputs as I found this categorisation to be unnecessary. All the knowledge types referred to in the original interviews then fitted easily into the new schema:

- **Embodied knowledge:** within the embodied category, I included personal knowledge of international examples, consultation, secondment, personal experience, practical experience, expertise, feedback, advice and representation. There were 30 instances of this knowledge referred to in the interviews.
- **Inscribed knowledge:** within the inscribed category, I included reviews, academic papers, reports, evaluation, letters, newsletters, awards, emails, written guides, DVDs, benchmarking, research, tool development, codes of practice, briefings, websites, leaflets, television advertisements and magazines. Respondents made reference to 70 instances of this kind of knowledge.
- **Enacted knowledge:** within the enacted category, I included events, committee participation, teaching, meetings, theatre performances, seminars, roadshows, workshops, speeches, conferences, training, media work, monitoring and networking. There were 62 instances of this knowledge referred to in the interviews.

This re-categorisation showed a policy community where embodied, inscribed and enacted knowledge types are all represented: each is discussed in detail in the following.

Embodied knowledge

"So if you are going to have a breakdown, have one [here], not [there]." (Towards a Mentally Flourishing Scotland [TAMFS] consultation, field note, 19 February 2008)

"Locally, what has worked well with Choose Life has been trying to plant a seed and let it grow – men's groups, men's mental health stuff is going on but is not joined up. We need to allow a network to develop around [population mental health work]." (TAMFS consultation, field note, 19 February 2008)

"We have no formal means of prioritisation, but if requests come in for work to be done, then it would be taken to the board and our host organisation for discussions about whether it was felt that it was a valuable and appropriate thing to be involved in." (Interview, 8 June 2007)

Each of these quotations deals with embodied knowledge – knowledge held in the bodies and minds of, in this case, service users, practitioners and advocacy workers. I have categorised embodied knowledge as including that gained through experience: as the preceding examples illustrate, in the case of the empirical research, embodied knowledge was comprised mainly of the personal experiences of service users and the practice-based experience of policymakers and practitioners. Embodied knowledge would typically be used to weigh up alternatives for action or to negotiate policy networks to influence change. It would also be used to draw attention to an area through recounting the negative impacts current processes have on individuals.

Looking at our case studies, our work on recovery demonstrated an important place for embodied knowledge in the development of recovery policy and practice (Sturdy et al, 2012; Smith-Merry and Sturdy, 2013). Recovery is generally described as the idea that individuals can expect a fulfilling life despite a diagnosis of mental ill-health, and is conceptualised as a personal process or journey that individuals are involved in to this end (Frese et al, 2009; see also Scottish Government, 2010[3]). Recovery has become a significant value shaping the operation of services for mental health in Scotland and is highlighted as a policy goal for both services and population health strategies (see, eg, the mental health services policy document *Delivering for mental health* [2006] and the *Mental health strategy for Scotland 2012–2015* [2012][4]). Our research found that embodied knowledge was used extensively in order to spread the concept of recovery through the policy, practice and service user community in Scotland. This is suggested by the following quotations:

> Audrey described her experiences of being diagnosed and treated and the effects that her medication had on her ability to work and to study. She came to feel that she no longer wanted to live under the shadow of medication. She felt she had been 'written off' and was depressed – 'who wouldn't be?' Being part of self-help groups and the Hearing Voices Network was a liberating experience and the start of a journey towards recovery. (Scottish Development Centre for Mental Health, 2002, p 5)

> "People from the Hearing Voices Network started talking about their experience of using services, how everything about their life had become symptomatic and diagnosis was reflected – they only lived through diagnosis and in some way people interact with them through diagnosis...."

The conference instigated a lot of self-reflection for service
providers." (Interview, 3 November 2009)

As these quotations demonstrate, the expression of embodied
knowledge by service users was a very powerful tool in spreading the
word on recovery. Personal recovery narratives were 'performed' at
training events and conferences, where the embodied knowledge of
service users worked to educate and inform parts of the mental health
practice community who did not already have an understanding of
recovery. The emotive content of their accounts, and the positioning
of recovery as an antidote to system-wide ills, made recovery-oriented
action in the field difficult to argue against and contributed to the spread
of the recovery message (Smith-Merry and Sturdy, 2013).

Another powerful use of embodied knowledge took the form of
Peer Support workers – who themselves have a lived experience of
mental ill-health – being placed as staff members within mental health
services. Peer Support workers modelled recovery for both service users
and staff in a way that allowed them to understand recovery beyond
the merely prescriptive and theoretical:

> "They now employ acute inpatient forum workers who are
> Peer Support workers and that has shifted things around
> a little. A user organisation is now placing Peer Support
> workers in acute units so they can assess patient experience
> and it has very much come from a local recovery network."
> (Interview, 17 September 2009)

The living embodiment of recovery is far more effective than a written
description of it. Here, the embodied knowledge of Peer Support
workers significantly disrupted the entrenched practices within the
mental health service and demonstrated the value of a recovery
approach (Smith-Merry et al, 2011). The fact that Peer Support workers
were paid members of staff further validated their embodied knowledge,
and this was a conscious government strategy that sought to elevate the
value of service user knowledge to make it valued in relation to the
practice-based embodied knowledge of other staff members (Smith-
Merry et al, 2011).

In the process of interviewing, respondents' thoughts and actions can
only really be expressed as words, which means that only the kinds
of knowledge they thought to mention were included in the analysis
of interview data. It is interesting that embodied knowledge was not
as frequently referred to in the interviews as inscribed or enacted

knowledge. This may be due to an inability on the part of respondents to see beyond formalised knowledge types and processes and to see value in personal experience. Individuals may only have mentioned those types of knowledge that immediately came to mind as 'traditional' forms of knowledge, leaving personal and experiential ways of knowing underrepresented in the analysis. Embodied forms of knowledge, that is to say, may be so embodied that it is difficult for individuals to see them as a form of knowledge.

Similarly, one stage of our work used ethnographic observation techniques in order to observe a consultation process for the Scottish Government's new population mental health strategy. Ethnographic methods use observation to understand the meaning and experience a particular process holds for participants and we used these methods to understand the interactions between and implications for participants in relation to knowledge use. We found extensive use of embodied knowledge as the main input into the consultation process during the consultation event stage of the consultation (Sturdy et al, 2012). The embodied knowledge present in the consultation took the form of discussions of participants' personal experience. Participants were mainly practitioners working in mental health and related fields and they expressed their knowledge most frequently as anecdotes about their practice-related experience. These observations regarding the importance of embodied knowledge are borne out by the extensive use of embodied knowledge in enactment processes, discussed later in this chapter.

Inscribed knowledge

Inscription makes knowledge portable. While embodied knowledge may be shared between individuals through conversation or by demonstrating practice, for it to be transported to a much larger audience, it must be inscribed in documents, videos or other artefacts (Freeman, 2006a; Freeman and Maybin, 2011). Knowledge is inscribed in ways that are relevant to the context in which the knowledge is to be enacted. Accordingly, within the sphere of Scottish mental health policy, we find a very wide range of forms of inscribed knowledge, including policy briefings, written guides, newsletters, television advertisements, academic journal articles and websites, each of which targets a different part of the policy community. The types of inscribed knowledge most frequently cited in the interviews were reviews and reports: this is not surprising, since reviews and reports are those inscribed objects that result from the main official processes of policymaking and so would most readily be associated as relevant outputs by other policy actors.

The reviews that our respondents referred to most frequently were those of the population mental health strategy, of mental health nursing (*Rights, relationships and recovery*, 2006[5]), and the review of mental health legislation carried out by the Millan Committee, which reported in 2001. Reports discussed included those dealing with forensic mental health, the national suicide prevention strategy and acute inpatient forums. Reviews and reports are made by government or other actors in the field in order to bring attention to an issue and make recommendations about changes needed:

> "The two big things [we've been involved in] have been evaluating Choose Life at the infrastructure development stage, and trying to learn what has been more or least successful in the development process.... The report provided recommendations on the next phase of the project." (Interview 1, 18 June 2007)

As this quotation illustrates, reviews and reports work to both describe a field and bring about action in and on it. These documents inscribe the results of extensive processes of enactment through activities such as policy consultations, service reviews and policy research. They also list priorities for further action and must therefore be structured in ways that can be understood and acted upon by services and policymakers in carrying out their jobs. Because they are handled as guiding documents, they carry more weight and circulate more widely than other forms of inscribed knowledge.

That the policy community know what to do with documents like reports or reviews is based on a history of practices that has been built up around these types of document. Much of the inscribed knowledge in reviews and reports is highly formalised, formatted in ways that can be read and understood by a particular audience. Sense-making of this kind – the process in which individuals understand, take up and use knowledge within set contexts – may itself be seen as a function of the embodied knowledge shared by actors within a particular community (Weick et al, 2005). Through being involved in the policy field, an understanding of the meaning and potential application of particular forms of formal inscribed knowledge such as reports and reviews is developed by practitioners and other individuals. These documents and their content make sense to this community, who, in turn, know how to use them.

Different forms of inscribed knowledge become easier to 'make sense of' when they are in circulation for longer, as more people come to share, and to share an understanding of, the knowledge they hold. Tools such as benchmarks were not seen as an important source of knowledge in the initial interviews we carried out in 2007, but by the time of the final interviews in 2010, this had changed, with a significant emphasis on this type of knowledge developing within the intervening three years (Smith-Merry et al, 2010). The growth of this type of knowledge was signified by the final report of a 'benchmarking project' issued in 2008, recommending the development of a set of indicators that would 'deliver improvement' in mental health services (Scottish Government, 2008). It aimed to do this through the development of a 'balanced scorecard approach', which is 'a strategic management and measurement system that links strategic objectives to comprehensive indicators' (Scottish Government, 2008, p 7). The balanced scorecard included 'strategic objectives' relating to cost, patient quality and efficiency, to which were attached specific mandatory indicators. In this way, the benchmarking project allowed new types of inscribed knowledge based around measurement and targets to seed and take hold in the Scottish mental health policy landscape (Coia and Glassborow, 2009). With the ability to measure came the circulation of new documents, including those that actively compared the mental health policy performance of different local health boards (Smith-Merry et al, 2011; see also Coia, 2009; Huggins, 2009). The circulation of these documents both signified and enforced the measurement of outputs and outcomes as a new way of thinking and acting in relation to mental health.

Enacted knowledge

> "It is not just good enough to produce a report, have information on a website or produce an event. There need to be networks which actively share this knowledge and are supported to do this and use the evidence in their everyday lives. We need to get better not just at knowledge transfer, but knowledge use." (Interview 2, 18 June 2007)

Enactments of knowledge, such as training sessions, conferences, networking, participation in committees, events and other meetings, were widely referred to in our interviews. This points to a policy community where policy knowledge is created and distributed through meeting and talking in both formal and informal settings. Our research points to interaction of this kind as a defining feature of Scottish mental health policymaking (Smith-Merry et al, 2008). The extent of this interaction can be visualised in Figure 2.1. Its seriousness and significance is reflected in the remark made by one of our respondents that "We are very, very serious about membership because we want to influence as much as we can…. [If] you miss a meeting you miss out." This focus on interaction in working groups, committee meetings and conferences demonstrates that within the policymaking community in Scotland, there is an emphasis on sharing and building as key processes. In turn, this implies an understanding of both policy and knowledge as processual and dynamic rather than static and inert.

Figure 2.1: The complex of meetings structuring interaction within the Scottish mental health system

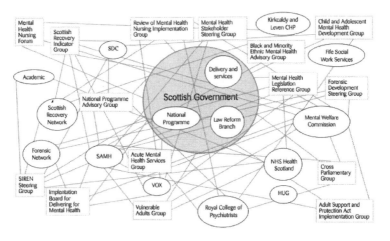

Source: Smith-Merry et al (2008).
Notes: HUG (Action for Mental Health); SAMH – Scottish Association for Mental Health; SDC – Scottish Development Centre for Mental Health; VOX – Voices of eXperience; SIREN - Steering Group (Suicide Information Research and Evidence Network Steering Group); Kirkcaldy and Leven CHP (Community Health Partnership)

Events, meetings and conferences serve as spaces where enacted knowledge emerges, and they function as critical moments in the development of mental health policy in Scotland. There are a number of key ways in which these meeting events function as knowledge points for the mental health community, including: building and maintaining the policy community; providing opportunities for personal and other connections; providing policy transparency; and allowing for the synthesis of both embodied and inscribed knowledge. Meeting events serve as ways for building and visualising the policy community through the process of inviting participation from different sectors or through the self-selection involved in open invitations. In engaging with counterparts of various kinds, participants are able to visualise the other actors and roles that are also involved in the policy creation process.

This creates a network between actors, which works towards the production of a policy community and strengthens the existing system of relationships upon which the policy community is built. This is because the events offer a chance for the embodied knowledge of the actors within the network to be enacted – they are able to talk to one another, discuss shared experiences and thus reinforce the bonds between the different actors. Involvement in meeting events by disparate members of the community also offers a chance for the policy development process to become 'transparent' and to break down the sense of alienation that members of the policy community may feel from the policy creation process. For the government, this assists in the validation of the policy development process because it provides an avenue for a larger number of voices to take part and thus 'own' the process through being implicated in the development of the policy. There develops a collective understanding of the policy to be implemented – a shared knowledge that helps to strengthen the policy community and aid in policy implementation.

The intangibility of much embodied knowledge means that, as discussed earlier, it is held in the minds and experiences of individuals, but is not easily inscribed. By bringing together disparate actors who may not come together in other forums, meeting events allow embodied knowledge to be enacted where it might otherwise be left out of a solely document-focused process. Most will bring together and enact both embodied and inscribed knowledge: embodied knowledge through the personal accounts of individuals and inscribed knowledge through the documents brought to and circulated within the meetings, such as reports, statistics, meeting minutes, research and so forth. In this way, they create a forum that allows for both informal embodied knowledge and more formalised inscribed knowledge to come together and be enacted to inform the policy creation process.

In our initial mapping, we described the types of groups that comprise mental health policy development in Scotland:

> There are 'steering groups', 'reference groups', 'implementation groups', 'interest groups', 'advisory groups', 'development groups' and 'working groups'. Many of the groups exist as 'short life working groups', a term the government uses to discuss a group that has been created

for a specific purpose and disbands once that purpose has
been fulfilled. (Smith-Merry et al, 2008, p 25)

These groups often merge into each other so that what might start out
as a development group for initial policy development is then replaced
by a reference group, and from there, a 'steering group' to aid in policy
implementation. The sense of collective purpose and legitimation of the
policy process brought about by involvement in these different meeting
events is thus sustained into the consolidation and implementation
periods of policy. It can be hypothesised that as a result of these effects,
the critical enactment function of meeting events facilitates a process
where the development and implementation of the new policy is less
contentious and more straightforward. A policy community is thus built
and sustained through continued communication brought about by
participation in the knowledge shared at these meeting events.

Discussion

So, how does the embodied–inscribed–enacted framework allow us to
make out new dimensions of knowledge where we could not before?
What does it add to our understanding of the field that my initial
mapping did not? In terms of the identification of a Scottish 'style' of
policymaking for mental health, it is the interactive processes of enacted
knowledge that emerge most clearly through this analysis. The original
mapping brought to light the multiple intersections of different policy
actors and organisations, but the concept of enactment helps to clarify
the central role of knowledge, including collective knowledge practices,
in policy. I discuss interaction here in more depth in order to illustrate
how this functions in practice.

One of our major case studies focused on the consultation process
put in place to develop the Scottish population mental health strategy
Towards a mentally flourishing Scotland (2008)[6]. Policy consultation
processes involve the organised elicitation and enactment of knowledge
through interaction for the express purpose of producing new policy. An
ideal type of consultation process involves the enactment of embodied
and inscribed knowledge. This follows several steps, which include:
policy consultation events that allow the embodied knowledge of
practitioners, service users and the general public to emerge around
the new policy through discussion in groups; the creation of written
policy submissions by interested groups and individuals, which are
submitted to government; reference group meetings that direct the
process, discuss the policy, interpret the associated submissions and

come up with suggestions about what the final policy should entail; and the determination of the content of the final policy documents by internal government bureaucrats, which are then signed off by the relevant minister.

In this way, policy consultation processes can be viewed as a series of interactions in which different forms of embodied or inscribed knowledge are enacted with the end result being a new form of inscription – the policy document. The embodied knowledge of the practitioners, for example, is articulated and expressed in consultation events, and the inscribed knowledge of organisations is articulated and expressed in the policy submission documents that are transferred to the government. The reference group and the internal government deliberations draw on both the embodied knowledge that their members and participants themselves hold, and the inscribed knowledge of those documents that they draw on (Smith-Merry, 2012). In turn, through the prescription contained in the recommendations, targets and benchmarks it puts forward, the policy document brings about new forms of embodied knowledge, as these technologies direct actors in the mental health system to act in new ways.

A major finding of our research, however, was that embodied knowledge – as represented in this case by service users' experiences and the practice-based experience of professionals and others – did not seem to travel well through the process of policymaking (Smith-Merry et al, 2009). The embodied knowledge that these actors expressed at the consultation events did not move out of the consultation event stage of the process and was not utilised in the final policy document. Certain kinds of knowledge, our findings suggest, could be embodied and enacted, but not inscribed. And because crucial stages of the consultation entailed or relied on inscription, this knowledge was absent from the final policy document.

However, we can also think about this a little differently. To assume that embodied knowledge was lost from the process is to see a linear progression from embodied to enacted to inscribed and back to embodied again. This is perhaps not a naive assumption to make, as a linear progression through these knowledge phases might be how an ideal consultation process is supposed to work. However, if we look beyond the ideal knowledge progression, we can see that the progression in this case also involved a shorter circuit: from embodied to enacted and back to embodied. Indeed, we were able to visualise a process of 'trading' of embodied knowledge taking place between participants in the consultation process, which helped both in initial sense-making and in the implementation of the resulting policy within local communities of practice.

This trading was most easily visualised within the discussion among practitioners attending consultation events (Smith-Merry et al, 2009). Here, practitioners would speak of their experience in relation to the themes being raised – thereby enacting their embodied knowledge – and others would do the same. This encouraged a dialogue of experience based around practice (Smith-Merry, 2012): because of the commonalities shared by the practitioners at the consultation events, they were able to take on the knowledge expressed by others and incorporate it into their own understanding of practice. Through this process, individual practitioners added to their repertoire of practice examples and enhanced their own embodied knowledge. This newly embodied knowledge could then be taken by these practitioners out into their work to create new ways of working.

New knowledge was thus being created in the consultation process, but through embodiment rather than inscription. As noted elsewhere, the consultation events worked to 'carve out a new space for policy action which would mean an easier transition to the new policy and a greater depth of policy awareness which would, in turn, lead to better policy implementation' (Smith-Merry, 2012, p 142). This was directly due to the enactment of embodied knowledge in consultation. The product of the enactment processes of the consultation was therefore not inscribed knowledge, but new forms of embodied knowledge, while the movement of much of the knowledge mobilised in the consultation process progressed not from embodied to enacted to inscribed, but from embodied to enacted and back to embodied.

It was a growing understanding of the utility of the embodied–inscribed–enacted framework that allowed for the exploration of this new perspective on practitioner knowledge. This awareness also alerted us to new ambivalences that were emerging around the role of embodied knowledge within the mental health policy sphere. Thus, according to one of our interviewees:

> "[It is] difficult for users to be assertive in the processes that are in place for their voice to be represented. You can get 'professional' service users. [This] happens both locally and nationally. There are real limits on how the user voice is heard." (Interview, 4 July 2007)

This quotation represents a view expressed by several of our respondents, who were critical of the way that the embodied knowledge of service users was enacted in Scottish policy (interviews, 8 June 2007; 22 June 2007; 4 July 2007). Where Freeman and Sturdy begin their exposition by suggesting that the most interesting questions about knowledge seem to be to do with the way it moves, the case of service user knowledge provokes instead the question 'What is about knowledge that sometimes prevents it moving?', since, as discussed earlier, not all types of knowledge can be easily inscribed. Similarly, not all embodied knowledge can be – or is allowed to be – enacted. This was true for service user knowledge at different stages of the research, with respondents noting that they were either excluded from policy processes or included in no more than a tokenistic way. The intangibility of the service users' embodied experiences is difficult to capture if it is not enacted in a way that promotes interaction and engagement with others. If embodied knowledge is not enacted, it just stays embodied and cannot move into other spheres. The enactment processes are thus critical to the transfer of knowledge through and between individuals, groups and sectors.

A principal obstacle to the inscription of embodied knowledge is that this form of knowledge may be *so* embodied that words to describe it do not come readily enough. As Mary O'Hagan (2004) noted with regards to the concept of recovery, the word 'recovery' is a 'useful container' for a set of actions and ideas, but what it is exactly remains beyond words. Defining recovery is difficult because its emphasis is on the lived experiences of individuals, and to create a fixed definition would be to impose an overly restrictive set of ideas onto a fluid concept: putting words to such complex and variable concepts inevitably involves creating a simulacrum. Of course, embodied knowledge must always be distorted when it is passed on in words or action. Freeman (2012, p 15) puts it thus:

> Policy makers make connections, with other actors and other ideas, as a message is passed on, stated and restated in one context and then another. Its reproduction, however, is highly contingent and always imperfect. We might think of it as a kind of translation: the knowledge brought to meetings is transformed as it is expressed in words; it is set down differently again in writing, as words on paper, and reinvented in the actions of professionals, practitioners, and public officials.

Such translation is necessary and unavoidable, as each actor will only understand another's knowledge in the context of their own embodied experience. As discussed earlier, our analysis of the consultation events also demonstrated that the embodied knowledge of practitioners was not readily transcribed into documents, and this meant that it did not impact upon the policy consultation process (Sturdy et al, 2012). However, the difficulty of inscribing service user knowledge is particularly problematic as it is this group whose knowledge should arguably be core within the consultation processes for new policy. The conventional orientation to inscription tends to reinforce the marginalisation of some types of knowledge from policy processes and, hand-in-hand with this, the identities and needs of those who hold that knowledge.

By contrast, the Highland Users Group (HUG) was cited by one of our interviewees as an example of the effective mobilisation of service user knowledge:

> "Branch meetings happen every two months. Branches are located throughout the Highlands and usually located at drop in centres or training facilities. At a branch meeting, the [HUG] project manager will attend and they will be informally structured. [The project manager] will give an account of what HUG has done on the people's behalf. They will have a couple of discussion topics. For example, recently, it has been on peer support, partly as a response to *Delivering for mental health*, and partly because of members' interest in it. There was also a discussion of child and adolescent mental health services, partly because of member interest and partly because there is currently a review of these services and the health board asked HUG to consult on this issue. They also look at local issues." (Interview, 22 June 2007)

From here, the project manager creates reports and newsletters and represents these views to others on official committees and through submissions for new policy. The process here is that the embodied knowledge of the service users is enacted at local meetings, this knowledge is then re-embodied by the project manager, who subsequently inscribes the knowledge in reports or enacts it through the processes of meeting events. This process is very different from that which leads to accusations of tokenism for more structured, official policy meetings. In official policy meetings, the tokenistic inclusion of service users is compounded because the forms of enactment and inscription that are generally deemed appropriate in such settings militate against the enactment and inscription of users' embodied knowledge. The forms of enactment and inscription made possible in the HUG meetings, however, facilitate such enactment and inscription. In this respect, the institutionalised and conventional character of different kinds of meetings, and the forms of action that are institutionalised in those meetings, has important consequences for what kinds of knowledge may be mobilised and represented there.

While the HUG processes were aimed at inscribing and transferring the existing embodied knowledge of service users, tools such as Peer Support and similar technologies such as the Scottish Recovery Indicator (SRI) or Wellness Recovery Action Planning (WRAP) can be viewed as technologies designed to bring about new forms of embodied knowledge within the practice community. SRI is a tool designed to track the extent to which recovery is being implemented in mental health services; WRAP is a planning tool used in order to develop plans to support an individual's recovery journey. The implementation and use of both SRI and WRAP were set out in *Delivering for mental health* (2006)[7]. These technologies create new institutionalised forms of therapeutic or administrative action that facilitate and privilege the enactment of certain kinds of embodied knowledge. The processes involved in using these tools force those involved to engage with recovery, speak about it and, in doing so, understand and take on the concept of recovery in their own lives and work (Smith-Merry et al, 2011). Inscribed in these tools, recovery is strengthened as an active form of embodied knowledge circulating in the mental health community in Scotland.

However, such tools have also been criticised by some respondents, who consider that the types of embodied knowledge they serve to reproduce is not 'authentic' recovery, because it is being implemented in the artificial organisational environment of services and policy (Smith-Merry and Sturdy, 2013). The tools were thus seen to be creating alien forms of embodied knowledge; real recovery could only come about as part of a personal journey in the context of peer support networks. Here, again, thinking through knowledge in relation to the framework allowed us to draw attention to enacted and embodied knowledge and helped to clarify the extent to which these policy instruments function to mobilise new forms of knowledge in the mental health practice sector.

Conclusion

While Freeman and Sturdy emphasise that knowledge is often stable, standardised and institutionalised, they also highlight its contingency and inconstancy. Only in reworking my data did I realise the extent to which my initial common-sense, inductive conception of knowledge only treated knowledge as static, assuming that it keeps the form in which it is created. However, knowledge is not static and the fact of its change is at the heart of some of the most significant policymaking instruments, for instance, the policy consultation exercise, where the embodied knowledge of actors is enacted and inscribed within the new policy. The utility of the embodied–inscribed–enacted framework thus lies in the fact that it allows for an emphasis on knowledge as dynamic, changeable and context-dependent. In doing so, it draws attention to the ways in which enactment, in particular, is often highly constrained by the institutional structures in which it takes place, and by those inscribed and embodied forms of knowledge that create these institutions. It thus also alerts us to the way that interaction within a particular policy setting structures the production, distribution and use of knowledge, determining which knowledge is prioritised and – perhaps more interesting in terms of this case study – which is marginalised or de-prioritised. Awareness of the importance of embodiment and enactment, and of the dual nature (under-determined but institutionally structured and constrained) of this enactment, helps to throw light on hitherto unilluminated aspects of the role of knowledge in policy.

In short, from my reanalysis of our original data, it is clear that conceptualising knowledge in terms of the embodied–inscribed–enacted framework is intrinsically valuable for understanding policy fields. However, I would also argue that it is the 'enacted' component of the framework that most sets it apart from previous attempts to categorise knowledge. It was this element that offered most for an analysis of the mental health policy field in Scotland, for it revealed the extent to which different forms of interaction determined the availability and mobility of knowledge. This is an important perspective if we are interested in promoting more meaningful policy change, as it tells us that it is by attending to these processes of interaction that we should address perceived problems with the marginalisation of some forms of embodied knowledge. Based on this understanding, the challenge for policy, practice and research is thus to design processes of meeting and inscription that are based on an understanding of the dynamics of different forms of embodied knowledge and how it operates in different contexts.

Notes

[1] Scottish Executive (2006) *Delivering for Mental Health*, Edinburgh: Scottish Executive (www.scotland.gov.uk/Resource/Doc/157157/0042281.pdf)

[2] In Scotland, the term 'service user' is used in the same way that the term 'consumer' is used in other countries.

[3] Scottish Government (2010) *Rights, Relationships and Recovery: Refreshed. Action Plan 2010–2011*, Edinburgh: Scottish Government (www.scotland.gov.uk/Resource/Doc/924/0097678.pdf).

[4] Scottish Executive (2006) *Delivering for Mental Health*, Edinburgh: Scottish Executive (www.scotland.gov.uk/Resource/Doc/157157/0042281.pdf); Scottish Government (2012) *Mental Health Strategy for Scotland 2012–2015*, Edinburgh: Scottish Government (www.scotland.gov.uk/Publications/2012/08/9714).

[5] Scottish Executive (2006) *Rights, Relationships and Recovery: The Report of the National Review of Mental Health Nursing in Scotland*, Edinburgh: Scottish Executive (www.scotland.gov.uk/Resource/Doc/112046/0027278.pdf).

[6] Scottish Government (2009) *Towards a Mentally Flourishing Scotland: Policy and Action Plan 2009–2011*, Edinburgh: Scottish Government (www.scotland.gov.uk/Publications/2009/05/06154655/5).

[7] Scottish Executive (2006) *Delivering for Mental Health*, Edinburgh: Scottish Executive (www.scotland.gov.uk/Resource/Doc/157157/0042281.pdf).

THREE

Knowledge moves: regulation and the evaluation of Portuguese schools

Natércio Afonso and Estela Costa

Introduction

This chapter explores the role and function of knowledge as a regulatory instrument. It examines how knowledge is produced and reproduced, thus performing its regulatory role within a specific policy process. It does so by means of a case study of the design and implementation of a programme of external evaluation of public schools in Portugal.

In a general sense, regulation is a form of policy. It is an expression of power, simply construed: it constitutes an attempt by one player to structure the behaviour of others. Now, in highly centralised countries like Portugal, the term 'regulation' is associated with the debate on reform and modernisation of public administration. It is imbued with a sense of governance rather than government, a 'new public management' where a priori direct control of procedures is replaced by a posteriori remote control based on results (Barroso, 2005). In the international context, Portugal offers a good example of the rise of 'post-bureaucratic' forms of regulation in education policy (Barroso, 2000; Maroy and Dupriez, 2000; Maroy, 2008).

Evaluation functions as a form of regulation in very specific ways. First, it shapes the behaviour of actors by measuring it against some standard, usually a specific level of achievement or a notion of best practice. This makes it very different from traditional bureaucratic forms of regulation, in which actors are governed by the application of rules. In evaluation, in other words, behaviour is considered wrong not because it is illegal, but because it is not effective. Second, and of particular interest here, evaluation entails the production and circulation of new knowledge and information: guidelines are drafted and examples of best practice set; data is collected and analysed; and performance is compared and assessed. Third, because information about organisational and professional performance is collected and processed by the actors themselves, often according to categories and standards set by their peers, regulation by evaluation is very often a process of self-regulation. In this way, evaluation forms an essential part of the cognitive framework within which the autonomy of actors such as these is exercised: the function of regulation is not simply to manage what they do, but to manage the way they think about what they do.

The empirical data used here were derived from an analysis of documents, primarily from the Portuguese Inspectorate's online database (which includes policy statements, planning documents, operational guidelines, school reports, national reports and conference minutes). In order to probe and expand upon the information they provide, interviews were conducted with an evaluation team, including two field inspectors and one external evaluator, who was a retired teacher. Likewise, a case study was carried out in a school where an external evaluation had recently been carried out. Information was collected from a range of interviewees: the director of the school and her staff management, and four department coordinators.

The making of the school evaluation programme

In 2005, following a landslide victory in parliamentary elections, a new government came to power in Portugal. The newly appointed Education Minister – an outspoken sociology professor – stressed the need to adopt evidence-based policy measures to rationalise and modernise the education system. A key element in this strategy was reinforcing and refining the system's evaluation structures to produce data to support policy decisions.

As part of this strategy, a new model for the evaluation of public schools was announced. A six-member team of experts – four academics and two senior civil servants from the ministry – commissioned the design of the model. This School Evaluation Working Group (SEWG) produced and tested an evaluation framework. The framework included indicators, criteria, data collection guidelines, reporting templates and scripts for conducting meetings, and drew on theoretical and institutional references from the scientific literature as well as the professional know-how of inspectors and evaluators. The ministry's Inspectorate General for Education (IGE) was then charged with putting the new policy into practice from 2006. By 2010/11, every public school was to be subject to evaluation. This required: a school self-evaluation document to be produced, an undertaking that entailed collecting and analysing a prescribed set of data; organising the evaluation team's school visit, including meetings and interviews with specific stakeholders; and preparing a final report to be published on the IGE's website.

But how did the SEWG know how to go about evaluating schools? Why was the programme of school evaluation deemed appropriate or even necessary? And what were the ideational and cognitive components of this new regulatory regime? They were essentially of two kinds: a technocratic understanding of evaluation combined with policy models from other countries.

The members of the SEWG brought together different fields of expertise and the experience of different sectors. The group comprised six individuals with diverse academic qualifications and professional backgrounds in higher education and public administration. Pedro Guedes de Oliveira, José Fernando Oliveira and Maria Antónia Carravilla were each professors or researchers at the University of Porto; Pedro Guedes de Oliveira and José Oliveira held doctorates in Electrical and Computer Engineering, and Carravilla in Production Planning. Cláudia Sarrico was professor at the University of Aveiro, having worked in management in the social and legal sciences and as a consultant in operational research, while Maria do Carmo Clímaco was a former English teacher with experience in higher education who had served as Inspector General of Education; both held PhDs in Social Policy from English universities. Finally, José Maria Azevedo was a senior government official with postgraduate qualifications in Education, Development and Social Change and in Management and Public Administration. He was also a former Inspector General of Education and was now providing strategic scientific advice to the Office of the Minister of Education in the Portuguese government.

Despite the diversity of their backgrounds, all the members of the SEWG had both national and international expertise in evaluation (see Barroso et al, 2008, p 114). Thus, of the three engineering professors: Pedro Guedes de Oliveira, the group's coordinator, was involved in the evaluation of public sector research and development (R&D); José Fernando Oliveira worked in the application of decision support methodologies for assessment and management processes in a university; and Maria Antónia Carravilla was involved in projects to support decision-making in evaluation of higher education courses. Of those who had trained in the UK, Claudia Sarrico had experience of assessing and managing the performance of public services in the fields of education and higher education, having published extensively in this area and having participated in several national and international projects. The former Inspector General of Education, Carmo Clímaco, had been responsible for coordinating and managing various teams in the area of curriculum evaluation, educational success and school performance and had also published widely. Having launched the national evaluation of schools programme, she had coordinated the 'School Quality Observatory' as part of 'Education for all – 2000' (PEPT2000, 1994). Her engagement with international organisations involved in school evaluation is also worth highlighting: she had represented Portugal in the Organisation for Economic Development and Co-operation's (OECD's) Indicators of Education (INES) programme and at the Standing International Conference of Inspectorates (SICI).

All of this experience informed the SEWG's approach to evaluation set out in its Final Report. It is specifically expressed in the best practice guidelines for school management, which emphasise the knowledge of evaluation models and theories of efficiency and efficacy. They place significant focus on 'quality' and on the qualitative aspects of pupils' learning, as well as on optimisation and improvement. Likewise, great significance is accorded to statistical data on school performance: the SEWG stressed 'the need to furnish the external evaluators with more quantitative information about the school they are visiting' (ME, 2006, p 6). It emphasises that the information selected by evaluation teams should be determined by evaluators' experience, but also by 'analysis of the literature regarding the factors that have an impact on school results and which are important for the evaluators to know in order to contextualise these results' (ME, 2006, p 6). The reference framework drawn up by the SEWG – which the evaluation teams expressly followed – is unequivocal on this point, specifying clearly its technical sources as well as the IGE's participation in SICI and its knowledge and understanding of approaches taken in other European countries.

The Portuguese IGE's participation in the SICI (see Chapter Six) testifies to its concern for international cooperation. SICI was established in 1995, bringing together inspection services from a number of European countries. Its activities focus on the exchange of experience, the development of partnership projects and the organisation of scientific and professional fora for the discussion of inspection methodologies and the professional training of inspectors. In introducing work planned for 2007, the IGE drew attention to the SICI meeting to be held in Lisbon in November, in the context of the Portuguese Presidency of the European Union, as well as the organisation of a workshop on 'Inspecting for Equality in Early Childhood Services' by the UK Office for Standards in Education (IGE/ME, 2007, p 7). The purpose of engagement of this kind was essentially that of knowledge exchange: to learn of other models and perspectives that might benefit the organisation and performance of the IGE, and to gather information that might raise the profile of inspectors in relation to the challenges they faced (Barroso et al, 2008).

The SEWG's Final Report also refers to initiatives taken by inspectorates in other countries, specifically in Scotland and Northern Ireland (ME, 2006). Scotland's school self-evaluation manual 'How good is our school?' (HMIE, 2007a) introduced new ideas that had been adapted to the Portuguese context, facilitating internal benchmarking and making comparison more stringent. The Final Report noted its 'huge popularity throughout Europe and the educational dynamism that has been brought about by giving schools the responsibility and the means to investigate their own quality' (ME, 2006, p 9). The Department of Education in Northern Ireland's document 'A process for self-evaluation' (ETI, 2001) similarly sought to support and develop a self-evaluation culture in schools. It was appropriated by the SEWG in drawing attention to:

> the way that evaluation is presented as part of the management of schools and the simplicity with which the different steps to be taken are described: the selection of key areas and the performance indicators, and specifically, the guidelines for schools to organise and prepare themselves for evaluation, so as to optimise the process in terms of overall performance, and minimise the negative effects that all evaluations may bring. (ME, 2006, p 9)

It was notable for being part of:

> a national strategy to improve education, which includes the evaluation of schools, assessment and improvement of the curriculum and educational services at different levels, improvement of the quality of initial and continuous teacher training and an overhaul of inspection methods so as to help guarantee quality. (ME, 2006, p 9)

In this way, the SEWG began to piece together elements of a framework for assessing the quality of Portuguese schools. The resulting model emerged from this confluence of projects and disciplines, professional training and practical know-how. Between them, the members of the team themselves had an advanced scientific and technical understanding of engineering, education, social policy, school inspection, R&D,

management and administration. The external vectors of influence on their work were of three kinds: international, sectoral and institutional.

The Effective School Self-Evaluation (ESSE) project run by SICI, which is important in assessing the consistency of self-evaluation by schools, is one example of international influence, among others. More broadly, the very idea of evaluation is invariably cast in what is the international, if anglophone, language of new public management: the SEWG's insistence on quality, and its talk of 'accountability', 'benchmarking' and 'best practice', all belong to a generalised discourse of 'modernisation', 'rationalisation' and 'efficiency'. In this way, what was international was also inter-sectoral: the evaluation methodology used in Portuguese schools drew heavily upon the European Foundation for Quality Management (EFQM) model, which is far from specific to education. As the SEWG reported:

> The 'European Pilot Project for Self-Evaluation of Schools' and its subsequent developments, the 'Total Quality Management' model or the EFQM ... has functioned as the framework for other self-evaluation developments such as the Common Evaluation Framework (CEF), both in public administration and in private organizations. (ME, 2006, pp 8–9)

Both sources of influence, however, only nourished a developing institutional appreciation of evaluation in Portuguese education. At the national level, an earlier school evaluation programme (the 'School Integrated Evaluation') had been carried out by IGE from 1999 to 2002. The work of the SEWG was not conducted ex novo, but is best thought of as a point of arrival in an ongoing process that began in the late 1990s and continued to be developed and reworked in subsequent programmes of Portuguese inspection.

The SEWG acted as a vessel for the reception and circulation of different kinds of knowledge about evaluation, a point of access for the international studies and institutional practices that had been variously internalised by the group members through their professional experience. It might be said that the logic of evaluation served as a technocratic common denominator of individuals and countries, disciplines and perspectives. However, its work was also an active process of synthesis and consolidation that shaped borrowings and inheritances to immediate purposes. What was imported from elsewhere was also reinvented in the process (Rogers, 2003).

In selecting from the scientific and international literature on school effectiveness, the SEWG placed particular emphasis on the qualitative aspects of pupils' learning, on the strategic aspects of optimisation and improvement and on the professional know-how of inspectors, principals and teachers. It openly distanced itself from more metric models of evaluation, which it treated as no more than management instruments. As the SEWG outlined, in its concern for accountability, it focused primarily on educational partners' search for fundamental answers about their performance, and less so on access to statistical data, which, in any case, is now widely available (see Barroso et al, 2008).

In Freeman and Sturdy's terms (Chapter One), the members of the SEWG brought almost incalculable embodied knowledge to the tables at which they drafted and deliberated the detail of the IGE's new evaluation policy for schools. They drew on a reservoir of related documents, reporting academic research and describing projects and programmes used in Portugal and elsewhere. A vast array of knowledge, in both embodied and inscribed form, provided the cognitive resources for their decisions. However, they still took decisions, made choices and had ideas that coalesced into the evaluation strategy they set out as if – as Garfinkel (1967, p 9) has it – for 'another first time'. That is to say, the moment of policy formulation is an enactment of a particularly significant kind.

The evaluation process

How is all this knowledge applied and used in the conduct of evaluations? We note that knowledge is a local phenomenon (Sturdy, 2008, p 1), structured within a specific context and holding significance for social actors based on their purposes and objectives in that context. It follows that our interest is not solely in knowledge 'inputs' – in this case, the knowledge incorporated in the instruments of evaluation – but also in the way that knowledge is processed in the course of the various activities that go to make up an evaluation. Here, again, our sense of the various and successive forms that knowledge takes – embodied, inscribed and enacted – provides the necessary heuristic for understanding the micro-transactions inherent in planning and carrying out an evaluation. It is used to describe how the 'policy technology' of indicators and guidelines, meetings, interviews, and reports moulds the way relevant actors, including inspectors, principals, teachers and pupils themselves, come to think of education and schooling and to perform their assigned roles in the regulatory apparatus.

As specified by the IGE, the work of an evaluator involves:

(i) participation in the initial training and a preparation session for each team member; (ii) full-time presence for two or three days in school visits; (iii) handing in of contributions to the team leader for the report, as well as a suggested classification; (iv) presentation of comments and suggestions about the versions of the report and replies to points made; and (v) participation in the annual evaluation of the process. (IGE/ME, 2009, p 12)

Evaluation teams are made up of two inspectors and one evaluator external to the IGE – a senior higher education teacher or researcher, a retired primary or secondary school teacher, or even a professional from another area (see IGE/ME, 2009, p 12). The external member is considered a precious resource that enables a crossing of viewpoints, leading to better identification of different aspects of the school that might be improved. While inspectors themselves are experienced in integrated evaluation, the role of the external assessor was deemed particularly important in supporting a new generalist approach. As an inspector pointed out:

> "[W]e had been recruited from different areas, but the idea in terms of the transformation of inspection was that the inspector should be more generalist. Hence, as well as the training we had, we did a postgraduate qualification in Inspection at the Catholic University with its own specific curriculum – we also had to have a lot of practical training on the various tasks of inspection, from the disciplinary area to financial issues. This gave us a lot of know-how in terms of 'general knowledge'." (Interview, 17 June 2010)

Of course, this generalist character makes the work as a whole more demanding:

> "One of the fundamental differences is that we have to master various aspects of the school ... everything that contributes to the school's being as it is. We used to work more in one area, like pedagogical or financial. Now it's the entirety of the process that counts. It requires us to know and to be inside the various areas of the school." (Interview, 17 June 2010)

Preparation

Each school visit is structured in three phases: preparation, a site visit and the final report. During the preparation phase, the evaluation team focuses on a set of documents provided by the school in order to give shape to their subsequent investigation (see Box 3.1). These include the Educational Project, the Curricular Project, the Annual Activity Plan and a set of internal regulations, as well as the Internal Evaluation/Self-Evaluation Reports. The 'School Presentation Document' requested from the school by the IGE is also submitted to careful scrutiny. In preparing this document, the school is invited to follow the format suggested on the IGE website. These guidelines specify the content and layout described as necessary to offer 'a global image of the school and its context', while also outlining the 'development priorities and targets, strategies to achieve them, results obtained and reflections they give rise to'.[1]

Box 3.1: Documents used in the External Evaluation of Schools, 2009/10

ME/IGE documents
- Dissemination leaflet on the External Evaluation of Schools and the global reports of the external evaluation programme
- Pilot project report (ME, 2006)
- Annual Reports (2006/07, 2007/08 and 2008/09)
- Reference framework for the evaluation of schools and groups (2009/10)
- Topics for school presentations (2009/10)
- Assessment scale (2009/10)
- Schedule and organisation of visits

School documents
- Curricular project
- Education project
- Internal regulations
- 'School Profile' (statistical data, socio-economic framework)
- Self-evaluation report

Each evaluator reads the school documentation, drawing up charts and categories from the information supplied:

"We dedicated the first day to reading the documents, each one of us individually, and we arranged a meeting on the second day to prepare the questions. This second day was basically about exchanging thoughts on the documents we had received and what questions they gave rise to. We used a chart, an Excel spreadsheet, in accordance with the Reference Framework." (Interview, 17 June 2010)

This stage of the process depends on good information management to filter the data, in order that only that which is relevant to the assessment is considered. There must be a "separation of the useful from the accessory ... as there could be two or three thousand pages of documentation" (interview, 17 June 2010).

From the school's perspective, producing the material required entails a collective analysis of the institution's structural documents and, hence, its identity. This is intended to lead to reflection on the life of the school and its evolution "in the last three to four years and the kind of thinking and conclusions drawn within the scope of the self-evaluation" (interview, 17 June 2010). However, in our case study, the degree of involvement in this activity by senior and middle management differed greatly. The former viewed the initiative as a resource to enable it to:

"have a more in-depth perspective, given that what is registered in writing is a positive or negative appraisal of that year, but then in subsequent years, the information ends up getting lost. If school issues were more documented and statistically processed so that afterwards they could be reviewed on a three or five-year basis, it would be much easier." (Interview, 30 June 2010)

Middle management, on the other hand, pointed to drawbacks, providing comments that were more impressionistic than factual:

"It seems to me that they evaluate according to what happened in the past.... If they really gather other information from the management, over the years, then perhaps this has some influence and may bias the evaluation from the start." (Interview, 30 June 2010)

Among the wider school community, meanwhile, there was greater acknowledgement of a learning process: "The fact we are building the educational project helps us to rethink what we want in a more conscious manner ... the evaluation contributed to this reflection" (interview, 30 June 2010). However the evaluation project is understood, the school's self-image must be condensed into a text of a maximum of 30,000 characters.

The site visit

Each school visit lasts for two to three days and includes a presentation by the school leadership with questions from the external evaluation team, an overview of facilities and interviews with different panels. It begins with a meeting between the school leadership and the evaluators in order to reach an overall appraisal of the documents and initial information provided, while identifying what further data might be necessary for their validation. This meeting can take different forms: it can proceed discreetly or be accorded significant focus by the school.

Inspection of a school's facilities includes observing its different services in operation, while asking "a question or two to a pupil or a staff member we come across" (interview, 17 June 2010). It is not intended as a formal visit, but an opportunity to get a snapshot of the everyday life of the school, in order to develop a broader sense of its pedagogy and organisation and to enable better judgements to be made about its different domains:

> "[W]e look at safety, in specific spaces such as the library and the laboratories to see the equipment and check the safety regulations are complied with.... At times, we are accompanied by the Head and call on one or two teachers. If the visit coincides with lessons, we take the chance to ask the pupils about laboratory experiments, whether they do them themselves or if they just observe the teacher doing them. We also visit the gymnasium and check the condition of things, and we talk to a Physical Education teacher."
> (Interview, 17 June 2010)

After that, a series of interviews is held, first with the school leadership, then with the self-evaluation team.

The interviews are conducted in panels organised by the school and are thought of as 'the essential method used by the external evaluation team to talk with the educational community and to gather information' (IGE/ME, 2009, p 13). Here, too, the process is informed but not determined by a standard template:

"We worked on the basis of the theoretical framework and then, depending on the reality of each school, we made the issues more concrete, trying to establish how they acted. Therefore, there is an adaptation of the theoretical framework to each particular school." (Interview, 17 June 2010)

One of the coordinators stressed, similarly, that:

"There was another point on which we did not have a very clear notion, which was not only associated with negative outcomes, but also with the question of 'quality of success', which was a concept that we had not, and we did not interpret the same way." (Interview, 30 June 2010)

The kind of embodied, experiential knowledge brought to bear in meetings and interview panels generally lacks the degree of formal coherence and consistency more characteristic of the document. Indeed, it is closely articulated with the subjective desires, aspirations and anxieties of the actors involved: "There is always a bit of nervousness, but we felt we were in a working environment that was receptive and collaborative", one manager said (interview, 30 June 2010). A coordinator noted the different styles of evaluators:

"Some raised issues in an inquisitorial manner, and we felt that there was a 'trick question' somewhere, which I think was unnecessary. But there were also other attitudes, more constructive, and I think that's also important." (Interview, 30 June 2010)

On the other hand, evaluators spoke of difficulties managing the larger panels: "Sometimes, you have to deal with the fact that one panel member or another wants to 'lead' and therefore we must try to give everyone the opportunity to participate" (interview, 17 June 2010). Another said that "I have already found some situations where people were, to begin with, rather suspicious. They exhibited a certain aggressiveness but then the situation loosened up" (interview, 17 June 2010). Different panels behave in different ways:

"In some, you can see that there has been almost no exchange of ideas about what goes on. Others have what they are going to say so meticulously prepared that we can see that messages had been passed between them about what they had to say." (Interview, 17 June 2010)

The pupil panels, by contrast, are often rich and spontaneous:

> "in defending their school and the fact they are there to show what they do. It can be seen from that that they feel in step with the school and that they view us as outsiders and people who need to be impressed." (Interview, 17 June 2010)

As one of the last panels, the interview with teachers is very important "because it allows us to cross-check a lot of the information we have collected and, in the end, this panel gives us the opportunity to confirm and clarify doubts" (interview, 17 June 2010).

Reporting

The final stage of the evaluation process is the drafting and presentation of a report, based on the template set up by the SEWG and adapted in accordance with the documentary and interview material gathered from the school. The draft draws on notes taken during the panels, "and then we cross with each other to confirm all the information" (interview, 17 June 2010). This is teamwork involving the participation of all its members in the making of the document: "We are particularly careful to do an internal reading to check that the ideas are clear, that there are no typos, that there is coherence" (interview, 17 June 2010). In synthesising different personal writing styles, a standard vocabulary and terminology is used, derived from the theoretical framework, which places the school at the centre of the analysis. Moreover, each report should be "properly grounded" (interview, 17 June 2010), based on arguments supported by evidence. The evaluators' appraisal is essentially mapped out "in terms of its internal coherence and the classifications" (interview, 17 June 2010).

In reputational terms, the significance of the report to the school is difficult to underestimate:

> "In our case, things went well. It [the final report] is published for everyone to see. If it had gone badly ... the public image of the school would have been questioned. If it had been unfair, that would have been catastrophic,

and a huge frustration for anyone giving everything to the school." (Interview, 30 June 2010)

This reputational risk is a function of the new knowledge and information generated about the school in the process of evaluating it, of course, but is also predicated on that knowledge being made mobile – and public – in inscribed, documentary form. Perhaps more positively:

> "[W]e are [now] more concerned to disseminate and illustrate what we do, and that used to be confined within the four walls of the school. Using the platform of the school, we have a blog, we are finally publicising our activity, with parents and with local authorities." (Interview, 30 June 2010)

Knowledge in the evaluation process

In this way, through its programme for the self-evaluation of schools, the ministry has a standard frame of reference for thinking about the quality of public schools in Portugal. Indeed, perhaps even more significantly, what it has standardised is the assumption that the quality and performance of schools is something that should be thought about. It has created a standard set of information about each school that makes one comparable with another and that makes each accountable for its performance in relation to others. What has been established appears rigid – a framework, an architecture or structure for the assessment and management of performance – and yet our case study is lit throughout by a sense of fluidity and uncertainty, both in the creation of the programme of evaluation and in its implementation.

In developing its new policy instrument, the ministry, through its IGE, has mobilised an array of knowledge about what evaluation is, but also about what education is and what a school should be and do. It has drawn on the various disciplinary backgrounds of the experts involved in its SEWG, on the experiments developed in other European countries and on its own experience of precursor and pilot initiatives. It invokes the everyday expertise of the school principal and her management team, teachers, pupils, and support staff. It gathers academic and policy papers, statistics, guidelines and rulebooks, job descriptions, memoranda, and reports. It requires all of these bodies of knowledge to be brought into relation with each other, in deliberation in meetings and in the consolidation and synthesis entailed in writing reports. In this way, the evaluation programme serves as an elaborate device by which different kinds of knowledge and expertise are funneled into and through the school. Our enduring sense is one of the inherent instability and mobility of that knowledge: the system is one of seemingly perpetual motion.

For all its technocratic aspect, evaluation endorses the knowledge embodied in persons: in chief inspectors, who know what is really going on at SICI; in teachers, who know how their school really runs; and in pupils, who know what they really do in and out of class. They may know what is in the documents, but they also know what is not in them. What is interesting, too, is the way embodied knowledge emerges in encounters and conversations with others, as well as with texts and artefacts. In the course of evaluations, moments of interaction are crucial for both the reconstruction of meaning and the production of new meaning, enabling the team to grasp the dynamics of and thinking behind the school. As one evaluator explained:

> "This happens, for example, in a school where we found nothing in terms of innovation ... through the intervention of a member of the community we were immediately given a vision that could not be gleaned from reading any of the documents about the innovative aspects of that school." (Interview, 17 June 2010)

The documents matter, of course. As the evaluation team points out: "we always work based on guidelines. The guidelines are usually produced by the central services" (interview, 17 June 2010). The guidelines draw on myriad others, including academic papers, policy statements and reports, and other guidelines. They generate, in turn, the school's account of itself in its rules and regulations, the minutes of its meetings, the job descriptions of its management team, and the reports and other statements it writes specifically for the evaluation. In this way, the self-evaluation of a school is realised not in individual documents, such as its Profile or its Final Report, but in the network of texts of which they form a part – and not only in texts and documents, but in artefacts and buildings, too: in the gymnasium the evaluation team visits, in the configuration of the playground and in the arrangement of chairs and desks in a classroom.

Knowledge is enacted, of course, in the conduct of every meeting, in the drafting of every document and in all the actions that follow from them. Working group discussions and panel interviews alike follow one course or another on the basis of what its participants know – for 'knowledge is what we think with' (Barnes, 1995, p 91).

What they know is called up in the instant of needing to know it, and deployed or not according to its holder's judgement of its validity and appropriateness in immediate circumstances. In the case of the External Evaluation of Schools, enacted knowledge emerges in a succession of fora: as the school management team drafts its Profile; in the inspectorate briefing sessions where the evaluation is planned; in the meetings and interviews carried out during the visit; and in the drafting of the Final Report and the further discussions that follow from it. It is this that gives us a sense that the most fundamental effect of evaluation is to put knowledge into motion. For all the new inscriptions it produces in documents, statements and reports, the most significant effect of evaluation is the obligatory enactment and re-enactment of the knowledge it entails. Evaluation, at least in the form we have studied here, does not necessarily require those evaluated to know anything new, but it does require them to know what they know: to express and articulate, revise and revisit, all of the taken-for-granted knowledge without which a school could not function and would not exist.

The evaluation process appears as a chain of enactments, of responding to questions and writing things down, almost always in collaboration and consultation with others. The enactment that is evaluation is an inescapably collective process. It may be this that accounts for the ambiguity it seemed to hold for its participants: the evaluation was variously constrained but creative, oppressive but liberating, routine but unpredictable. It is this uncertainty that we explore in the last part of this chapter.

Regulation and re-enactment

The purpose of evaluation, as a regulatory instrument, is to make actors newly aware of what they do. This is especially true of self-evaluation, which is designed to inculcate a heightened degree of reflective self-awareness among managers and professionals. One inspector revealed that:

> "We're not going to control, we will not tell the school what to do, but to see how the school works ... our intention is to get people to show what they do, to question them and lead them to reflect." (Interview, 17 June 2010)

Another expected to see "a reflection of the school ... how the school has reflected on their reality and what is being done to improve the results, because this is what is intended" (interview, 30 June 2010). And the evidence of our case study is that evaluation does indeed work in this way. As panel members acknowledged, "the questions they asked made us reflect on things which we often don't realise are being carried out in the school.... It makes us reflect more together about school procedures and ways of running the school" (interview, 30 June 2010). Some said that the effect of the IGE's intervention had been to alert them to aspects of their work that they had not previously valued, including "the work of cooperation that we have been involved in and which has been intensifying" and "the articulation that now we have with the pre-school and other cycles" (interview, 30 June 2010).

It is crucial to the regulatory function of evaluation that with increased reflection goes an increased sense of responsibility. As one of our respondents commented:

> "It was above all an added concern, because we are aware of the work that we are doing; we have been at this school for a long time and we have done a lot of work. Now we feel that anything that is not right will be written down and published as a label that says the school is not a good one … this is an added responsibility....When we left the panel, we were a little anxious, but afterwards, we had the sensation that we were in fact doing a lot, only we don't question it." (Interview, 30 June 2010)

This is burdensome, even troubling to some, as when they spoke of the 'nervousness', 'concern' and 'anxiety' brought by the added sense of accountability they felt the evaluation process had vested in them.

Whether reflexivity and responsibility bring any increase in autonomy is difficult to determine and that is perhaps because, in a sociological sense, it is undetermined. The flow of knowledge in and through the school is carefully channelled by the formal requirements of the evaluation. This 'cognitive scripting' leaves actors with the freedom to *act*, though it requires them to *think* in very specific ways, that is, in ways that will give appropriate content to the categories according to which they will be evaluated. A school or any part of it may be innovative, exceptional, unique or simply different if it can justify those qualities in terms set by the evaluation.

Something similar holds at the different stages of development and implementation of the evaluation programme we have reviewed here. In the national and international context in which it worked, there was nothing that required the SEWG to design its programme one way or another. What it proposed was specific to education in Portugal, but recognisable to its peers in other sectors and countries. The programme for the External Evaluation of Schools was new, but normal; that is to say, that the knowledge it comprised, like all knowledge, was subject to an almost infinitely extended process of social validation. In turn, the enactments of evaluation – the draftings, discussions and deliberations that take place in schools – are re-enactments of those enactments made by the SEWG that set the frame of reference. They unfold sequentially, over time, as documents are drafted and redrafted, successive meetings are held, and different stages of the process are completed. A school learns what it is by learning how to describe itself in the terms set by the evaluation. In this sense, the process of evaluation is also a process of education.

Accounts and assessments of school performance are achieved only through repeated rehearsal of the cognitive script set by the SEWG. Each enactment of it is no more – and no less – than a re-enactment of an external frame of reference. Its precepts are reproduced necessarily imperfectly, but they are necessarily reproduced. As a governance mechanism, self-evaluation has a tolerance or affordance that more direct or bureaucratic regulation does not. It harnesses the specific dynamic of knowledge that is both locally specific and generally or socially validated, and it is this that makes it seem at once both unpredictable and inescapable.

Note

[1] See: www.ige.min-edu.pt

FOUR

Knowledge, policy and coordinated action: mental health in Europe

Richard Freeman and Steve Sturdy

Introduction

Between 12 and 15 January 2005, a World Health Organization (WHO) Ministerial Conference on Mental Health in Europe took place in Helsinki, attended by over 450 delegates and observers. Approximately half of the 52 member states of WHO Europe were represented by their respective health ministers; the others by ministerial delegates. Most country delegations also included psychiatrists and departmental heads with responsibility for mental health services. Additionally, the participant list included representatives from the Council of Europe, the European Commission and selected local and international non-governmental organisations (NGOs), as well as service user and carer groups. In the course of the conference, the delegates joined in signing the *Mental health declaration* and *Action plan for Europe* (WHO Europe, 2005a, 2005b).

After Helsinki, the *Declaration* and *Action plan* were disseminated widely, and quickly became a touchstone for subsequent developments in mental health policy in Europe. Their implications were discussed at other meetings, such as that of the Leaders of European Psychiatry that took place a few months later, and a number of follow-up conferences were held on specific issues, led by WHO-designated collaborating centres such as those in Lille and Edinburgh. Bilateral initiatives were undertaken with specific member countries in Eastern Europe. Meanwhile, in October 2005, the European Commission issued a Green Paper on mental health (European Commission, 2005) that was a direct outcome of WHO's inter-ministerial conference, and which led to further rounds of consultation and new projects across the European Union (EU). WHO, for its part, invested in a survey intended to show how member states were enacting the priorities outlined in the *Declaration* and *Action plan*. The resulting report on *Policies and practices for mental health in Europe* (WHO Europe, 2008) was meant to establish a 'baseline' against which continued progress might be measured, thereby providing a renewed impetus for the policies laid out in the *Declaration* and *Action plan*.

In acting in this way, WHO was behaving as a typical international policy organisation. As Michael Barnett and Martha Finnemore put it, international organisations:

> (1) classify the world, creating categories of actors and action; (2) fix meanings in the social world; and (3) articulate and diffuse new norms, principles, and actors around the globe. All of these sources of power flow from the ability of IOs [international organisations] to structure knowledge. (Barnett and Finnemore, 1999, p 710)

But what is this knowledge? What is it that international organisations create, fix, articulate and diffuse? How is it achieved? And how does it work as a means of power in policy? In this chapter, we set out to retell the story of the *Declaration* and *Action plan* (previously recounted in Freeman et al, 2009; Freeman, 2012; Sturdy et al, 2013) by highlighting the crucial role that all three phases of knowledge – embodied, inscribed and enacted – played both in the drafting and official endorsement of these policy documents, and in determining how they were subsequently implemented in particular national settings.

The making of the *Mental health declaration* and *Action plan for Europe*

Where to start our analysis? There is no single, unequivocal starting point for any narrative of the making of WHO mental health policy, which can be traced back at least as far as the birth of WHO itself. For present purposes, however, as good a place to start as any would be with the decision, in 2000, by Marc Danzon, Regional Director of Health Services at WHO Europe, to organise an inter-ministerial conference on mental health. Danzon's role as champion of this initiative is significant, since he himself embodied substantial knowledge about mental health in Europe. He had begun his career as a child psychiatrist in France, and thus acquired first-hand experience of front-line mental health service provision, before moving into public health insurance work and then into WHO Europe. There, he served as Regional Director of Communications and subsequently of Health Services, with responsibility for the mental health programme. Consequently, Danzon possessed not just extensive factual knowledge of mental health and public health policy, but also practical knowledge of how to navigate the health bureaucracies of WHO Europe and its various member states. Not least, he was personally acquainted with policymakers across Europe, including the Minister of Health and Social Services in Finland, Maija Perho, whom Danzon knew as a friend as well as a colleague. Crucially, Danzon knew that Perho had a deep personal interest in the cause of public mental health, and he put that knowledge to good use when he persuaded her not just to host the inter-ministerial conference in Helsinki, but also to provide the administrative support that would be vital for making it a success.

Embodied knowledge was also strongly represented on the conference Steering Committee. This included knowledge of mental health policy and practice in different member states, provided by members from Germany, Slovakia and the UK and by a representative from Mental Health Europe (an association of national NGOs). But, importantly, the Steering Committee also included detailed procedural knowledge of how to run an effective intergovernmental conference. In addition to project officers from the Finnish Ministry of Health, which had previously hosted an EU Conference on the Promotion of Mental Health and Social Inclusion, the organisers recruited representatives from Greece and Belgium, which had organised and hosted previous EU Presidency conferences on mental health, as well as representatives of the European Commission (which agreed to co-organise the main conference) and the Council of Europe. The Committee membership thus embodied both factual knowledge and practical know-how, both of which were brought to bear on the planning of the conference. That knowledge was duly enacted: at first discursively, in the Committee's discussions about how best to organise the conference in order to secure their desired aims; and then practically, in the running of the conference itself.

The deliberations of the Steering Committee also proceeded in dialogue with the work of WHO's Regional Committee for Europe, the administrative body that determined the overall agenda and organisation of WHO's activities within the region. In September 2003, the Regional Committee considered an agenda item on 'Mental health in WHO's European region'.[1] The Regional Committee's actions under this item reveal the role of another kind of knowledge in the preparations for the inter-ministerial conference. Like the conference Steering Group, the Regional Committee included substantial embodied knowledge, in the person of subject experts and experienced administrators with both factual knowledge of mental health policy and procedural knowledge of how to take forward the WHO agenda. But, in addition, the Committee was concerned to invoke and discuss the knowledge inscribed in a number of earlier documents, including the 2001 *Athens declaration on mental health and man-made disasters, stigma and community care* (WHO Europe, 2001) and WHO's own *World health report* (WHO, 2001) of the same year, which testified to the increasing burden of mental health problems in Europe. The final action of the Regional Committee under this agenda item was to draft and approve a new document, WHO resolution 'EUR/RC53/R4: Mental health in WHO's European region', which not only re-inscribed knowledge culled from the previous documents, but also outlined the agenda for the 2005 inter-ministerial conference. In this way, the Regional Committee not only enacted a formal endorsement and justification for the Steering Committee's plans for the forthcoming conference, but also inscribed that endorsement in a permanent documentary record that would outlast the transient actions of the Committee itself, and would provide an enduring point of reference to which future actions could be referred.

In June 2004, Regional Adviser for Mental Health Matt Muijen, in consultation with the Steering Committee, began drafting yet another document that would eventually become the *Mental health declaration* and *Action plan for Europe*. This was a labour-intensive process, which involved not just referencing the knowledge inscribed in a range of other policy documents, but also heeding the advice of other knowledgeable actors. In total, the *Declaration* and *Action plan* would pass through 19 different versions. The early drafts were clearly meant only for internal discussion. But after version nine, the document was formatted to resemble an official WHO document and circulated more widely for comment. In September 2004, WHO hosted a meeting of international NGOs and user and carer groups to review and comment on the document. The knowledge that these new actors embodied, and that they voiced in their contributions to that meeting, proved crucial: the draft *Declaration* and *Action plan* changed considerably at this point, adopting a much more aspirational approach than had been reflected in previous drafts. Two months later, a meeting of key representatives of member states in Brussels went through the document line by line, making further changes of wording, but retaining the substantive amendments made in September. The final text of the *Declaration* and *Action plan* was thus the outcome of multiple interactions between a group of highly networked actors occupying strategic (but not central) positions in national health systems, professional bodies, and national and international organisations. In the course of those interactions, the participants collectively elaborated, negotiated and finally came to a working agreement on how best to articulate the knowledge that they embodied – including not just their knowledge of mental health research and policy, but also their lived experience of planning, providing and using mental health services. Played out in a series of meetings and other communications, the work of producing the *Declaration* and *Action plan* thus involved multiple inscriptions, enactments and re-inscriptions of that embodied knowledge.

Once the overall direction and content of the conference had become clear, the Steering Committee also set about commissioning and reviewing a series of working papers from authors in a range of countries, the purpose of which was to provide substantive detail about why the recommendations and aspirations laid out in the *Declaration* and *Action plan* were necessary, and how they might be fulfilled. The working papers were issued as background or briefing papers for conference participants, and were published in full in the conference report. The Steering Committee also commissioned and convened a series of developmental 'pre-conferences' at which members of other projects and organisations had the opportunity to present their respective knowledge of mental health policy and practice. The Steering Committee thus ensured that the presentation of the *Declaration* and *Action plan* at the Helsinki conference was backed up by a wealth of additional knowledge, inscribed in the working papers and enacted in the various pre-conferences, which reinforced the message of the *Declaration* and *Action plan* and the urgency of putting them into action.

The Steering Committee's strategy proved eminently successful. In effect, the proceedings of the Helsinki conference served to enact a wealth of knowledge. This included the embodied knowledge of the Steering Committee, as they oversaw the running of the conference, as well as that of the various conference speakers. But it also included, in the various presentations and discussion sessions, enactment of the knowledge inscribed in the working papers, the reports of the pre-conferences and, importantly, in WHO resolution EUR/RC53/R4 and, in turn, the various other policy documents that the resolution cited. The conference culminated in a final action to collectively endorse the *Declaration* and *Action plan*. In a signing ceremony that played out the formal and ceremonial procedures of the WHO and its partner organisations, the delegates enthusiastically added their names to the document, thereby lending their authority, if not their authorship, to the knowledge inscribed within it.

Putting the *Declaration* and *Action plan* into action

Getting the member states to sign up to the *Declaration* and *Action plan* was one thing; getting them to act on it was another. One step in that direction was the decision to undertake a 'baseline' study of mental health policy and provision in the various member states, against which progress in implementing the *Declaration* and *Action plan* could be measured. This initiative originated with WHO's Regional Adviser for Mental Health, Matt Muijen, who suggested it to Markos Kyprianou, the European Commission's Commissioner for Health and Consumer Protection, during one of their conversations at the Helsinki conference. The Commission subsequently provided a grant to fund WHO to undertake the study (interview 1, 18 November 2008). Here, again, the experienced public official's embodied knowledge of who to approach was crucial in getting this initiative off the ground.

The study itself involved the production and distribution of a new document – a detailed questionnaire that, in its final form, included 90 questions, covered approximately 1,000 variables and was nearly 50 pages long. The first draft of the questionnaire was produced by WHO's Regional Office for Europe, where officials were able to draw on long experience of undertaking similar surveys of mental health provision in different countries. The new questionnaire drew on earlier surveys, but was redesigned to reflect the structure of the *Declaration* and *Action plan* by asking "What is it [in those documents] that can be turned into a variable and to an indicator eventually?" (interview 2, 18 November 2008). After pre-testing in four countries – Belgium, Italy, Poland and the UK (England and Wales) – in October 2006, the draft questionnaire was presented to a consultative meeting in Vienna of WHO's mental health 'counterparts' – experts nominated by the ministers of health from each of the member countries to liaise with WHO's Regional Adviser for Mental Health. At that meeting, "We again had the text of the questionnaire on the big screen and went through it question by question, participants made comments that were added with track-changes and after the meeting, we produced an updated questionnaire incorporating the comments" (interview, 25 February 2009). Like the *Declaration* and *Action plan* before it, the questionnaire used in the baseline study thus incorporated elements drawn from previous inscriptions, revised in the light of WHO officials' embodied knowledge of how earlier instruments had been used and how they might be adapted to current needs, and in light of the detailed face-to-face interactions among a group of embodied experts over how the new questionnaire could be employed in their own countries. In effect, that knowledge was inscribed into the questionnaire, insofar as the questionnaire served to define what should be seen as constituting mental health provision, what more needed to be known about such provision in different countries and what parameters were to be used in collecting and reporting on it. Some questions were even added for which counterparts knew no data was available, on the grounds that:

> "we would like to put [these questions] in to mark the fact that we should have this information and we don't. It might be something that we have further on. But we would like it there for us to be able to officially say 'we don't know that'." (Interview 2, 18 November 2008)

As a knowledge instrument, the questionnaire was intended to assist not just in the production of new positive knowledge, but also in the identification of 'known unknowns'.

Once completed, the questionnaire was distributed among national coordinators – usually, the counterparts – within the member countries, who, in turn, distributed it to individuals charged with collecting the relevant data. The knowledge inscribed within the questionnaire thus travelled from the WHO offices to many different locations within Europe, to be put to use in the work of generating new knowledge of local mental health services. However, the WHO officers appreciated that dissemination of the questionnaire was not alone sufficient to ensure that the right data would be collected: the knowledge inscribed in the questionnaire could not, in itself, determine how that knowledge would be enacted locally in light of respondents' own embodied knowledge and interests. Consequently, the central research team were careful to cultivate personal relationships with those responsible for generating the data: "What we decided from the beginning was to have a very personal approach to each country, so we never sent an email starting 'Dear All...'" (interview 2, 18 November 2008). By such means, the researchers were able to motivate their respondents: "By discussing directly with each [region], they were more likely to get involved and collect the data" (interview 2, 18 November 2008). But, in addition, they were also able to coach their respondents in good data-collection practices. Data collection was "a partnership process" (WHO Europe, 2008, p 6), a "dialogue" (interview 2, 18 November 2008), in which respondents were asked to indicate their data sources, which were cross-checked with other secondary WHO and similar international sources, with discrepancies and outliers followed up. "As a side effect, some countries discovered how to collect data for themselves" (interview 2, 18 November 2008). In effect, by cultivating personal relationships with local respondents, the central researchers were also able to pass on something of their own embodied knowledge as to how to do research.

As respondents enacted that knowledge to complete the questionnaire, they generated a huge quantity of new knowledge of local mental health services, which they inscribed in the response documents they returned to the researchers. The researchers then had the task of consolidating the responses into a single final report on *Policies and practices for mental health in Europe* (WHO Europe, 2008). Here, too, the researchers' own embodied knowledge was vital: not just their formal knowledge of statistical and other analytical techniques, but also their understanding of the circumstances in which the data had been generated. They continued to interact with their respondents, drawing on their experience to challenge what they sometimes identified as anomalous returns, but also taking care to filter the data they used "based on what they felt was politically correct from [the country's] side" (interview 2, 18 November 2008). In so doing, they were also mindful of the uses to which the knowledge inscribed in their final report might be put: "[P]rofessionals can use that in the lobbying in the country with the decision makers in health" (interview 2, 18 November 2008). In effect, by taking the knowledge sent to them by local respondents, analysing it and re-inscribing it in a single synoptic document, the WHO researchers created yet more knowledge that could, in turn, be used in various policy actions in member countries.

Meanwhile, the *Declaration* and *Action plan* were being enacted in national policy in various member countries. In order to appreciate some of the processes involved in that enactment, it is convenient to take an illustrative example from a single national setting. In Chapter Eight of this volume, Bori Fernezelyi and Gábor Eröss examine the case of Hungary, one of a number of European countries that routinely contract so-called Biennial Collaborative Agreements with WHO. These Agreements specify what funding the country will receive from WHO and other sources and, in return, set national priorities for cooperation with WHO across the whole field of health policy, including specifying expected results. Prior to the inter-ministerial conference in Helsinki, mental health had rarely figured among Hungarian policy priorities. Following Helsinki and the signing and publication of the *Declaration* and *Action plan*, however, an agreement to produce a National Programme for Mental Health was written into the Biennial Collaborative Agreement between Hungary and WHO for 2006/07. The Agreement specified that the National Programme would be based on the priorities indicated in the *Declaration* and *Action plan*. But, as Fernezelyi and Eröss show, the way those priorities were subsequently interpreted was profoundly influenced by the politics of mental health within Hungary itself (see also Fernezelyi and Eröss, 2009).

Crucially, insofar as mental health figured at all in Hungarian health policy, it was dominated by psychiatrists, whose principal concern was to modernise and expand what they saw as the woefully inadequate provisions for institutional care of the mentally ill in their country. These predominantly psychiatric interests largely determined the way that the *Declaration* and *Action plan* were incorporated into national policy. Plans to formulate and implement a National Programme developed only slowly following the initial promise of the 2006/07 Biennial Agreement, and it was not until late 2008 that a full version of the National Programme was drawn up and put out for consultation, concluding with a consensus conference held in March 2009. The resulting National Programme document was heavily inflected by the knowledge and interests of its psychiatrist authors. The aims and methods inscribed in the WHO *Declaration* and *Action plan* clearly emphasised the importance of preventive and community-based mental health initiatives rather than the psychiatric treatment of the mentally ill. However, while the Hungarian document ostensibly addressed all the same topics and issues, it made only one explicit reference in more than a hundred pages to the *Declaration* and *Action plan*. Moreover, the whole emphasis of the Hungarian document was strikingly different from the WHO publications, overwhelmingly equating mental health provision with psychiatric care, and making only minimal reference to community-based services and the involvement of service user groups.

As this shift in priorities from the *Declaration* and *Action plan* to the Hungarian National Programme makes clear, the act of interpreting previous inscriptions in the light of local embodied knowledge is far from predetermined by the content of those inscriptions themselves. However carefully a document may be drafted, and however strictly the concepts it represents may be defined, the precise meaning of such a document will nonetheless always be open to multiple interpretations. Moreover, which of those interpretations ultimately prevails will depend upon negotiation and the exercise of political power. This was certainly the case with the Hungarian National Programme. While critics at the consensus conference objected that the overwhelmingly psychiatric understanding of mental health incorporated in the consultation document was distinctly partial, they were mostly persuaded that the Hungarian psychiatric services were in such a dire state of disorder, and funds for other kinds of initiatives were so limited, that the only thing to do was endorse the National Programme as it stood. In this instance, then, enactment of the *Declaration* and *Action plan*, and their re-inscription into the documents that defined a new national mental health programme, was profoundly informed by local politics, which ensured that a particular professional group was able to gain almost exclusive control over that enactment and to ensure that it conformed closely to their own knowledge and experience of mental health service provision, while remaining compatible with WHO terminology.

Embodied, inscribed and enacted knowledge in WHO

Our analysis of the events surround the drafting, endorsement and enactment of the WHO *Declaration* and *Action plan* endorses the view of WHO as an organisation whose activities depend fundamentally on its power to mobilise knowledge (Barnett and Finnemore, 1999). However, it conceives of that knowledge in a rather different way from previous commentators on international organisations, who have been concerned primarily with the mobilisation of technical evidence and information in policy. For one thing, it draws attention to the very different forms or phases of knowledge that are all equally crucial for WHO's activities. For another, it emphasises the dynamic processes by which that knowledge is transformed from one phase to another, in ways that sometimes serve to fix the meaning of that knowledge across time and space, but at other times lead to quite dramatic changes in meaning. Let us start by reviewing the different forms or phases of knowledge that figured in our narrative.

First, the knowledge embodied in a host of individual actors was plainly crucial both in the planning and achievement of the Helsinki conference and in the enactment of the *Declaration* and *Action plan*. This included factual knowledge of the incidence and burden of mental ill health and of the measures taken in different countries to prevent or treat it. But it also included know-how – for instance, how to organise a high-profile ministerial conference, how to legitimise action within the bureaucratic structures of WHO, or how to gather data – as well as knowledge of who was who in mental health and policy, and of what powers they possessed and what resources they could mobilise. Without such knowledge, the conference would never have got off the ground. This may seem like a trivial point: without embodied knowledge, *nothing* would ever happen. But it is one that often seems to be forgotten by those who seek to understand such sophisticated activities as policymaking and implementation. In fact, such apparently mundane knowledge as how to draft a minute of a meeting or whom to approach for funding may itself require a sophisticated understanding of the policy process, and may be crucial to the success or failure of that process.

Second, the story we told about mental health policy could not have happened without the knowledge inscribed in documents. Again, this plainly included factual knowledge of various kinds, inscribed in the research literature and in various WHO and other reports on mental health. But it also included knowledge relating to the policy process itself, regarding what had been decided, what was seen to be desirable or legitimate, and what might be achievable. Documents such as WHO resolution EUR/RC53/R4 and, indeed, the *Declaration* and *Action plan* itself played a vital role in the policy process by recording and communicating the outcomes of meetings and the decisions taken by WHO and other institutions. In this regard, their qualities as inscriptions were crucial for how they fulfilled that role. Unlike the embodied memories of those who had participated in the decision-making process, which were inevitably partial and fallible, documents possess a much greater degree of fixity, and can be more faithfully reproduced and disseminated. This makes them invaluable as a tool for coordinating action, be it within a single institution like WHO or across the much wider spread of national institutions and actors that WHO sought to influence. Documents such as the *Declaration* and *Action plan* provide a fixed point of reference against which subsequent actions can be compared. Moreover, such documents commonly refer to one another, both as a means of consolidating the legitimacy of the decision or actions they record, as we saw in the case of WHO resolution EUR/RC53/R4, and as a means of coordinating different kinds or areas of action. This has important implications for how we think of the relationship between documents and policy. WHO's emerging policy on mental health in Europe cannot be identified with any single document, even ones as pivotal as the *Declaration* and *Action plan*. Rather, insofar as that policy resides in inscriptions, it is to be found in the rhizomic interconnections of different documents and texts (Freeman et al, 2012).

Third, both embodied and inscribed knowledge became visible in our narrative chiefly when they were enacted – when they were expressed or mobilised in action, be it in speaking or writing or some other kind of action, such as running a conference. Our narrative spans a host of actions of one kind or another, all of them involving enactment of embodied knowledge and many also involving inscribed knowledge. Some of these were evidently the actions of individuals, for instance

Danzon's original decision to organise an inter-ministerial conference on mental health. But many of the actions that we describe were plainly collective and *interactive*. Meetings, especially, were crucial sites where many different kinds of embodied and inscribed knowledge were brought together and enacted in discussion and debate.

Such actions and interactions often, in turn, gave rise to new knowledge. Indeed, some actions were expressly conducted with the aim of generating new knowledge. The design and distribution of the baseline survey, and the work of data collection and analysis, involved the enactment of both embodied and inscribed knowledge for the purpose of producing systematic knowledge of mental health services across Europe. But other kinds of action, too, resulted in new knowledge, even if this was not explicitly recognised as an aim or an outcome. In particular, meetings and the discussions and negotiations that took place within them were often the site of new knowledge production. In the case of the Steering Committee convened to organise the Helsinki conference, for instance, members brought their own embodied knowledge – of mental health and policy, but also of how to organise effective intergovernmental meetings – to the meetings. They also drew heavily on examples, research findings, recommendations and so forth inscribed in previous documents. Perhaps most importantly, in the course of their meetings, they *enacted* their embodied knowledge and elements of the previously inscribed knowledge through speech and argumentation. As a result of these discussions, they developed a new, shared understanding of what the conference sought to achieve and how best to achieve it. This new knowledge, embodied in the Steering Committee members, could then be re-enacted in other places, including in other committees and ultimately in the running of the conference itself. Meetings could also result in new inscribed knowledge; indeed, in many cases, meetings were convened specifically for the purpose of inscribing or re-inscribing knowledge. This was the case, for instance, with the meetings convened to consider the various drafts of the *Declaration* and *Action plan*. These meetings were deliberately organised to provide an opportunity for service users, as well as mental health and policy specialists, to enact the very different kinds of experiential knowledge that they embodied. Following intense discussions, the new knowledge that emerged was ultimately enacted in the work of drawing up and agreeing a new, substantially revised version of the *Declaration* and *Action plan*, which would, in turn, become the basis of further discussion at the Helsinki conference and beyond.

It is worth stressing that the knowledge that actors brought to meetings, be it embodied or inscribed, rarely determined what went on in those meetings in any simple way. Meetings commonly involve arguments, contestations and negotiations, the course of which is often open-ended and unpredictable. To put it another way, the enactment of knowledge in meetings proceeds in interaction with other actors – inter-enactment, perhaps – with their own knowledge and their own aims and interests. Such collective enactment commonly involves an element of interpretation or recasting, the outcome of which may differ significantly from the knowledge with which the meeting started. Indeed, it is the very open-endedness of such interactions, and the possibility of unanticipated outcomes, that makes meetings such a powerful site for generating new knowledge, as we saw in the case of the redrafting of the *Declaration* and *Action plan*. Of course, not all meetings lead to novelty: the Helsinki conference, for instance, was convened not as an opportunity to contest or negotiate the knowledge inscribed in the *Declaration* and *Action plan*, but in order to enact official approval of that inscription. However, even then, the outcome was not preordained. In the event, the conference proceeded smoothly along its largely ceremonial course from opening presentations to official signing. That it did so was largely due to the organisers' knowledge, not just of mental health and policy, but also of how to organise a successful inter-ministerial conference, and how best to stage-manage the presentation of the knowledge embodied in selected actors and inscribed in supporting documents. Unlike the drafting meetings, the Helsinki conference was carefully organised so as to minimise the opportunities for interpreting the knowledge that went into it. That it succeeded is testimony to the organisers' own embodied knowledge of how to run a conference.

The importance of interpretation in the enactment of knowledge is particularly apparent if we consider the role of inscribed knowledge in the development of WHO policy on mental health. Earlier, we emphasised the importance of the fixity and stability of inscriptions such as documents, and particularly what this means for their usefulness as tools for coordinating action at a distance. However, we must also emphasise that while documents themselves may enjoy a high degree of stability and mobility, there remains considerable room for interpretation when those documents are used as a basis for action. Recall, for instance, the questionnaire drawn up for the purpose of conducting the 'baseline study' of mental health services across Europe. Despite the knowledge and care that went into compiling that questionnaire, it is clear that respondents in member countries often differed markedly in their own knowledge of how to use it as a tool for data collection. Consequently, careful oversight was necessary to ensure that respondents enacted the survey in ways that permitted a degree of comparison and generalisation across the region as a whole. In effect, the successful enactment of the baseline study was only made possible through continuous interaction between the survey's organisers, with their embodied knowledge of what the survey was meant to achieve, and the survey's respondents, with their own embodied knowledge of local circumstances.

The issue of interpretive flexibility is even more apparent when we consider how the recommendations inscribed in the *Declaration* and *Action plan* were enacted in Hungary. As we have seen, Hungarian actors acted on those recommendations in a way that departed significantly from the intentions of the original authors, by interpreting the call for new mental health initiatives as a call for improvements in psychiatric service provision. In this instance, while WHO action was sufficient to spur Hungarian policymakers into action, WHO officials were unable to enforce their own interpretation of the *Declaration* and *Action plan*, and had little choice but to accept a psychiatric appropriation of their own agenda. In summary, inscribed knowledge has only a limited power, in itself, to determine action. Rather, the enactment of inscribed knowledge necessarily involves embodied knowledge of how to interpret the relevant inscriptions. Moreover, that enactment commonly takes place in interaction with other actors, the outcome of which, like all interaction, is inherently under-determined and depends upon a host of factors, including, but not confined to, the knowledge that informs that interaction.

In conclusion, our study of the development of WHO policy on mental health enables us to make a number of points about how we should observe and think about the role of knowledge in policy. It makes clear the importance of embodied knowledge, including both factual knowledge and know-how, and underlines the key role of meetings as sites where actors can bring their embodied knowledge for enactment in debate and discussion. It makes clear the importance of inscribed knowledge, particularly policy documents, in providing a fixed point of reference for coordinating policy action among widely distributed policy actors. Above all, it makes clear the importance of enacted knowledge, not just as the means by which embodied and inscribed knowledge is realised in discourse and practice, but as an essentially open-ended interpretive process through which new knowledge, both embodied and inscribed, may be generated.

This brings us back to the point from which we started, namely, the observation by Barnett and Finnemore (1999, p 710) that the power of international policy organisations such as WHO flows from their ability to create, fix and diffuse knowledge. The story we have told in this chapter serves at once to endorse, but also to complicate, this observation. If policy is anything, it is the coordination of action. Plainly, both embodied and inscribed knowledge have an important role to play in the work of coordination. Inscribed knowledge, in particular, possesses the qualities of fixity and diffusibility that Barnett and Finnemore see as vital to securing such coordination. However, as we have seen, embodied and inscribed knowledge are not alone sufficient to ensure coordination, precisely because the way that they are enacted is always open to interpretation. Knowledge, be it embodied or inscribed, is a resource that may inform action but that does not determine it. Consequently, if we are to understand how action may be coordinated across time and space, we cannot attribute this to the effects of embodied and inscribed knowledge alone. Ultimately, the coordination of action by policy is achieved through the same social processes as lead to the coordination of everyday action, namely, through face-to-face interaction, negotiation, sanctioning and coercion, and through the willing or reluctant efforts of individuals to align themselves with what they take to be the intentions and expectations of others. Coordinated action is necessarily knowledgeable action; but it is also social action, and must be understood as such.

Note

[1] EUR/RC53/7: Provisional agenda item 6(a) 'Mental health in WHO's European region', Regional Committee for Europe, 53rd session, Vienna, 8–11 September 2003.

Part Two

Embodied, inscribed and enacted knowledges

FIVE

'We know who to talk to': embodied knowledge in England's Department of Health

Jo Maybin

Introduction

This chapter illuminates the significance and character of embodied knowledge in policymaking through a case study of work practices of civil servants in England's Department of Health (DH). It describes the distinctive importance of embodied knowledge to the ways in which civil servants construct understandings of the objects of national health policy, and the possibilities for their transformation. It sets out how civil servants identified to whom they should turn for knowledge, and offers an analysis of the in-practice principles guiding whose knowledge was permitted to contribute to policy formulation.

The second half of the chapter offers an account of the distinctive properties of embodied knowledge in this context, providing an analysis of why this form of knowledge was so appealing to the civil servants, as well as the ways in which embodied knowledge could prove problematic. The conclusion returns to the embodied–inscribed–enacted framework to argue that the strength of this heuristic for analysing policymaking in this context lies in the way in which it allows a foregrounding of embodied knowledge, together with a recognition of the primacy of interaction, or, more specifically, 'inter-enactment', for determining the significance and meaning of that knowledge in the case of any particular policy.

The analysis that follows draws on a case study of civil servants working in the Policy and Strategy Directorate of England's DH in 2010/11 (Maybin, 2012). The study is situated in a sub-field of interpretive policy analysis, which is concerned with understanding the work practices of policy actors (Wagenaar and Cook, 2003; Wagenaar, 2004; Colebatch, 2006; Colebatch et al, 2010; Freeman et al, 2011). It offers an ethnographic account of how knowledge was deployed in the everyday work practices of civil servants engaged in formulating high-profile national health policy in England. Data collection comprised 60 hours of interviews and meeting observations, together with documentary analysis.

The research focused on mid-ranking civil servants, who are often charged with leading on the formulation of policy documents, though it also included interviews with and observations of more junior and senior staff. The study included interviews with and observations of 'analyst' civil servants, who are trained in economics and statistics, as well as mainstream policymaking civil servants; sources given in footnotes in the following text distinguish between these two categories. In order to secure observation access to the DH, and to protect the identities of the participants, all references to individuals and to policy content that might identify actors have been removed from the data. In order to make quotes comprehensible, I have in some cases added equivalent phrases or names to replace those I have redacted; these are contained in square brackets.

The majority of the policies discussed in interviews and meetings were examples of what Page and Jenkins have termed policy 'production' work, which focuses on producing a draft statement or document as a one-off task (Page and Jenkins, 2005, p 60). A significant minority fell under the category of policy 'maintenance work', in which civil servants are 'making or recommending day-to-day decisions about how a particular scheme or set of institutions should be handled ... maintenance jobs have no end point' (Page and Jenkins, 2005, p 60). For further details on the case, and the study methodology, see Maybin (2012).

Overnight experts

When the civil servants in my study started work on a particular policy document or programme, they were typically entirely new to its subject area, and they were often moving between policy areas at least every one to two years. This was especially true of those on the fast-stream training programme, which institutionalises this type of regular and frequent movement between posts within the DH, but it was also the case for many of the mid-ranking civil servants I spoke to. For example, one mid-grade analyst, who had started as a fast-streamer, had been through six different postings within the DH in less than four years, working on a wide variety of different subject areas:

Interviewer: "I'm interested in some work that you did where you started on the topic or project area and you really knew nothing about it before you started. I don't know which of your experiences might be the best example of that?"

Respondent: "Almost all of them." (DH analyst, interview, 23 June 2011)

More junior staff members have the support of their senior colleagues when starting out on new topic areas, but mid-grade and more senior civil servants described having to very quickly take on the full responsibilities of a 'policy lead' on a subject to which they were often completely new: "[T]o be honest with you, when I moved to [this] post, it was straight in, you know I was kind of drafting submissions [to ministers] in the first week, so you really have to get your head around [the policy issue]" (DH policymaker, interview, 28 August 2011). Policy leads are positioned within the DH as in-house experts on their particular policy area, and many were aware of the tension between this positioning, and their relative lack of knowledge of an issue at the start of their postings. Although they treated their fellow policy leads as knowledgeable, when the question of their own expertise on a policy issue came up in interviews or the meetings I observed, the civil servants always found a way of distancing themselves from the term: "I just have to convince them that I'm an expert [*laughs*]" (DH policymaker, interview, 24 March 2011); "[us], the so-called policy experts in the area" (DH policymaker, interview, 4 August 2011); "I'm no expert on [this area]" (civil servant, field note, 10 May 2011); "You know, we are not experts in many technical areas, actually, in fact, it doesn't even have to be technical" (DH policymaker, interview, 4 August 2011).

The civil servants varied in the extent to which they found this positioning problematic, and in the strategies they adopted to manage the tension. But, crucially, all of the participants had confidence in their abilities to get hold of the relevant issue-specific knowledge that they did not themselves possess, and having these skills seemed more important to them than possessing that knowledge itself:

> "[O]ne of the nice things about the civil service is that actually the skills are more transferable than a lot of people recognise, quite frankly. They are transferable, and you get, you find yourself working on things that you think … 'I don't know anything about that', but it's not necessarily the knowledge base, because you can learn that … the skills are

fairly, as I said, transferable." (DH policymaker, interview, 28 August 2011)

People, more than paper

So, how did the civil servants learn about the policy issues they worked on? The principal forms in which knowledge about policy issues was mobilised in this context was through interactions with people, and through reading documents. As one civil servant put it: "[A]ll of my knowledge is the product of speaking to doctors and professors and academics and you know, reading, essentially" (DH analyst, interview, 23 June 2011).

People transpired to be the dominant source for this type of knowledge among the civil servants I spoke to. There were some exceptions to this, some participants (more often analysts than policymaking civil servants) liked to read themselves into a subject first, then go to speak to people. But for most others, when a civil servant needed to understand a new topic area, they would start and continue their knowledge development through relatively informal conversations with others. Here are some examples:

> "Like everything we do, it was sparked by government or others saying 'We should do something for [this social group]' or whoever. And our task is to think, what are the things you can do in order to do it? So, then you have discussions with [people from that group] and other [government] departments and build up the knowledge as you go along." (DH policymaker, interview, 24 March 2011)

Interviewer: "So when you were given this piece of work, how did you familiarise yourself with what the issues were, what needed to be done? What were the kinds of things you were reading, or people were you talking to?"

Respondent: "Well fairly early on we made a visit to [Liverpool] to see what was happening there and understand a bit about how things worked in [that part of] their hospital and how it worked in practice. Some discussions with other officials [in the DH] who had had some kind of involvement with the bits of work that had happened at an earlier stage. You know the fact that this guy [Joe Brown] in the South East had done some stuff on it meant that we, I think at a fairly early stage, had some kind of initial meeting with him." (DH policymaker, interview, 16 June 2011)

> "The first thing I did was ring all the big academics, because I'm interested in academia ... I spoke to a few people, finding out what's going on. I actually went to visit an amazing professor in [the west]." (DH policymaker, interview, 15 July 2010)

> "[T]his is a classic policy development role that I've not done before. So I am very terrified. Very much wanting to use all of my contacts, not only in the Department but also [from outside] to inform and build that thinking." (DH policymaker, interview, 15 July 2010)

This preference for engaging directly with individuals rather than texts, for drawing on embodied rather than inscribed knowledge, was exemplified in the civil servants' attitude to formal public consultation exercises as a knowledge source. Public consultations involve civil servants publishing a call for (usually written) responses to a series of questions about a policy in development, which generates responses from stakeholders, researchers and members of the public.

Such exercises were referred to by less than a third of the interviewees in their descriptions of policy development, and received only one mention in all of the meetings I observed. Those who did describe them presented them as a process that had to be completed, a hoop to be jumped through, rather than a source of insight or intelligence on the policy issue at hand. But while I saw no evidence of formal consultation exercises themselves having a significant impact on the content of policy, the civil servants did value the opportunity these exercises presented for identifying contacts that they could go to speak to about an issue, and for gaining a sense of the views and position of those contacts in advance of such conversations. For example:

> "I took the judgement that I didn't have enough time to go through the responses, and just used the Department's response [to the consultation responses received]. But I did search the originals from local authorities and PCTs [primary care trusts] or trusts to look for people we could contact." (DH policymaker, interview, 20 July 2010)

"So, if we want to win their hearts, bringing them into [this policy], we need to understand where they're coming from.... You can't enter into dialogue with any of these organisations or, indeed, any key stakeholders without understanding [laughs], you know, what are your issues?... [F]or me, the main bit was really to understand those who I was going to have to work with." (DH policymaker, interview, 4 August 2011)

In this way, formal consultations served as a prelude to informal consultation. This underlines the extent to which the civil servants felt that face-to-face interactions gave them more of what they needed than did written texts: they had a bespoke document from these respondents that (at least in theory) related to the particular issues and questions the civil servants were contending with, and yet the civil servants still wanted to go to speak to the respondents personally.

Which people?

People were thus a critical knowledge source for the civil servants. But which people? Who was seen as knowledgeable? Who was permitted to contribute their knowledge to policy development? And why were those particular groups and individuals consulted, and not others?

One of the most striking characteristics of the civil servants' work practices was the extent to which they drew on one another for their knowledge of policy issues. When I asked interviewees how they 'got up to speed' on new topic areas, they frequently referred to conversations with fellow team members and their immediate predecessor in a post. As their work progressed, they would draw on other policy leads or analysts in the DH who were either technically responsible for a particular policy area or who had developed expertise through past experience on the topic. I put this observation to a senior civil servant:

"[A]bsolutely, that's how the Department works, we know who to talk to. When I need to talk about, I don't know, heart disease, I don't go and think 'Who do I go to outside?', I go straight to the heart disease team. Mostly, 95% of the time, they will tell me what I need to know, the other 5%, they will go and access it for me. So that's the way it works, internal networks. But I think it's a really interesting observation, because we worry so much about where we get the expertise from and we probably worry too much

about that. You know, we have it, or we have access to it."
(DH policymaker, interview, 2 March 2011)

Internal policy leads, and individuals who had worked for some time on particular subjects, were treated as something like human filing cabinets on a topic; they were the first point of reference for knowledge on an issue. During meetings, when civil servants decided that they needed more knowledge on a particular area, rather than agreeing that one of them would read up on the issue, they would invariably decide to invite someone from the DH with the relevant responsibility or experience to contribute to the next meeting.

Policy leads would also be spoken about as if they were synonymous with their topic area. For example, in one meeting I observed, a participant mentioned a particular type of hospital and queried how it would relate to the issue in hand. A colleague replied, "that's not around this table" (field note, 25 January 2011). That phrase seemed to connote both that the policy lead for foundation trusts was not part of this particular working group, *and* that the policy area itself was not one that was an explicit part of the working group's remit or programme. In this way, the policy lead and the topic area for which they were responsible were sometimes talked about as one and the same thing. These practices stood in tension with the fact that policy leads were often relatively new to issues and recognised the lack of their own issue-specific expertise (as described earlier).

Although using internal colleagues as sources for such knowledge was very common, identifying these internal contacts who were not part of a particular policy team took work on the part of the civil servants, and involved drawing on informal peer networks. For example:

Interviewer: "In terms of internal people, how did you know who it was who had done stuff? How did you know who to go and ask?"

Respondent: "Erm ... that's probably quite a good question. I think that probably a fair bit of it relied on the recollection of particular individuals. So, like [my director] will remember having had quite a lot of involvement in [that type of] work generally.... So I think it was probably, probably just, I don't think it happened systematically that we were necessarily aware of what had taken place beforehand, just the links between different people. So I think because of the way the Department works, it's not likely that there would have been other bits of work going on that we would never have found out about ... but I suppose it's not impossible." (DH policymaker, interview, 16 June 2011)

Interviewer: "How did you know who to talk to?"

Respondent: "It was about, umm, kind of networking, so I tended to network through my analytical colleagues, who I have quite a wide sort of network of, to find out who the right people in policy to speak to are. So I kind of go a bit backwards, because policy leads would often speak to policy teams to find out who the analysts are, rather than vice versa.... So, then, that's how we sort of generated names [of policy leads]. And then where you, where we couldn't identify people through people that we knew, it was just a process of searching through, we have a big directory that gives people and their responsibilities." (DH analyst, interview, 23 June 2011)

> "I think in terms of some of the peer networks you have, it's kind of informal, so it will depend on whether you have links to other analysts and other policymakers in the Department whether you can actually get access to that [information] or not." (DH policymaker, interview, 2 March 2011)

As the second of these interviews suggests, there was a staff directory the participants might have used, and yet this was rarely mentioned, and when it was, it was seen as a last resort. More valuable was the embodied knowledge of colleagues about the embodied knowledge of other colleagues.

The participants were also regularly engaging with contacts from outside the DH to develop their understanding of issues. These included individuals from the following groups: professional representative or membership organisations, such as the British Medical Association (BMA), the Royal Colleges, the National Health Service (NHS) Confederation and the Local Government Association; academia; health policy think-tanks, such as the Nuffield Trust and The King's Fund; patient charities, such as Diabetes UK and Rethink; NHS staff, including GPs, hospital staff and commissioners; third-sector service provider organisations; DH-appointed clinical advisors; DH-appointed committees or working groups with a specific remit, or who provide a generic sounding board for policy development (these groups comprise individuals from a range of backgrounds, for example, in one case: "clinicians, a lawyer, ethicist, patient representatives, charity representatives" [DH policymaker, interview, 4 August 2011]); other government departments; and non-departmental public bodies, such as the health care quality regulator.

How and why did the civil servants turn to these groups, and select particular individuals within them to converse with? In a similar way to their identification of internal colleagues, the most common way of identifying or selecting people to speak to was by past personal contact, or 'contacts of contacts'. More senior interviewees, in particular, would describe, for example, personally knowing "some of the main authors" (DH policymaker, interview, 28 August 2010) of research papers as a result of their experience in that field, or being able to visit a particular type of hospital "through a friend" (DH analyst, interview, 2 March 2010). Most of the interviewees identified people through the recommendations of colleagues within the DH, and sometimes of other external contacts. The following account was typical:

> "I reckon actually usually it's a case of getting [contacts] from asking other people. Because it's the sort of whole six degrees of separation. It doesn't take many people – if there's someone worth talking to, someone will probably know. And that's the way I would do it. Always that. Which is basically just asking people, 'Who else might be good to talk to about this?' And there's obviously, cause there's a lot of people in DH who know, you know, people like [Dan Jones], just like knows pretty much everyone in [public health], you say 'I really need to talk to someone like this, who do you think might be a good idea?' And even if they're not the best people, they'll then be, you'll then speak to them and they'll say, 'Ah, who you should be really speaking to is …' So it's lots of, it's kind of personal contacts, I think." (DH analyst, interview, 15 July 2011)

In the meetings I observed, I saw first-hand this practice of sharing contacts:

Civil servant 1: "We've been down a number of blind alleys, this has taken us too long."

Civil servant 2: "Is there someone we should be bringing in too?"

Royal College representative: "Regulators, the HPC [Healthcare Professionals Council], their chief exec ... and head of legal ... and [a local part of the NHS]. I wouldn't speak to [X] because they're just a Quango [quasi-autonomous non-governmental organisation]." (Field note, 10 May 2011)

Charity director: "We're looking for guidance on who the key organisations are that we should be keeping in touch with. So we'd like input on that. We've got a list of third sector groups that we'll give you."

Civil servant: "Be really good to get that so that we can feed it in. We can probably add to it." (Field note, 11 May 2011)

Being well-connected, in the sense of having lots of contacts both within and outside the DH, was seen as a real asset in terms of career progression in the DH, and individuals described how they or colleagues had been moved on to particular projects because of the contacts they brought with them. An important part of the embodied knowledge civil servants brought to a project was knowing who the 'big names' and 'main players' are on some particular policy issue. Having the knowledge and skills to access appropriate embodied knowledge was a critical asset in this role. But what kinds of embodied knowledge were considered appropriate? How can we make sense of the ways in which the civil servants selected and identified some knowledgeable individuals and groups over others?

There are three sets of theoretical resources that can help us to understand the organisation of embodied knowledge in this context, relating to: civil servants' preference for 'cognitive proximity'; the potentially innovative information flows enabled by 'weak ties' with contacts of contacts; and the relationship between the influence and authority of an individual or group and the power of their knowledge claims.

Cognitive proximity

Why did the civil servants go to colleagues, or to contacts of colleagues, for their knowledge? Why was this type of proximity a criterion for selecting between potential knowledge sources? One possible explanation can be drawn from studies of organisational learning, which, building on Simon's (1955) concept of 'bounded rationality', emphasise the extent to which comprehensive information searches are time-consuming and costly. Authors in this field have described the tendency of organisation members to draw on what is familiar and cognitively (if not spatially) proximate, something Cyert and March (1992, p 61) referred to as 'local' rather than 'general' scanning.

More generally, theories of communication suggest that we find it easier to communicate with people who share similar frames of reference to us; in Basil Bernstein's (1971) terms, when the civil servants are conversing with one another, they can use 'restricted' language codes, which are relatively short and take for granted (and, indeed, remake) shared understandings and meanings about the world they reference. By contrast, when communicating with outsiders, the civil servants must be more explicit and detailed in their communication, using 'elaborated' codes that make it possible for the outsider to understand what it is that they are saying. There may be a sort of ease and efficiency in talking to colleagues who share a similar frame of reference that is absent in conversations with outsiders.

However, I would suggest that there is another, perhaps more foundational, reason for the civil servants selecting internal colleagues, and contacts-of-contacts, as sources: the importance of trust. During the development of policy, when civil servants work tirelessly to construct fragile coalitions of agreement around policy options (see Maybin, 2012, ch 6), the civil servants cannot share privileged information about policy in development with people who are minded to share the information they receive more widely, use the information themselves to damage the DH's reputation or sabotage the policy's progress. This trust is not assumed, but rather has to be earned. Being a close colleague with a shared interest in a policy's success and maintaining the DH's reputation, or being a contact of such a colleague, provides the civil servant with grounds for being able to speak openly with that person; hence the reliance on contacts of contacts for identifying outsiders to speak to.

Weak ties

Although the use of 'contacts of contacts' by the civil servants seemed, in one sense, to serve as a substitute for cognitive proximity and trust in the process of identifying sources of knowledge outside the DH, another way of looking at such relationships is as an example of 'weak ties', which, in fact, link civil servants to different and potentially innovative sources of information and knowledge (Granovetter, 1973, 1983). Writing in the 1970s on the diffusion of information through social networks, sociologist Mark Granovetter identified the 'strength' of particular kinds of so-called 'weak ties' for explaining the bridge between micro and macro social patterns of information-sharing.

In Granovetter's theory, the relative strength of a social tie is defined by: the amount of time two individuals spend in contact; the emotional intensity and mutual confiding involved in that contact; and the reciprocity of the services they offer to one another (Granovetter, 1973, p 1361). Strong ties tend to be concentrated within a group – if you have a strong link with an individual, they are likely to have strong links with others in your group – weak ties, on the other hand, 'are more likely to link members of *different* small groups' (Granovetter, 1973, p 1376, emphasis in original), with the advantage that those individuals 'are more likely to move in circles different from our own and will thus have access to information different from that which we receive' (Granovetter, 1973, p 1371). Particular weak ties provide 'bridges' across network segments (Granovetter, 1983, p 229); conversely, 'individuals with few weak ties will be deprived of information from distant parts of the social system and will be confined to the provincial news and views of close friends' (Granovetter, 1983, p 202).

Granovetter's account is a reminder of the way in which using a contact of a contact – or, at least, a contact of that contact of a contact – can, in fact, lead to conversations with people who are significantly removed from the world of the DH. This potentially opens up the kinds of knowledge, experience and mindsets that the civil servants are drawing upon to those beyond the immediate community of the DH. Significantly, weak ties are still *ties* of some form and they thus still offer the civil servants some grounds for trusting that their interlocutor will not use the information they share to sabotage policy formulation efforts. However, by definition, this trust is not as strong as it is with those with whom the civil servants have strong ties, principally, their close colleagues.

Authority and influence

Where the civil servants were not identifying potential interlocutors through the recommendations of colleagues, they were choosing them on the basis that they were a 'big name' and a 'major player' in a particular field. This seemed to refer to the extent to which an individual or group had the capacity to impact on the 'success' of a policy, both in terms of how it would be received and framed in public discourse, and in terms of supporting its implementation; hence the influence of large membership organisations such as the BMA. The knowledge claims of some individuals were also given credence on the ground that the individual was an authoritative voice on that topic. The claims put forward by such individuals or groups were considered worthy of attention by virtue of the authority of their holders. As one civil servant working on health policy in the Cabinet Office told me, "if someone is risk-averse, they will just use the ideas of those who are authoritative, the Le Grands" (Cabinet Office policymaker, interview, 16 November 2009) (the reference is to the London School of Economics and Political Science Professor Julian Le Grand, who had served as health adviser to the Blair administration).

The notion that the authority of knowledge might be tied up with its creator or promoter is well-established in the sociology of knowledge. Here is Pierre Bourdieu articulating this point:

> What creates the power of words and slogans ... is the belief in the legitimacy of words and of those who utter them. And words alone cannot create this belief.... In the struggle for the imposition of the legitimate vision of the social world, in which science itself is inevitably involved, agents wield a power which is proportional to their symbolic capital, that is, to the recognition they receive from a group. (Bourdieu, 1991, pp 170, 238)

This recognition of authority is also mutually reinforcing: when a civil servant draws on the ideas of a reputable academic to shape a policy, they are, in turn, strengthening that individual's claim to authority. Nigel Gilbert put forward a similar argument in a theorisation of referencing practices in papers for academic journals (Gilbert, 1977). In an article entitled 'Referencing as persuasion', Gilbert suggests that scientists include references in their articles to authoritative papers in their field because, 'inasmuch at this work has already been accepted a "valid science", it also provides a measure of persuasive support for the newly announced findings' (Gilbert, 1977, p 116); the author is 'trading on its acknowledged adequacy' (Gilbert, 1977, p 116). In turn, by including a reference to such a work, the present author 'can be seen to be making an assertion about his own opinion concerning the validity of the findings of the cited papers, and is thus contributing, albeit only in small measure, to the overall consensus of his research area' (Gilbert, 1977, p 117).

A similar phenomenon is identified by Katherine Smith in her study of the use of evidence by policymakers working on health inequality policies in England and Scotland (Smith, 2008). Smith draws on Latour and Woolgar's (1986) model of 'cycles of credit', in which the credibility of a scientist's ideas, and his or her ability to promote those ideas (eg in reputable journals), becomes bound up with their credibility as a scientist. The more the scientist is able to produce credible ideas and publicise them, the greater is his or her individual credibility and, hence, the likelihood that he or she will secure resources such as research funding, which enable the scientist to develop and publicise further ideas, and enhance his or her credibility.

It is notable that knowing how to seek out embodied knowledge was itself a form of collective, embodied know-how shared among the civil servants. It was nowhere written down, but was rather learnt through watching other civil servants at work, through sharing stories of past policy development and through *doing*: through being put in a situation in which the civil servants had to quickly grasp an appropriate foundation of knowledge on an issue.

Why people?

So, why were people such significant sources of knowledge in this context? What was it about embodied knowledge in particular that made it so appealing, or useful, to the civil servants? In the course of my study, I identified five key characteristics of the kinds of knowledge people bring that were particularly valuable to the civil servants. Embodied knowledge was distinctive and valuable because: it included accounts of how policies, systems and organisations work in practice; it appeared to be less censored than written accounts; it was often very current, while documents become dated almost as soon as they are published; it was synthesised, and editorialised, and drew upon years or decades of experience and accumulated knowledge; and it comprised different perspectives and mindsets that offered new ways of seeing issues. In the following sections, I elaborate on each of these claims, before identifying some of the disadvantages of embodied knowledge in this context.

How systems work in practice

In health services research, written descriptions of how policies, systems or organisations work in practice are hard to find, and where they do exist, they are almost always already out of date. Yet, understanding the practical mechanics of arrangements in the health and social care system seems vital to understanding, analysing and developing policy intended to improve its functioning. Descriptions of how someone with a particular kind of condition moves through different services, or how in practical terms the DH actually gets local NHS organisations to do things, or what hygiene rules mean for the routines of staff in hospitals are difficult to come by unless you can speak to people who have some kind of involvement in such processes.

The DH meetings I observed often involved presentations or descriptions by civil servants and outsiders that provided basic accounts of how particular services or organisational relationships work in practice. These would often simply be informal oral accounts, as the following excerpts from interviews indicate:

> "Sometimes, it's not the most senior people who can give you the best [information], you know, it's the people who know how it's done on the ground. So, you know, if you're trying to understand that.... So we did a visit to [Milton Keynes] as part of the [X policy], and it was talking to all the people who are managing [these] services. Actually, you wouldn't have got the same richness of understanding how the system works if you'd spoken to more senior staff." (DH analyst, interview, 15 July 2011)

> **Respondent:** "[this other government department] tend to not understand the distinction between the Department of Health and the NHS – they think that if they put a certain amount of pressure on a certain part of the Department of Health, or the Department of Health in general, that that would result in something happening in the NHS. That's not the case."

> **Interviewer:** "So, was part of what you were having to do at that meeting explaining how that relationship works?"

> **Respondent:** "Yeah – there was quite a lot of that, yeah." (DH policymaker, interview, 16 June 2011)

Where meeting participants were using PowerPoint presentations, these would invariably involve some kind of organigram, flow chart or other kind of diagram to describe the working of a service or a system. Of course, sharing such images does not require face-to-face interaction, but meetings seemed to be the place where they were displayed, perhaps because this enabled their creators to frame and caveat them as they saw necessary.

Less censored accounts

One of the strong appeals for civil servants of orally reported knowledge was that it seemed to them to be less censored than written accounts, to somehow be more *candid* and *real*. The civil servants themselves believed that they could elicit more open and honest responses from colleagues and outsiders through informal meetings, site visits and chats than they could through formal consultation exercises. Here are some examples:

> "And I think ... a lot of the time in health ... it's the things that people don't write down that are quite important. So, erm, because it's such a sort of thing about people, and the interaction between people.... And when people aren't, aren't [following some policy guidelines], they aren't necessarily going to sort of come back to consultation and tell you in writing why they wouldn't [follow them], because of course they're supposed to [be doing so].... I would almost characterise it as there's a verbal exchange of, you know, it's sort of, it's like having a verbal history that a lot of these things are passed on and people know about them but they don't necessarily write all of them down." (DH policymaker, interview, 11 August 2011)

> "And so doing something over a cup of coffee can be so much – because it's not something that's formal, you know, we have all of our formal routes and our governance processes and that stuff, but we don't have to formalise everything. So having a conversation with somebody to understand where they're coming from doesn't need to be a minuted meeting with a room booked. Actually, let's sit in the [café area], let's do that. And I think I get, I receive so much more from people that way, that's real, as opposed to it being something that's very guarded." (DH policymaker, interview, 28 August 2011)

> "I always find it quite helpful to meet people on a face-to-face basis at the outset as well, because I think it kind of gives you the opportunity to build up a more friendly working relationship, which certainly works better for me.... I think it gives you the opportunity to get more information as well out of them. I think if you reduce the formality, they tend to be more relaxed, they tend to be more open about

what's good, what's bad, what's working, what's not and so on." (DH analyst, interview, 27 July 2011)

In terms of my own search for knowledge about the practices of civil servants, I also felt that some of the conversations I witnessed in meeting observations (eg about the existence of bad practice or about internal tensions surrounding a policy's development) would never be committed to paper. Knowledge shared orally seems to be considered less *risky* than knowledge that is written down. Documents might get into the wrong hands, and oral reports can be more easily denied or reformulated.

Up to the minute

Another advantage of the knowledge that people bring is that it can be the most up-to-date account possible of some state of affairs. This is important to the civil servants who are devising programmes intended to act upon the world now and in the future, not on the world as it existed in the latest year for which published data or research are available. It is also particularly important in the context of a continually evolving policy and political environment, to which the civil servants must try to connect their particular area of policy responsibility in order to secure its currency and influence. When I asked interviewees about the purpose of a particular meeting or a series of meetings, updating one another on 'what's been happening' often featured in their responses, and in the meetings I observed, the civil servants would always give colleagues or external individuals accounts of the latest developments in policy formulation and implementation on their particular patch:

> "We're in a period of political turbulence and are currently having a pause in the legislation. There are four work-streams, one of which is being led by [X], who we all know.... The areas which look likely to change are around GP consortia's constitutions and Monitor's role. We're waiting with bated breath. The Bill has to pass this session if it is to get passed." (DH senior civil servant, field note, 10 May 2011)

> "There are some fairly existential discussions going on at the moment about whether the [new body will take on that particular function]. It seems inevitable that it will.... I'll actually be joining in some of that work, so I'll be able to

bring along more insights on what's happening next time."
(Civil servant, field note, 22 August 2011)

"So that's a very quick run-through of what's happening [in
our area] – in some cases, as we speak." (Civil servant from
another government department, field note, 26 July 2011)

"[W]hen we put the consultation together, one of the
almost stumbling blocks we had was how we fitted in with
the commissioning board in the future. That was being
developed as we were developing our consultation. So I
spoke to one person and they said, 'Yeah, it would be good
to speak to X,Y and Z'." (DH policymaker, interview, 16
May 2011)

Documents have the quality of being frozen in time; they cannot give
an indication to their reader of what may have changed since they
were written (or they can do so only in very vague terms) – people
are better placed to know what is happening *now*.

Synthesised and editorialised

A further advantage of seeking knowledge from people is that they
have already digested, synthesised and effectively editorialised what
may be years of accumulated experience and learning on an issue.
This was especially true of outside 'experts', but was also the case for
some internal colleagues who had worked on a topic for a number
of years. This digested knowledge represents an invaluable resource
for civil servants who are seeking to quickly understand an issue, to
identify its most significant themes, questions or tensions, and to do
so under considerable time pressure. The meetings I observed often
involved someone giving a one-line précis of entire bodies of research
or experience, for example:

"Research tells us that it's not [this group's] conditions that
are different but they have a different set of cultural needs.
And some want people [from their background to speak to]
and some don't." (Civil servant, field note, 11 May 2011)

These one- or two-liners had, in turn, been picked-up from interactions
with 'experts' in the field. This seemed to be a form of embodied
knowledge that became encapsulated into these phrases, which would

then be carried over to and repeated in other interactions. As a junior civil servant said to me at the end of a meeting involving experienced practitioners: "I just really hear things in meetings like that and then say them in other meetings where they seem relevant" (field note, 27 June 2011).

Perspectives and mindsets

Individuals were valued not only for the bodies of knowledge they carried, but also for their distinctive ways of seeing and thinking about issues. These mindsets, or perspectives, seemed to be the product of a combination of a particular educational background, a particular professional experience and/or belonging to a social group, with an associated identity and life experience. They ranged from critical thinking skills grounded in logic, to seeing questions from the viewpoint of protecting or furthering the interests of a particular group. Here are some examples:

> "The benefit of [you] being in the room is that you've got a unique perspective that's different to the mental health perspective, and that's the value of what's in this room." (Chair, field note, 27 June 2011)

> "So, the brief I was given was … 'We want you to bring [this particular] lens to all of the policy thinking'. … So very much trying to tease out from [this outside group] what they might be able to help with and contribute to this process. Because they look at this stuff very much through – 'We want [X] in our communities, so therefore what's [this] strategy going to give us towards that?' So that's very much about getting external insight into my thinking as well." (DH policymaker, interview, 28 August 2011)

> "I think we've got a lot of pretty motivated people [in our team] who are intelligent and are capable of thinking things through quite critically, quite honestly, quite openly and then passing that on. Which I quite like because I struggle with … people who don't challenge stuff, or don't have the capability or don't display the capability for critical thought on things and I think that's something that's good in our team at the moment. It's very rare that you will say something and it will just be let go because people are either

too apathetic to disagree with it or whatever it might be."
(DH analyst, interview, 27 July 2011)

"What we are bringing [to the policy team] is a set of perspectives, questions and possible answers, as well as a body of research knowledge." (DH policymaker, interview, 15 September 2010)

Although these various quotations refer to very different forms of knowledge, what links them is that they provide distinctive ways of appraising proposals.

The civil servants valued interacting directly with individuals in possession of these bodies of knowledge, critical thinking skills and distinctive perspectives, so that the insights they gave could be applied specifically to the particular questions and issues that they were engaged with. In this context, there is something important about the act of *interaction*, in combination with the qualities of embodied knowledge and the particular perspective or 'thinking skills' that individuals may bring to such conversations. I take up this point in the conclusion.

Problems with embodied knowledge

While embodied knowledge was highly valued and relied upon by policymakers in this context, it did also have distinctive disadvantages over other knowledge forms. As Freeman and Sturdy identify in Chapter One, first and foremost is the problem of people moving on. Individuals leave project teams, or organisations, and take their embodied knowledge with them. This was a particular issue for the DH at the time of my field research, as concurrent government programmes to reduce overall public spending and to reduce the role of the DH in running the health service had instigated a significant restructuring of the DH, including plans to reduce its size (Department of Health, 2010; HM Government, 2010). A voluntary redundancy programme was already in operation during my fieldwork, and participants were starting to feel the absence of knowledgeable colleagues. For example:

"[T]here are people in my team for example who left in March. And I think we probably do get a bit, you know, there were handover notes and things like that, but definitely a lot of the knowledge and experience is kind of, sometimes, just is lost when it happens, certainly, or you don't think

very much about the transfer." (DH policymaker, interview,
16 June 2011)

Interviewer: "That's all my questions. I don't know if there's
anything else you want to say to me, if you've felt, 'She should
really understand X if what she's interested in is knowledge and
how it works in the Department'."

Respondent: "I think maybe the knowledge management
thing is the trickiest to get your head around because it is, we're
constantly told it's really important, especially as people are leaving
as they are at the moment. You know about the admin-funded
and programme-funded workers and that sort of thing. And
there's people also going on voluntary severance schemes as well.
So when they leave, they obviously take some knowledge with
them. And if you haven't got that, or they've filed it in a strange
way, then you almost have to start again, which is no good for
anybody and is a waste of money." (DH policymaker, interview,
16 May 2011)

> "When stuff comes in from [this academic] say, on mental
> health, I don't know how to interrogate it, so I take it to
> [James] in mental health. But [James's] job isn't going to be
> there anymore, so I don't know what I'll do then [*shrugs*]."
> (DH policymaker, interview, 24 March 2011)

Echoing the way in which the internal staff directory was a last resort
when seeking out a particular internal contact, handover notes and
the electronic knowledge management systems holding archives of
notes and correspondence were seen as inadequate by comparison
with being able to access a person, and their embodied knowledge. But
such inscriptions had a stable presence and longevity, characteristics
that could not be guaranteed by their embodied counterparts.

A further potential weakness of embodied knowledge related to its
authority. While this form of knowledge was highly influential in the
development of civil servants' understandings of policy issues and the
subsequent shape of policy content, it could only be used to account
for or *justify* policy development where its holder was seen to be
sufficiently authoritative, and often where their knowledge had been
somewhere inscribed in a text that could be referenced. Embodied
knowledge was persuasive when encountered first-hand, shaping how
the civil servants came to understand a policy issue (and hence also

the possibilities for its transformation). But when it came to building a robust case for a policy, which might survive scrutiny by parliament, the media and external stakeholders, the civil servants would marshal only the claims of authoritative individuals and, more commonly, authoritative forms of inscription, including cost–benefit analyses and evidence from large-scale academic research projects.

Giandomenico Majone's account of 'evidence' as information or data that is marshalled by analysts to explain or defend courses of action as reasonable is apposite here (Majone, 1989). Majone emphasises the role of argument and persuasion in decision-making, and defines rationality 'not in instrumental terms, but as the ability to provide acceptable reasons for one's choices and actions' (Majone, 1989, p 23). That the grounds for justifying a decision might be different to the way in which the decision was reached (a distinction between knowledge for 'discovery' and knowledge for 'justification') is, according to Majone, entirely reasonable and, indeed, in keeping with knowledge practices in that bastion of rational inquiry, the natural sciences. In this context, embodied knowledge was powerful for 'discovery', but less so when it came to 'justification'.

Conclusion: embodied knowledge and 'inter-enactment'

Embodied knowledge about policy issues was highly valued and relied upon by the civil servants in this case study. This suggests that in order to understand the knowledge that is reviewed and enrolled in the formulation of any particular policy, researchers would do well to start with examining who civil servants are speaking to in the course of their daily work. The civil servants' practice of identifying these individuals via contacts of contacts itself relied on the embodied knowledge of colleagues, and, more abstractly, upon their own and their colleagues' shared embodied *know-how* (Ryle, 1949) about what makes for an appropriate embodied knowledge source in this context.

However, collating information on which individuals were consulted by policymakers in some particular case, and why, can only take us so far in understanding how that embodied knowledge informed the development of policy. As Freeman and Sturdy describe in Chapter One, embodied knowledge is necessarily indefinite, and undetermined; in their terms, it 'must be enacted to be realised'. A clear finding from my own case study, which echoes the conclusions of reviews of the evidence-based policymaking literature (Innvær et al, 2002; Hanney et al, 2003; Nutley et al, 2007), was that *the* most important form of enactment of embodied knowledge took the form of *interactions* between civil servants and their colleagues and outside interlocutors. This is not the only form that enactment of embodied knowledge might take: the civil servants might have spent their time listening to talks or lectures, or reading transcripts of oral evidence to parliamentary committees. However, instead, they sought out meetings, chats, catch-ups and site visits.

The critical advantage of interaction as a means of realising embodied knowledge in this context was that it was a form of *inter-enactment*: it enabled the bringing together of some individual's embodied knowledge about a particular policy issue with the civil servants' own knowledge about the requirements of the policy formulation process. The function of the interaction was in enabling this first form of knowledge to be re-rendered in terms that served, or could be made to fit with, a proposal that was considered viable in *policy* terms. In this context, in order for a policy proposal to succeed, to be made to happen, it had to be coherent with other government policies, with the minister's preferences and with the views of powerful stakeholders (see Maybin, 2012, ch 6). When the civil servants spoke to others to learn about a policy issue, they were not only trying to develop an understanding of an issue, but also to rework this understanding in terms that enabled a policy proposal to meet those in-practice requirements for success.

Thus, the strength of Freeman and Sturdy's triptych in supporting an analysis of this case is in enabling both a centring of the importance of embodied knowledge to the ways in which civil servants learnt about policy issues, *and* a recognition of the importance of enactment, and, in particular, *inter*-enactment, to making sense of the ways in which knowledge is woven into policy.

SIX

Reconstructing school inspectorates in Europe: the role of inscribed knowledge

Sotiria Grek

Introduction

Although education in Europe has always 'travelled' (Lawn and Grek, 2012), until recently, school inspectors were firmly rooted in particular national contexts, and derived clout from their local and authoritative standing as education 'connoisseurs'; their embodied expertise in making evaluative judgements on the quality of schooling is perhaps the best example of such knowledge in the field of education. However, this seems to be rapidly changing; inspectors are not alone any more:

> Inspectorates are today only one among many institutions and organisations that produce evaluative material on schools, teaching and learning. The place, role and status of inspectorates can no longer be taken for granted. The quality of their products and services will increasingly be compared with other sources and could be challenged by other evaluators.... Like all public services, external evaluation of schools will increasingly be challenged to show its value for education and for society at large. Failing this challenge will endanger the future of inspectorates, as they will be failing to deliver the information and analyses that our societies need.[1]

Indeed, recent decades have seen a transformation of school inspectorates and inspection regimes in Europe, from professional dominance based on expert connoisseurship, to a much less certain position in a world of competing agencies and new challenges on what inspection is expected to achieve. So, how have inspectorates adapted to this new situation in such a way as effectively to consolidate their position in this new state of affairs? In order to answer this question, I examine why European inspectors are leaving their local 'knowns' and are now voluntarily and actively looking into new 'unknowns'. The chapter focuses on the role of documents, through the close examination of the influential school self-evaluation policy that was first developed in Scotland and then subsequently travelled to a number of European and other countries. The chapter will give particular attention to the role of the 'How good is our school?' (HMIE, 2007a) document as the main instrument both for the establishment of quality indicators for the measurement of school performance and as an evaluation toolkit that was to be taken up by other countries almost intact (eg the German version 'Wie gut ist unsere Schule?' [Stern and Döbrich, 1999]).

The chapter argues that the tripartite schema of embodied, inscribed and enacted knowledge is particularly useful in relation to the study of international policy communities, their formation and their workings, as it signals a new level of 'political work' (Smith, 2009): that of exporting, internationalising and then importing afresh one's local/national knowledge once it has successfully gone through the international 'test' and is therefore still relevant and future-proof. This is exemplified well through the Scottish self-evaluation policy, which has travelled and travelled again during the last decade in Europe (Jones and Alexiadou, 2001; Ozga and Jones, 2006), as we will see later. Despite the self-proclaimed developmental and bottom-up approach declared by the Scottish Inspectorate when it first introduced the policy in the early 1990s, self-evaluation was only successful and, in fact, realisable through the pertinence and dominance of the inscribed knowledge that exemplified it – that is, the 'How good is your school' document and all its different versions that followed its initial publication in 1992. To a large extent, and as I will show further later, self-evaluation travelled precisely due to the fact that it came with a very prescriptive and clear manual – a document. This is because instead of the complexities, nuances and implicit meanings of expert judgement – almost exclusively the mode of inspection in the past – inscriptions, especially in the form of data, indicators and benchmarking, are highly explicit and, hence, portable. However, before we move into detail on the role of the text, it is important to offer a brief historical excursus on school inspections, their function and their role.

'I speak for myself alone': inspection as a historic and contemporary function

Initially invented by European states in the 19th century, inspection aimed at enabling surveillance and control of sites and practices of a public nature; the school, the prison, the factory and other public institutions had to somehow be governed from a distance. Inspectorates became the means for governments to achieve this indirectly and from the centre, and, therefore, according to Clarke, inspectors came to represent:

> a form of embodied expertise, with powers of access to otherwise closed settings (whether the prison or the school), and a responsibility to report publicly on their findings. Inspection is then, from the outset, a very particular form of governmental practice, involving distinctive boundary crossing powers, based on a conception of expert observation and inquiry, and discharging defined sets of public responsibilities through investigations and reports. (Clarke, 2011, pp 1–2)

Interestingly, inspectors represented state power, yet had to be independent; hence their continuous branding as Her/His Majesty's Inspectors. Independence related to their ability to offer expert judgement in regard to the quality of the education system, a system that was heavily stratified in most European countries into an elite secondary school education and a mass primary education. Having no other method of knowing and controlling the system, inspectorates represented the means for its oversight, which 'relied on a strong collegiate tradition and shared experience (as well as internal guidelines) to achieve reliability and common practice' (Maclure, 1998, pp 21–2).

White, suited, middle-aged men in their majority, and protected by their club-like separateness and 'independence', inspectors were able to mediate between institutions, from the school, to the local authority and the ministry (Lawn, 2011). Their power did not derive from the limited number of standard observations they made; on the contrary, most of their work relied on their expert judgement and experience: 'I can comment formally upon any breach of the regulations concerning such matters as opening or closing, registers, the premises, or the holding of religious instruction; but beyond this *I speak for myself alone*' (Allen, 1960, p 237, emphasis added).

For most of the 20th century, inspectorates continued with their independent mission to know and control schools; they brokered this knowledge through notes, files, reports and letters (Allen, 1960), and the main tools of their craft were judgement, comparison and experience. Increasingly, they found themselves advising on government policy; in fact, they became an important node in its production, being involved through an advisory role all the way from planning to implementation.

In the UK, a change to their influence and role started to slowly occur around the late 1980s/1990s when, for the first time, voices against their established and well-recognised position began emerging: on the basis of what evidence were they judging schools? The rise of the evidence-based policy paradigm meant that inspectors had to face the new reality of measuring and evaluating education performance; this was now to be done through the production of data. Statistics and numbers, examination test results, as well as other quantitative and qualitative data – required to be collected by all schools – were added to their toolkit. In what was slowly emerging as the audit state of the late 1990s/early 2000s, 'performance' became the new way for New Public Management (NPM) to name the problems of control at a distance and the proposed solutions to them. Following Clarke (2008), NPM involves 'the cult of efficiency' in which market mechanisms displace the state, services are outsourced to hybrid public–private organisations and responsibility for self-management, choice-making and the management of risk is increasingly devolved to individuals and families and away from state institutions. Good management – following best practice – is assumed to follow from these developments, but there are problems of coordination and control, and also of rising expectations (Clarke, 2008). These problems are partly addressed by data use (Grek et al, 2009) and through the repertoire of evaluation and accountability mechanisms and agencies that has developed since the 1980s, and which is often termed NPM.

The nature of NPM has changed over time, but one of its essential characteristics is its development from private sector models and assumptions, especially those promoting the auditing of performance and ensuring the use of explicit formal measurable standards of performance and success, along with a preoccupation with managing risk (Lapsley, 2009). NPM thus translates quality into measurable, statistical and standards-based systems of measurement that are installed in advance of the activities that they measure: they set the parameters within which such processes may unfold. NPM has increased scrutiny of public sector delivery through increased inspection, audit and regulation in order to embed performance management within the public sector.

As a result, inspection moved centre stage again, albeit with a renewed mandate: to assure that schools were improving their performance and that, at any given time, they had the numbers and spreadsheets to prove it. While schools became more and more capable and expert at evaluating themselves, the inspector's role was one of externally evaluating and, in many cases, simply validating the schools' own audits.

However, one size does not fit all – the English experience has been different from the Scottish, and the latter also different from those of other nations. The question that arises is: how have inspectorates managed to retain and, if anything, consolidate their role in this new policy environment? Since 'speaking for themselves alone' seems to be insufficient, inspectors needed to speak with one voice. However, before they achieved that, they would have to speak to one another; self-evaluation became the primary means through which European inspectors met and began to collaborate. The next section will discuss what self-evaluation is, its beginnings and more recent developments.

School self-evaluation and the role of inscriptions

Given this context, School Self Evaluation (SSE) represents an element of a larger policy paradigm shift. SSE is about creating a school evaluation framework that claims to bring about constant comparison and improvement, broadly focusing on answering two key questions about educational practice: (1) 'How good are we now?' – in order to identify strengths and development needs in key aspects of teachers' work and the impact it has on learners; and (2) 'How good can we be?' – in order to set priorities for improvement.

As a key text makes clear, the shift in responsibility is reliant on, and produces, a holistic approach to evidence and learning: 'schools are not islands. They work with other schools, colleges, employers and a number of other services' (HMIE, 2007a, p 55). SSE is used as a tool to encode school knowledge, create consensus and promote specific values that relate to the creation of self-managed and self-sufficient individuals (both teachers and pupils). In other words, as schools learn self-evaluation, so they are asked more and more to do it themselves. The coding enables this shift and apparent 'light touch', while co-opting schools further into the new networks of knowledge production. Furthermore, as schools do more, they produce more and more new knowledge about themselves, which becomes productive for the constant improvement not only of the individual school, but for the governing of the system as a whole. But how is this achieved?

'How good is our school?' (HGIOS) (HMIE, 2007a) is the key text that guides and promotes self-evaluation practices. It is based on a quality framework for self-evaluation common to all public services, which seeks to support the integration of knowledge across different services; in effect, HGIOS is a long list of quality and performance indicators that schools are asked to consider (indeed, *have to* follow) when they do their self-evaluation and, crucially, when they fill in their self-evaluation forms to be inspected and checked by Her Majesty's Inspectorate of Education (HMIE). The Scottish school national quality assurance and school development system is based on a combination of inspection of schools by the HMIE and self-evaluation by schools using the HGIOS quality indicators (HMIE, 2007a). HGIOS was developed by the HMIE, which, in turn, is responsible for monitoring the HGIOS quality framework that encourages schools to develop and use their own knowledge about themselves to conduct ongoing self-monitoring and self-evaluation, leading to school improvement. Inspectors are, then, key actors in both the development and close monitoring of the self-evaluation agenda, as well as its reform – HGIOS, as the bible of self-evaluation, is the product of the Scottish inspectorate, which found in it a solid basis on which to adapt its role and function within a largely hostile evidence-based policy world in which their own subjective connoisseurship seemed quite dated and obscure. In effect, the inspectors have retained their role in the process by taking responsibility for the business of inscription. The school inspection framework, along with schools' self-evaluation, is designed to provide the Scottish government with reliable data about the health and performance of the sector, as well as to inform policy development. Moreover, as suggested earlier, the self-evaluation approach is designed to change the culture of schools as organisations, by committing them to constant knowledge production from which they and the wider system can – indeed, must – learn.

Changes in 2008 to the school inspection regime followed on from the introduction of a new version of HGIOS in autumn 2007. 'How good are we now?' (HMIE, 2007b) is the updated version of 'How good is our school?'. A key change in inspection that has supported the growth of self-evaluation has been a move away from the use of attainment data along with inspection visits and towards the use of the self-evaluation/self-monitoring processes that are now a constant requirement on schools. This shift emphasises the schools' responsibility for their ongoing quality monitoring, evaluating and reporting processes. This is a shift that is intended to signal a move away from 'hard' governance towards a softer, more attractive approach that draws participants in (Lawn, 2006). Schools are discursively constructed as learning organisations, where teachers and school leaders are responsible for constant self-monitoring and self-evaluation and for improving their school's performance and attainment levels for learners within the context of responding to the ever-changing and complex demands of their communities and society. The quality framework documented in HGIOS and used by both the inspectors and schools extends the scope of assessment and evaluation so that the interrelationship of different aspects of a school's provision is highlighted. This more holistic view of school performance includes different kinds of knowledge gained from learners, staff, parents and community surveys. As a consequence, organisational managers and members are expected to identify and act on dissonant knowledge that highlights a lack of shared meaning or knowledge across the organisation: all aspects of the knowledge production process have to be brought into alignment, they need to play their part in constructing a seamless narrative and they need to be seen to be guiding action. The inspection element requires schools and teachers to demonstrate how this knowledge has changed their practice for the better.

The self-evaluation process asks schools to evaluate their performance in terms of impact and outcomes and to identify priorities for action leading to improvements and innovation. The quality framework in HGIOS includes a revised set of quality indicators that guide the process of self-evaluation. There are three key domains against which schools must assess their performance: (1) successes and achievements; (2) the work and life of the school; and (3) vision and leadership. The next section provides a closer look at HGIOS as the key inscription that attempts to marry the knowledge claims of a governance system that promotes bottom-up evaluation with the requirement of adherence to external benchmarks and indicators (albeit in reduced numbers).

The role of inscriptions: 'How good is our school?'

As indicated earlier, self-evaluation in schools is synonymous with the HGIOS framework, which was first established in 1992 and most recently updated in 2007. Schools are required to use the 'quality indicators' outlined in HGIOS in order to describe, quantify and measure their performance, which is to then be externally judged on a regular basis through inspections of schools carried out by HMIE. The definition of 'quality indicators' by HMIE effectively defines what should be regarded as 'quality' in education. Thus, the HMIE is able to define what is evaluated – and therefore what is valued in education.

Here, rather than look at previous versions of HGIOS, we focus on an examination of the most recent one in 2007, which reflects 'the developing context' of recent policy developments, such as the 'Curriculum for Excellence' (Scottish Government Curriculum Review Group, 2004), as well as the Scottish Executive's vision statement for Scotland's children (Scottish Executive, 2006). From the Foreword, it is made clear that the focus is now on impacts and outcomes, as 'self-evaluation is not an end in itself. It is worthwhile only if it leads to improvements in the educational experiences and outcomes for children and young people, and to the maintenance of the highest standards where these already exist' (HMIE, 2007a, p 2). It is not a policy that is meant merely for internal implementation; it has an international dimension, as, according to the Senior Chief Inspector, it builds on good practice within and outside Scottish borders. It comes as part of a wider framework, the so-called 'Journey to Excellence', and provides 'sets of tools which can be used to bring about continuous improvement in learning' (HMIE, 2007a, p 2). Therefore, although schools are encouraged not to use the framework of quality indicators as 'checklists or recipes', the idea of offering teachers specific tools for evaluation is well-embedded in the policy culture surrounding the self-evaluation movement in Scotland. The quality indicators become tools for pedagogic practice since they provide teachers with a new language, a new framework of what is to take place in the classroom; evidence of its impact can then be produced and communicated at any point – the need to always be ready to be accountable is also emphasised. In fact, the significance and reach of the quality indicators is meant to be far wider than the classroom. According to HGIOS, and as we have already discussed in our previous work on integrated children's services in Scotland (Grek et al, 2009):

> Schools and pre-school centres are now part of a wider partnership of professionals, all of whom deliver a range of services to children. This edition of 'How Good is Our School?', therefore, has evolved by adopting a framework for self-evaluation common to all public services and structured around six questions which are important for any service to answer. (HMIE, 2007a, p 3)

This is particularly important as it highlights the ways in which a policy instrument like HGIOS, initially created to produce specific knowledge about school effectiveness, is now to be used across a range of 'services' for children and young people – effectively, self-evaluation has become the key policy regime for accountability across public services in Scotland.

HGIOS heralds new ways of working for teachers, where teamwork and peer review are an important aspect of becoming a reflective practitioner; it recommends that all staff engage in professional discussion and reflection based on 'shared understanding of quality and a shared vision of their aims for young people' (HMIE, 2007a, p 3). Self-evaluation is the new professional practice that needs to be part of the working practices of all staff, leaders and teachers alike – it becomes the major vehicle for learning and teaching: 'self-evaluation becomes a reflective professional process which helps schools get to know themselves well, identify their agenda for improvement and promote well-considered innovation' (HMIE, 2007a, p 3).

HGIOS and self-evaluation more generally, then, are not only of interest as a significant policy shift in terms of the assessment of school effectiveness, but also indicate a new relationship between knowledge and schools as educational establishments. Ultimately, self-evaluation as a governing regime replaces discussions of pedagogy and epistemology in schools with a new focus, that of a continuous self-awareness of weaknesses and strengths and a disposition towards constant comparison and improvement. This is systematically promoted through all HGIOS publications; words starting with 'improve' are to be found in 189 instances in the 2007 HGIOS text, a 57-page document where at least half of the pages are images. This emphasis on self-awareness and continuous improvement of oneself signals a new emphasis on the relationship between knowledge and schools. Schools are not to be viewed as beacons of wisdom and enlightenment, as older value systems described them, where knowledge could be externally viewed as something that lies 'out there' waiting to be found and explored: rather, knowledge becomes more of an internal process of 'self-awareness', self-management and self-improvement. That self-evaluation is not simply a self-assessment exercise for teachers, but increasingly a way of being for all, pupils, parents and teachers alike, is documented in HGIOS. It is a moment of transformation of inscribed into embodied knowledge: 'The evaluative activities involved [in HGIOS] are similar to those which we encourage pupils to engage in as part of their own learning process. Taking part in them creates a community of learners' (HMIE, 2007a, p 7).

Indeed, self-evaluation is promoted as a professional process that should not be mechanistic or bureaucratic – it is a guide to practice, 'alongside other sources of guidance such as curriculum advice, research into learning and pedagogy and studies of leadership styles and approaches' (HMIE, 2007a, p 6). In terms of its specific characteristics, HGIOS argues that teachers need to be 'forward-looking' and 'promote well-considered innovation', as well as 'peer evaluation' (HMIE, 2007a, p 7). In particular, teachers are asked to be active in:

- commenting on each other's work, for example plans and assessments;
- engaging in cooperative teaching and discussion; and
- visiting each other's classroom to see how particular developments are going, to experience different methods of teaching or to confirm our views of learners' progress. (HMIE, 2007a, p 7)

Teachers are asked to organise their work and gather evidence (so that nothing 'slips through the net' [HMIE, 2007a, p 8]) in order to always be in a position to answer the questions laid out in Figure 6.1.

Figure 6.1: The 'How good is our school?' framework

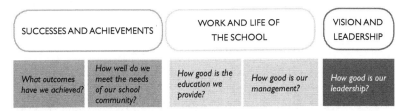

Source: HMIE, 2007a, p 14

Gathering evidence is a continuous task – a task which has to be central in all aspects of school life; teachers have to gather evidence through observation as they teach, and they have to gather evidence when they mark coursework. They gather evidence through test results and they also gather evidence on school trips; they take notes and they take photos. They count and they sketch; they share notes and they exchange them. Above all, evidence has to be accounted for; it has to exist either on paper or in electronic form; it has to be traceable and it has to be available constantly. In the new inspection framework, inspection is not a one-off event; it is a continuous process of self-assessment and audit. According to the HGIOS framework, this approach allows for celebrating best practice, or, in the case of weaknesses, these 'can be tracked down by focusing on some of the indicators' (HMIE, 2007a, p 15). This approach is called a 'proportionate approach', since it 'enables you to focus on areas of priority rather than routinely covering all aspects of the school's work in turn' (HMIE, 2007a, p 15).

There are 30 quality indicators under the following headings:

- Key performance outcomes
- Impact on learners
- Impact on staff
- Impact on the community
- Delivery of education
- Policy development and planning
- Management and support of staff
- Partnership and resources
- Leadership
- Capacity for improvement (HMIE, 2007a).

The self-evaluation procedure set out in HGIOS requires schools to look at each aspect of provision and ask: how are we doing? How do we know? What are we going to do now? For each indicator, the school is expected to gather evidence in order to evaluate performance on a six-point scale, from 1 (unsatisfactory) to 6 (excellent). A range of relevant themes are developed for each indicator and its key features, as well as 'illustrations' of what a level 5 (very good) evaluation would be, as well as level 2 (weak).

Again, as discussed earlier, the focus is on how well 'the school knows itself'; strong emphasis in the level 5 illustration is on 'improvement', whereas at level 2, lack of consensus, teamwork and rigour of data are seen as detrimental to effective self-evaluation. In terms of what kinds of information teachers need to gather, what is proposed is a 'triangulation' of quantitative data with people's views and direct observation (see Figure 6.2).

The role of the HMIE is central here; they are the ones who prescribe what kinds of knowledge has to be collected and documented and they are also the ones who have the authority to either validate a school's self-evaluation report or question it – if the latter is the case, then further inscriptions are required and further controls are put in place.

Figure 6.2: Using indicators and sources of evidence

Source: HMIE (2007a, p 12).

Travelling texts: 'How good is our school?' and the Standing International Conference of Inspectorates

An interesting element of the SSE approach is the way in which it is presented as essentially 'Scottish': as somehow encapsulating elements of Scottish practices and approaches that reflect particular choices and priorities. In this sense, it is referencing a hinterland of supposedly shared purposes that may derive ultimately from principles of the Scottish Enlightenment and from Calvinistic Protestantism. By this, it assumes that improvement through self-knowledge and effort is both possible and desirable – indeed, self-improvement is a duty.

This branding of SSE as the 'Scottish approach' has undoubtedly helped in its rapid take-up within and beyond Scotland, as it has been successfully exported to many other European countries (including England), which are looking to Scotland for examples of how to train more 'self-aware' and thus self-managed teachers. Inscriptions are, then, particularly important in terms of policy learning and 'externalisation'; when becoming international, policies return home reinvigorated, more widely accepted and unquestioned than ever before (Steiner-Khamsi, 2002). In other words, the scrutiny of scrutiny at the level of the international is what makes a policy shift solid and impervious to resistance or doubt. Hence, apart from achieving international prestige and recognition (and policy elites like the HMIE are always in need of these kinds of power displays), previous knowledge and policy constellations become far easier to mould and recast into new relationships and valued/devalued knowledge forms. Through the systematic efforts of the key knowledge actors – the Scottish Inspectorate – revised and improved versions of the self-evaluation policy paradigm point towards further refinement of the tools and show the intricate ways in which new knowledge categories and processes of knowledge production begin to matter, especially at times of financial crisis and shrinking budgets in the public sector. This is largely exemplified through the increased involvement of Scottish inspectors with a European association of inspectors, the Standing International Conference of Inspectorates (SICI).

SICI serves as a forum for exchanging experience in relation to inspection systems and wider education issues across Europe. Initially founded as the 'Conference of School Inspectorates in Europe' by the Organisation for Economic Co-operation and Development (OECD) at the instigation of the Netherlands in 1985, quality assurance and evaluation have been of prime interest to the organisation from its launch. In 1997, Douglas A. Osler, then Her Majesty's Senior Chief Inspector (HMSCI), was elected President of SICI; during his time, SICI grew through the organisation of workshops, the development of a descriptive study on the supervision and inspection of schools in Europe, the compiling of a critical analysis of school inspection in Europe, and the instigation of mutual projects based on joint visits or joint inspections. Osler, in his speech at the International SICI Congress in Utrecht in 2000, spoke about 'The future of school inspectorates in the 21st century', stressing the need to focus on continuous improvement for the first time. According to Osler, 'it is not sufficient in terms of school inspection just to write a report – it is also necessary to supplement each and every evaluation with a proposal for improvement'.[2]

Since 1995, SICI has been involved in a number of interesting studies and exchanges of expertise in inspectorates across Europe. In this chapter, the focus is mainly on SICI's work in relation to the concept of self-evaluation and the role that Scottish actors played in the development of the project, in an attempt to map some of the interactions between the national context and European developments. In particular, the 'Effective School Self-Evaluation' (ESSE) project has been one of the most significant projects SICI has undertaken. Funded by the European Commission (Socrates 6.1), the ESSE project ran for two years (2001–03) and had the following aims:

- identify key indicators for evaluating the effectiveness of school self-evaluation;
- develop a methodology for inspecting school self-evaluation;
- identify the weaknesses of school self-evaluation across countries and regions;

- produce an analysis of how self-evaluation and external evaluation can most effectively be combined; and
- produce case studies of effective self-evaluation in practice.

Thirteen European countries and regions took part in the project, which comprised mainly a questionnaire survey, as well as documentation and personal contacts. The combined use of these sources led to the development of a draft case study for each participating region, which was later sent to the respondents in order to check the accuracy of the information supplied. The questionnaire dealt with a series of issues such as: the statutory position of self-evaluation in the different countries/regions; benchmarking; indicators, standards, criteria and conceptual frameworks to evaluate the quality of school self-evaluation; stakeholders in the school self-evaluation process; the role of the inspectorate; external inspection of the quality and effectiveness of the schools self-evaluation process; and other similar areas (European Commission–SICI, 2001).

Chris Webb, from HMIE in Scotland, was the manager of the project. According to Erik Nexelmann, the Head of Division in the Danish Ministry of Education, the SICI ESSE workshop in Copenhagen in 2005 was a 'milestone in the ESSE project'.[3] Webb stated that the project took its starting point in the European Union's strategic target for 2010 to be the most competitive, dynamic and knowledge-based economy in the world. According to Webb, this target required a modernisation of education systems in Europe; it called for inspectorates across Europe to play a role in encouraging transparency, quality evaluation and self-evaluation. Webb also stressed that 'school self-evaluation does not exist in a vacuum, but in a context where external support and benchmarks are important'.[4] For Webb, this external support can be found in the form of statistical data for comparison, sets of quality standards and training in self-evaluation methods. Webb characterised schools with 'high capacity' as those that promote leadership, reflective and systematic self-evaluation, and systematic tracking and evaluation of pupils' progress. Finally, the ESSE project manager stressed the need for balance between self-evaluation and external evaluation, 'to prevent schools ... resorting to self-delusion'.[5]

The final report from the project outlines the 'ESSE framework', which provides the rationale behind self-evaluation and sets out the quality indicators, which range from level 4 (very good) to level 1 (unsatisfactory). These indicators are applied in what are described as the following 'key areas':

- Key Area 1 – Vision and strategy
  - QI 1.1 Aims and values
  - QI 1.2 Strategy and policy for self-evaluation and improvement
- Key Area 2 – Evaluation and improvement of key inputs
  - QI 2.1 Staff/human resources
- Key Area 3 – Evaluation and improvement of key processes
  - QI 3.1 Policies, guidelines and standards
  - QI 3.2 Planning and implementation of self-evaluation activities
  - QI 3.3 Planning and implementation of action for improvement
- Key Area 4 – Evaluation and impact on outcomes
  - QI 4.1 Evaluation and improvement of key outcomes
  - QI 4.2 Impact of self-evaluation on improving key outcomes

The report provides guidelines for conducting evaluation visits using the framework of quality indicators, explores the balance between internal and external evaluation, and contains country reports that set out the strengths in self-evaluation in the countries/regions that participated in the project. Finally, the report features case studies of effective school self-evaluation.

The Scottish contribution to the ESSE project has been crucial. This is not only to be seen in the similarities of the recommendations of the final project report with quality indicators set in the HGIOS reports, but, crucially, through the personal contacts and travelling of ideas and people from Scotland to the other participating countries. According to a Scottish policy actor describing the position of Scotland within the European education space, and specifically in relation to the concept of self-evaluation:

> "Well, we feed back to people. We find a lot of the time we are … this sounds slightly odd, but we're actually giving more than we're necessarily taking out. Partly because of the sort of area of work in which we are … particularly with the accession nations that we're actually, in a sense, ahead of the game in Scotland … we have, for instance, presented on what we do in Scotland. And that's caused considerable interest and they've come back to us and asked for more.… Well on the entire self-evaluation system in Scotland.… So how, you know, how inspection fits with evaluation. Some of these countries have inspectorates, some don't. So they're always interested in that relationship. They're interested in what the expectations of schools are." (Interview, 10 March 2010)

Apart from the informal contacts and exchanges, there was evidence of more formalised, contractual 'consultancy' work, through which Scotland has been spreading the 'self-evaluation' word around in Europe:

> "There is a lot of ... European links. And, for instance, and the visits to Scotland and the relationship will be of a number of different kinds. Some will be straightforward. A contract between us and, say, Malta and the Czech Republic to provide various services which involves staff development training." (Interview, 10 March 2010)

In relation to the role of inscribed knowledge, a senior inspector discussed the persuasive power of the HGIOS text:

> "I think the thing that attracted so much attention to the system here was just the way that HGIOS was produced as a very – school-focused, schools found it easy to use, accessible, written-for-schools system – an easy way of capturing data – and so HGIOS has been very much discussed and the momentum often translated – whereas other inspectorates – and, you know, in England – have tended to produce things that were written as inspection guidelines." (Interview, 25 February 2010)

Discussion

This chapter has discussed the self-evaluation policy and its instrument, HGIOS, as a means of encoding school knowledge, creating 'compatibilities' – in this case, a shared 'project' of self-improvement – and promoting self-managed and self-sufficient individuals (both teachers and pupils) in a decentralised, inclusive system. In other words, schools and their teachers and pupils become members of learning organisations, embedded within the larger learning organisation of the local authority and of government itself. The coding of knowledge through inscriptions enables flows of knowledge within and across new networks of knowledge production. Furthermore, as schools and learners do more, they produce more and more new knowledge about themselves, which produces the constant improvement not only of the individual school, but also of the governing of the system as a whole.

Although data are crucial to the new governance, and reconstitute knowledge in governing form, the 'data dream' of infinite interoperability is disrupted by incompatibilities, by the inert mass of accumulated information and by the continued need for processes of brokering and translation of knowledge into action. The development of self-evaluation may be understood as an attempt to address these problems, as well as the immediate financial crisis, by enrolling communities of practice in processes of constructing compatibilities through an emphasis on learning and self-evaluation. Further, the rise of knowledge-based professions and the brokering of knowledge by knowledge managers – in this case, the HMIE – are both central in the development of knowledge-based governance.

As a result, inscriptions, in the form of manuals for assessing perceived quality, have been a major force in the reconfiguring of school inspections in Europe during the last decade through the work of the Scottish inspectorate and of the SICI. In the introduction, I explained why European inspectorates are increasingly faced with new challenges that, in some ways, not only question their traditional authority in delivering school assessment, but also sometimes threaten them by rendering them obsolete. On the one hand, they are faced with increasing school autonomy in relation to schools' own evaluation of learning and teaching, with schools (at least in some contexts) enquiring about the extent to which the inspection process offers anything more than a disruption to the life of the school. On the other, due to the proliferation of data (produced by other actors and 'centres of calculation') and the broadening of learning lifelong and life-wide, they themselves increasingly need to appear fresh, cutting-edge and outward-looking. In addition, as already suggested, working in new neo-liberal or quasi-market contexts, they are not the sole providers of data and expertise to governments anymore, while they are faced with the novel challenge of working for a new clientele, parents, as well as demanding and knowledgeable school governors who demand their expert help. Therefore, this chapter focused on how previously powerful, largely disconnected policy communities now need to come together to redefine and modernise what they do – and, above all, protect their internal, local standing by seeking support and ideas externally. If inspectors have traditionally been the embodiment of external control in the life of the school, inscribed and encoded comparative data now have an important bearing on the ways that inspections are being enacted.

However, in what more detailed ways has the embodied, inscribed, enacted knowledge schema been helpful in analysing this reconstruction of inspectors as professionals? The chapter argues that it has been particularly useful as a heuristic tool for locating, analysing and explaining the transformations of the knowledge manifested through the rise of self-evaluation policy in Scotland and its subsequent travel to multiple other European countries. First, the chapter discussed how the previous embodied knowledge of the classroom connoisseurs began to be questioned: either directly, through cost-cutting exercises, or indirectly, through the emergence of the evidence-based policy paradigm and new practices such as the Open Method of Coordination. Data, indicators and benchmarks, as systematically collected through instruments like HGIOS, brought with them not only a large number of new actors expert in applying them to educational settings, but also a new logic – that judgement from now on would only be one aspect of the evaluative activity and that it had to be founded on some kind of standardisation or other. Mode-2 knowledge production (Gibbons et al, 1994; Nowotny et al, 2001) describes fluid and networked knowledge systems, through which knowledge, when inscribed and encoded, can travel. European inspectors quickly needed to come to terms with this new condition, and so they did. Inscribed knowledge became very important in their efforts to create a common language, and HGIOS quickly became the vehicle and the language of translation and communication. At the same time, the international stage on which these processes took place became important – the notion of 'Europe' offers these policy communities a degree of meaning and solidarity that is vital in encounters between complete (and powerful) strangers.

Indeed, the examination of the case of HGIOS presents an argument for the role of inscriptions in the governing of the European education space and attempts to offer a way of approaching Europeanisation in education through the lens of data production and flows. Any extension of the scope and scale of the central monitoring and soft governance of European education systems is predicated on standardised, mobile knowledge; that is, on inscription. That was as true of the nationalisation of education as it is of its Europeanisation. The work and role of the Scottish inspectorate is a telling example (and certainly one of many) of the ways that the incessant production of inscribed data is now used to collect and monitor performance in education. It is part of a larger argument which suggests that these inscriptions, and the preoccupation with quality assurance and evaluation that drives their production and use, can be understood as a form of 'fabrication' of European education and, indeed, as the principal form of its governance. As Ozga et al (2011) have discussed, regulation in late-modern society is so complex that it is no longer possible for the nation-state to govern without producing a number of counterproductive effects (Pierre and Peters, 2005). The nation-state often copes with its lack of capacity for governing by introducing indirect regulation and seeking a coordinating rather than direct regulating role. Underscoring this ambiguity in the actions of the nation-state, Sassen (2007) writes that nation-states participate in setting up new frameworks sustaining globalisation while these frameworks destabilise the nation-state's governing capacity. SICI, and more generally the increased inclination of inspectorates in Europe to work together and share knowledge and practices, is a representation of this; the engagement with the global, in this case, 'Europe', requires the new construction of an 'imposed consensus' entailing 'specific types of actual work, not merely decision-making' (Sassen, 2007, p 37). The construction of indicators, tests and manuals for inspections and the collection and processing of these inscribed data are examples of 'actual' work that builds this kind of agreed, yet imposed, consensus.

This, as we have seen earlier, is demanding work, requiring constant attention and effort to build and maintain new relationships, with struggles and dissent around the meaning of data always possible. Inscriptions exist within a growing mass of accumulated information in different forms, and from different sources that are not always compatible or standardised. As Porter (1995, p 29) has pointed out, 'there is a strong incentive to prefer precise and standardizable measures to highly accurate ones. For most purposes, accuracy is meaningless if the same operations and measurements cannot be performed at other sites'. Porter continues to suggest that this is particularly the case when the measures are going to be put to work outside the statistical or scientific community, for example, as in policy work. The political use of numbers, Porter adds, 'creates and can be compared with norms, which are amongst the gentlest and yet most persuasive forms of power in modern democracies' (Porter, 1995, p 45). Furthermore, if the numbers are accepted as valid, and, here, 'technologies of trust' operate because of the role of experts in the construction of statistical indicators, then, as Porter (1995, p 45) argues, 'the measures succeed by giving direction to the very activities that are being measured'.

To conclude, this chapter set out to explore the ways that inscriptions, collectively produced, are operating to shape and influence policy in European education systems. This raises interesting issues about the relative openness or receptiveness of these systems to the combined effects of data production and transnational networking in promoting new forms of governance of education in Europe. It showed how inspectors downplayed – or at least encoded – their own embodied knowledge in favour of producing standards (the HGIOS quality indicators) on the basis of which schools were asked to collect and report on the gathered intelligence about more or less all aspects of school life. Inspectors then made two more important moves: first, building on the basis of their former status and authority, they secured their position as the only ones able to validate or reject the school's self-reported and self-presented reality; and, second, they took SSE to the international stage only to bring it back home much stronger than ever before. The making of standardised knowledge through collectively inscribing data was crucial to both these moves. Since the processes that create indicators and rankings are characterised as 'technical' or 'scientific', they represent what Latour and Woolgar (1979, p 51) have called an inscription device, which constitutes that which it purports to represent. Inscriptions thus become 'a rhetorical technique for "black boxing" – that is to say, rendering invisible and hence incontestable – the complex array of judgements and decisions that go into a measurement, a scale, a number' (Rose, 1999, p 208).

Acknowledgements

This chapter was developed in the course of the KNOWandPOL project (see Preface), but some of its data is also derived from the ESRC (Economic and Social Research Council) research project 'Governing by inspection: school inspection and education governance in England, Scotland and Sweden'. Many thanks to colleagues contributing to the discussions around this chapter, and especially Professors Jenny Ozga and Martin Lawn.

Notes

[1] *SICI Newsletter*, no 30, December 2004, p 18.

[2] *SICI Newsletter*, 2000. Available at: http://www.sici-inspectorates.org/ww/en/pub/sici/publication/ newsletter_archive.htm (accessed 23 June 2008).

[3] 'SICI Workshop on Effective School Self-Evaluation (ESSE) – report of the SICI Workshop held in Copenhagen, 20–21 January 2005'. Available at: http://www.sici-inspectorates.org/ww/en/pub/sici/publication/workshop_reports_sihce_2006.htm

[4] 'SICI Workshop on Effective School Self-Evaluation (ESSE) – report of the SICI Workshop held in Copenhagen, 20–21 January 2005'. Available at: http://www.sici-inspectorates.org/ww/en/pub/sici/publication/workshop_reports_since_2006.htm

[5] 'SICI Workshop on Effective School Self-Evaluation (ESSE) – report of the SICI Workshop held in Copenhagen, 20–21 January 2005'. Available at: http://www.sici-inspectorates.org/ww/en/pub/sici/publication/workshop_reports_since_2006.htm

SEVEN

Enacting knowledge in a European project

Maria José dos Santos Freitas

Introduction

We live in a world where both policy and practice increasingly transcend boundaries well beyond those imposed by geography and national borders: a world of cross-national partnerships, projects and plans. In this world, European Union (EU)-funded collaborations (EU projects) go beyond incorporating policy partners and local policy actions in project design: EU projects are primary sites for generating knowledge that informs the EU policy process. But what happens when people get together to work together on an EU project? How do they *know* what to do? The answer to this question is that *they do not know*. Any proposal, agreement or contract that brings people together provides nothing more than an opportunity for negotiation – an opportunity for enactment. This chapter is about enacting such an opportunity in a research-oriented EU project.

People in a newly established EU project may be surprised to find out that what they have set out to do is from the outset undetermined, or fuzzy at best. The uneasiness arising from *not knowing* is common, and is tackled by adapting to the idea that they still have to *create their knowing together.* An EU project comes alive when its partners begin to translate the project's design from formally written words into concrete human actions. In other words, partners become knowledgeable about their project by collectively engaging in sense-making interaction. It is through interaction that the enactment of available knowledge takes place. In this sense, the project is not the knowledge people bring to it, but the knowledge they, as partners, 'enact' or 'perform' or 'practice' or 'do' within and throughout the project. It takes partners months and years of joint meetings, debates, readings, writings and emails to grasp the building process inherent in the knowing endeavour. Their project *becomes* the words repeated in joint conversations, the opinions expressed by the partners involved in discussions, the shared views articulated in collaborative texts. In this way, a project is a generative space in which people with diverse background 'knowledges' get an opportunity to build a way of doing things together over time and space; ultimately, they *become* a group, as their knowledges become collective knowledge.

We are only beginning to learn about the social and cultural processes that shape EU projects – the same processes that construct the shared meanings that make the EU's structures and activities possible in the first place. Our conventional understanding of bureaucracy (Weber, 1947 [1924]; Morgan, 2007) might lead us to think of participation in a EU project as something clear, well-ordered, grand and, not least, prestigious, as a locus of advanced public policy and scientific knowledge generation. While this view may have some merit, it is also a source of frustration for inexperienced partners and veterans alike, if and when their ordinary assumptions about knowledge and organisation are undermined (interview, 6 July 2009; field notes, 18 January 2010; interview, 20 April 2012). My contribution to the account of knowledge explored in this book is to present an empirical illustration of knowledge not as an object, but as a practice created in interactive social processes. Those interested in issues of knowing in practice – or enactment – note specifically how difficult it is to 'see' social constructions as they happen (Sandelands and Srivatsan, 1993; Yanow, 2000), and this is what I want to articulate: the collective construction of knowing as it unfolds. The term 'collective construction of knowing' implies an unfolding of knowing – a process, a knowing of a particular sort – a creative, dynamic, provisional and situated knowing. It also picks up on the learning that emerges through identity-building in participation (Lave and Wenger, 1991), which is made possible through social interaction.

Cook and Brown (1999, p 383, emphasis added) suggest neatly that 'for human groups, the source of new knowledge and knowing lies in the use of *knowledge as a tool for knowing* within situated interaction with the social and physical world'. This chapter offers an in-depth account of how social actors (EU project partners) enact knowledge (following the project design) by interacting in a situated context (a three-year project in different transnational settings) to generate new knowledge (in documents and practices). I show how the social and cultural processes in which learning takes place not only shape the generation of new knowledge, but also create particular knowledge practices (Lave and Wenger, 1991; Schön and Rein, 1994). My task, then, is to puzzle out the enactment of a single project in a research programme and, in doing so, to highlight the constructed character of knowledge: in situated action *enacted* together by people. For 'It is the job of social scientists to find out just how members accomplish phenomena we routinely gloss as "practice" or "an organization"; and the pivotal question asked – always – is, "How is this done?"' (Miettinen et al, 2009, p 8).

Knowledge as social practice

My conceptualisation of knowledge as social, (inter)active, process-oriented and situated (Brown and Duguid, 1991; Blackler, 1995) challenges rationalist notions of knowledge as something individual, static and acquired (Nonaka, 1994; Grant, 1996). My perspective also advances a practice-based view of knowledge (Miettinen et al, 2009), whereby knowledge and knowing are embodied in social practice (Higgins and Mirza, 2012). Practices like having meetings, planning activities, making agreements and developing a report are produced in a continuous flow of collective human action and behaviour developed through negotiation and renegotiation by those who participate in them; these practices form the building blocks for learning (Gherardi et al, 1998). In exploring them, I make use of the literature that explores knowing, learning and practice in organisations (Gherardi and Nicolini, 2003), which is founded on social-constructionist notions of knowledge as a process of formation and transformation of ideas, methods and ways of doing through human action in particular social environments.

The view of organisations as processes or systems of meaning (Weick, 1969) that give form and character to collective human interaction makes it possible to address questions concerning practice: how different understandings of practice are translated into meaningful forms of interaction. Most of the conventional literature in organisational studies investigates knowledge from an individual and cognitive perspective, but there are some who have taken a view of learning and knowing as a collective process, including Brown and Duguid (2001), Gherardi and Nicolini (2003), Schatzki (2006), Wenger (1997) and Yanow and Tsoukas (2009). Their work develops a practice-based perspective on knowing and learning in organisations that is being taken up more and more by scholars representing an array of academic and practice backgrounds and who share social-constructionist assumptions about knowledge:

> [For these authors] organizational knowledge cannot be conceived as a mental substance residing in members' heads; it can instead be viewed as a form of distributed social expertise: that is, knowledge-in-practice situated in the

> historical, socio-material, and cultural context in which it
> occurs. (Gherardi and Nicolini, 2003, p 205)

For Brown and Duguid (2001), organisational learning is not only socially constructed, but also greatly improvisational, while the learning involved in acquiring organisational knowledge also includes a social process of identity formation. This suggests that each knowledge-generating activity can produce different outcomes that channel further action, reflecting the roles that different actors take and how they contribute to the situation. Although learning is an activity commonly attributed to individuals, Cook and Yanow (1993) argue that the concept of culture helps us to understand that an organisation as a whole can be said to learn. They use the vivid examples of playing in a basketball team, performing as part of a symphony orchestra and crafting classical flutes to ask how an organisation learns 'to do what it does, where what it learns is possessed not by individual members of the organization but by the aggregate itself' (Cook and Yanow, 1993, p 378). In doing so, they draw attention to culture as a group attribute of 'values, beliefs, and feelings together with the artifacts of their expression and transmission, that are created, inherited, shared and transmitted within one group of people and that, in part, distinguish that group from others' (Cook and Yanow, 1993, pp 378–9). This perspective returns to an exploration of how a group of people, which can be seen as an organisation in a broad sense, acts together to learn what is required to produce something together.

The generation of new knowledge, then, is not the isolated application of techniques or the product of some innate quality, but an interactive process of people talking, exchanging, clarifying, synthesising and creating in a social context.

An EU project

This chapter uses material from an empirical study of the members of an EU project that received funding through the European Commission's Seventh Framework Programme (FP7, 2007–13). The project was a transnational, collaborative research project of scientists, technicians and networkers from 10 organisations in four EU member states (the Netherlands, Italy, Bulgaria and the UK), in which each organisation contributed a specific kind of expertise (see Table 7.1). The project set out to bring together people from the scientific and technological development communities working on sanitation to study knowledge brokerage on sustainable development in sanitation – across countries and across disciplines. Some of the scientific partners had expertise in knowledge brokerage, and some were experienced in issues of sanitation.

Table 7.1: EU project partner organisations

	10 organisations with three kinds of expertise		
Four countries	*Scientific*	*Technical*	*Networking*
The Netherlands	1. A university research department	6. A water company	9. An international water association
Italy	2. A research centre (non-profit) 3. A national research council (public)	7. A municipality	10. A section of the Council of European Municipalities and Regions
Bulgaria	4. An independent research centre (NGO)	8. A municipal water supply and sanitation company	
United Kingdom	5. A university research department		

In comparison with other EU projects, this one could be classed as a small project as it involved only four countries – but it was not small in terms of its social make-up. The scientists and technicians included social scientists with different academic backgrounds in sociology, physics, science, technology and society (STS), information science, water, and spatial engineering and statistics. Taken together, group members comprised university-based academics, private and public sector researchers, politicians, civil servants, water company and water policy professionals, project managers, technical engineers, biologists, doctors and public administrators, men, women, Southern Europeans, Eastern Europeans, Western Europeans, young academics, old-world professors, experienced EU project participants, and new EU project participants. It was this combination of people with all these available *knowledges* – fuelled by distinctive national and personal histories – which came together to create new knowledge through the project.

The very origin of this project exemplifies the social processes and improvisation involved in its construction. More specifically, it was made by and between people in discussion over time, rather than appearing fully formed by one person all at once. The project's topic emerged more than a year prior to its formal start. It started with an idea from someone in the Italian research organisation and it was progressively shaped by a series of personal exchanges, including people in Brussels involved with EU-level research. The development of the idea was supplemented by exchanges with some scientific partner organisations with whom the Italian organisation had previously collaborated.

The members of the Italian research organisation led much of the application process. They wrote most of the project description and sought out the scientific partners, who then brought in technicians from their respective countries and networks. One Italian scientist described the search for partners like this: "[W]hen you have to set up a project, you are in a hurry. You try to find the best partners, but you have the partners you find" (interview, 8 July 2009). A Dutch scientist explained: "Someone knows someone; someone does answer the phone, the other doesn't answer the phone and then there is a lot of juggling to partly use your network and grab whoever you can grab" (interview, 15 July 2009). This suggests that availability and timing played a role in deciding who should become a partner. The development process leading to this research topic and partnership – along with the extensive time span between its development, write-up and official start-up – meant that by the time the project's initial meeting was convened, relatively few people knew each other or had read the full EU project description that was part of the application. As a result, the kick-off meeting not only served to introduce people to what they had committed themselves to do vis-a-vis the Commission, but also served to familiarise the newly established partners with each other – the people about to create the project.

As one of them recalled, that meeting set up a pattern of social interaction that was to sustain the project throughout:

> "[F]rom the very first meeting … and the dinner, it has been very important that people, most of the people, get along very well in the project and really enjoy seeing each other at meetings and things. And, I think that helps keep the project afloat. I think you can also see the difference, I mean, the partners most involved in the project, the most active in the project, are also the partners that have most personal, um, have the better personal relations and enjoy having dinner and drinks together. I don't know how that relationship necessarily works – the work and the, sort of, personal

getting-along – but there is definitely a correspondence between the two." (Interview, 24 January 2011)

From paper to practice

The structure and design of the project (see Figure 7.1) provided the setting in which to understand the project as an organisation 'in becoming' and to observe what Weick (1969, p 1) describes as 'processes which create, maintain, and dissolve social collectivities'. As an organisation – a temporary one – the project had few levels; it was a flat organisation with a scientist as the one main authority figure. A Dutch university team headed by one principal scientist led and coordinated it. His formal responsibilities included overall responsibility for all aspects of project management, development and contact with the project officer of the European Commission. The other EU partners reported to him. By design, scientific partners held leading positions in the project and had regular formal input to its different elements

Figure 7.1: EU project organisational chart

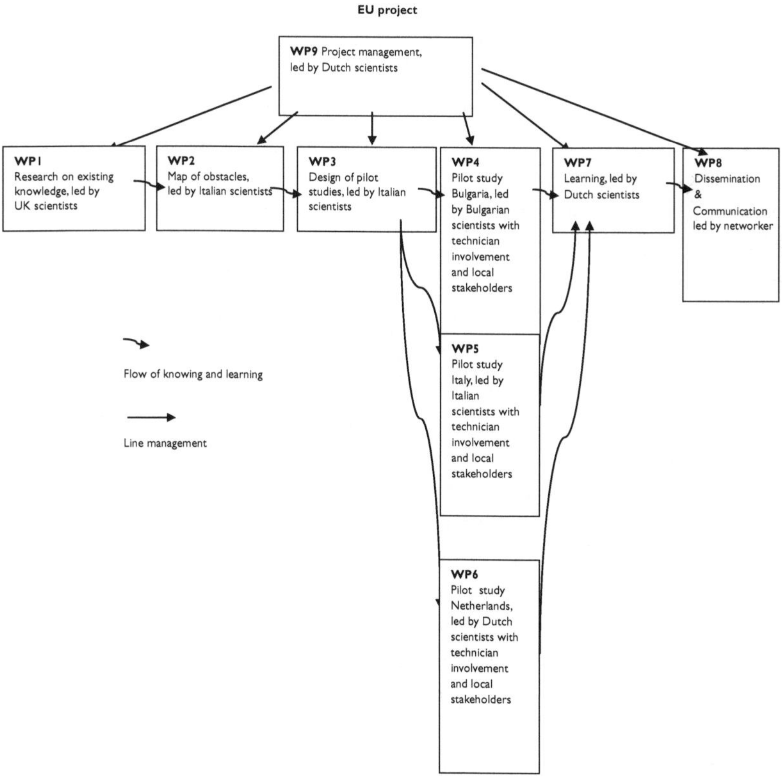

and activities. The flatness of the organisation, combined with its transnational nature, provided space for individual partners to work independently and build formal and informal contacts with others.

The project was divided into nine work packages (WPs), which are specific parts of the project framework. The WPs were transformed into specific actions for learning, which built successively upon preceding actions led by a scientific partner. The first and second WPs concentrated on an inventory of existing knowledge, as well as challenges for research in different EU countries. The results were fed into WPs three through six, which pertained to the development and implementation of three pilot studies: one in the Netherlands, one in Italy and one in Bulgaria. WP seven consisted of gathering the lessons learnt from the pilot studies and using these along with previous learning opportunities to develop a position paper with policy guidelines. WPs eight and nine ran throughout the project and dealt with communication/dissemination measures and project management, respectively.

In order to visualise how situated learning was brought about by the project design, I identify three phases in that learning: a transnational phase, a local phase and a final one that combined both transnational and local learning practices. The first phase comprised WP1, WP2 and WP3, in which partners had to learn to act collectively. It created a substantive basis through empirical research that resulted from a series of negotiations between partners about their research. This included very practical issues like: choosing the type of tools to use to generate data, including interviews and questionnaires; selecting where to look for data and from whom, whether experts, networks or countries; choosing forms of data presentation, entailing discussion of tables, graphs, text, format and style; and identifying writers such as WP leaders or other interested and available partners. This was also the phase in which four out of five partner meetings took place: the face-to-face sites for social interaction that occurred in the different partner countries and included field visits to each of the three sites hosting pilot studies.

The second phase of the project combined WP4, WP5 and WP6 in local learning practices. It presented a different level of learning than the first phase, comprising the implementation of local pilot studies in which the scientific partner in the project engaged with local stakeholders in sanitation to address a common interest in sustainability. Although it was comparatively short, this phase extended the learning potential of the project by drawing on insights from local experts. The resulting reports, written by the scientific partner of the respective study country, were disseminated and their learning compared in the EU project group.

I call the last phase 'learning practices combined' as it rounded up the results and achievements of the practices partners developed transnationally and locally to arrive at the substantive lessons learned in the project. Elements of practice were bundled and translated into a final knowledge product – a booklet – to symbolise the knowing and learning that took place.

The following is a segment taken from a discussion in a partner meeting, which serves to illustrate the enactment of knowledge in the project (audio transcript, June 2009). It demonstrates that people did not come together in this project to do what they already knew how to do, but that they had to go through a process of learning what the project was by doing it. The discussion details the generation of issues and ideas that went with considering how to do a literature review.

> **Partner 1:** "So, how I see this work? [We] will establish a framework to delimit the extent of the review. I think what will happen is … a quick sweep of literature and … come up with boundaries of what we should be looking at; share that within the group … to comment, to amend, to add to as you see fit…. Once we have agreed on the scope of the literature review, we would prepare a checklist to guide the review."

> **Partner 2:** "What is a checklist for a literature review?"

> **Partner 1:** "It is by no means a detailed checklist but … highlighting the main things to look for; it is then easier to integrate and consolidate the four different products that come out of it. *Obviously, you will do it, as you do it anyway* [emphasis added]. So it is by no means prescriptive, it is just to assist in the analysis of consolidation."

> **Partner 3:** "Maybe what we can do is to work together to produce some sort of 'analysis grid' … we will not need to have a summary of a whole book, but we can focus on the issue that is interesting."

> **Partner 4:** "That it is a good plan, to make a checklist – or whatever you want to call it – and of course we may share, and someone may add to it…. Basically, I was assuming that we would do all of this in English. It doesn't make much sense to summarise the Dutch literature in Dutch."

Partner 1: "At every stage [we should use] – a consortium approach ... share everything. So, for example, with the checklist ... you can make comments, amendments and all the rest of it. The flipside of that is that we have to be responsive, if we ask for comments within a week, please give them within a week."

Partner 5: "The checklist could help us within our own organisation to sharpen what we want: what is important for us, what we can obtain, and what we can give and then have the interviews. I don't know exactly when this is going to be but ..."

Partner 6: "I am also thinking, you said you want to delimit the extent of the literature review. Interviews [with the three water partners] can help you with that because now, we discussed in the first half of the morning, [what] the three [water] partners want to get clear: what are their problems and goals? And that could be used as a guideline ..."

Partner 4: "Yes, but not if this [interviewing the three water partners] leads to further postponing the start of the literature review."

Partner 6: "Yes, that is a problem."

This segment exemplifies the enactment of knowledge in the way that partners took their literature review – which at the time of the meeting was only written on the EU application form – and gave it meaning by discussing it in smaller components like a 'checklist' – in the context of what they were doing together. The moment of enactment entailed making suggestions, presenting queries, contemplating options, identifying challenges and signalling caution.

Face-to-face interaction

The learning process in the project was inherent in the activities it required (Nicolini et al, 2003). These tied members of the project together by gathering knowledges available within the group and putting them into practice: this process consequently *performed* the collective (Gherardi and Nicolini, 2002, p 422). It was face-to-face activities that revealed the social processes of the project and the impact these had on knowing and learning. The core face-to-face activity was the transnational partner meetings, which were eventually named 'steering committee' meetings. There were five of these: two in the Netherlands (June 2009 and September 2010), one in Bulgaria (September 2009) and two in Italy (January 2010 and October 2011). There were also two additional 'seminar' meetings in Brussels (December 2010 and September 2012), which targeted European stakeholders (see Table 7.2). In contrast to these two seminars, the transnational partner meetings were sites for collective meaning-making: moments in which the immediate partnership met specifically to talk and listen to each other speak. It was where partners considered progress, gave each other direction, made commitments, set targets and tabled their differences. The meetings made for on-site identity-building. Interestingly, they did not feature explicitly in the project design – they came into being early on in the project as partners voiced the need to meet to develop their work together. They were slotted into WP9 under the heading of 'steering committee' and were thereafter referred to as 'steering committee' meetings; they were the only occasion for direct, face-to-face interaction among all the members of the transnational partnership. Their significance for knowledge creation rested in their participatory character, which called for the involvement of all those in attendance to negotiate their work collectively. In this way, steering committee meetings were sites for nurturing the trust and sense of belonging required for developing 'ownership' in the collective endeavour.

The steering committee meetings were attended regularly by the scientific partners and networkers, but less so by the technicians. Who attended the meetings varied; meetings never achieved full attendance of all 10 formal partner organisations. Depending upon the time and location of the meeting, there were 15–20 participants, including guests from the hosting city. The latter were primarily local water issue technicians and politicians, who had the role of welcoming and leading the project partners on field trips to the water sanitation sites of the pilot studies. These field trips were opportunities for familiarisation and reflection: partners were bussed to specific locations intended to expose them to the local ways of 'doing sanitation' in Bulgaria, Italy and the Netherlands. They provided snapshots of the contexts in which the project worked. Partners were able to meet, listen to and interact with local experts as they explained the challenges they faced.

Another type of face-to-face activity was the parallel pilot studies: one in Bulgaria, one in Italy and one in the Netherlands (see Table 7.3). There was no pilot study in the UK. The pilot studies sketched out in the initial project design had to be rethought and renegotiated during a steering committee meeting in the Netherlands, due to changes in local settings after the writing-up of the project idea and new insights

Table 7.2: EU partner attendance at meetings

Meeting	Partner country	Type of partner			Meeting purpose
		Scientists	Technicians*	Networkers	
Kick-off Meeting, June 2009 (NL)	Netherlands	✓	✓	✓	Partners met for the first time; first collective, face-to-face discussion on the project
	Italy	✓			
	Bulgaria	✓			
	UK	✓			
Steering Committee Meeting, September 2009 (BUL)	Netherlands	✓	✓	✓	Partners met to discuss project work; meet practitioners: water partners; visit local waste water site
	Italy	✓		✓	
	Bulgaria	✓	✓		
	UK	✓			
Steering Committee Meeting, January 2010 (IT)	Netherlands	✓	✓	✓	Partners met to discuss project work; meet Italian water partners; visit local water reservoir
	Italy	✓	✓	✓	
	Bulgaria	✓			
	UK	✓			
Steering Committee Meeting, September 2010 (NL)	Netherlands	✓	✓	✓	Partners met to discuss project work; visit local water sanitation plant
	Italy	✓		✓	
	Bulgaria	✓	✓		
	UK	✓			
Seminar, December 2010 (BEL)	Netherlands	✓	✓	✓	Public presentation of project and knowledge product
	Italy	✓		✓	
	Bulgaria				
	UK				
Steering Committee Meeting, October 2011 (IT)	Netherlands	✓	✓	✓	Partners met to discuss project work
	Italy	✓		✓	
	Bulgaria	✓	✓		
	UK	✓			
Seminar, September 2012 (BEL)	Netherlands	✓	✓	✓	Public presentation of main knowledge products
	Italy	✓		✓	
	Bulgaria		✓		
	UK	✓			

Notes: *The Bulgarian and Italian technical representatives were members of a municipal authority without a water sanitation/technical background.
NL – The Netherlands; BUL – Bulgaria; IT – Italy; BEL – Belgium.

– halfway into the project – into what was feasible given the available knowledge and time frame.

The purpose of each study was to address a local challenge in brokering for sustainable development in sanitation. All three were led and implemented by the national scientific partner from the EU project in cooperation with the nationally designated water partner and local stakeholders. Unlike the steering committee meetings directed at the partners engaged in the transnational learning components of the project, the pilot studies were the expression of local-level activities for learning. The social interaction that took place was local and embedded in the native language of each locale: it followed local norms and took place within local spheres of influence. As a result, each pilot study addressed concerns and used approaches to fit its local context, but all three shared the aim of generating and addressing forms of knowledge brokerage that promoted sustainable water sanitation. The nested learning captured in each pilot study was brought into the transnational domain by way of three individual pilot study reports made available to all partners across the project and then reworked to contribute to WP7.

While partners worked in their national and institutional settings, they used a form of distance learning supported by a computer-based project management and communication tool that provided opportunities for cooperation and communication. Although not face-to-face, this also fostered social interaction since it was the main vehicle for sharing draft documents and commenting on substantive matters. It was used to post travel and meeting plans and to voice organisational queries; it was a question-and-answer forum as well as a photo repository for project events. This kind of communication was supplemented by personal telephone and email contacts, personal letters, and Skype exchanges. These tended to address incidental and sensitive issues: a telephone call to voice a concern and/or stimulate a specific action, for example, or a formal letter to a mayor in deference to local protocol, or a Skype meeting to progress a WP task. The enactment of knowledge was both direct (in face-to-face meetings) and indirect (via information and communication technologies), stimulating the social processes required to generate the words, images and relations leading to knowledge products like a map of technologies, a wastewater directory, reports, newsletters and policy guidelines.

Table 7.3: Local pilot studies

Bulgaria	Italy	The Netherlands
The Bulgarian scientific partner (a sociologist) led and implemented the Bulgarian pilot with the cooperation of the municipal civil servants and an engineer from the local water supply and sanitation company. The main purpose of the pilot was to improve the connection of small enterprises into the municipal sewage system by conducting research on the current challenges in the sewage system and by bringing together local public and private stakeholders to discuss the challenges identified.	The main Italian scientific partners (sociologists) led the pilot, implemented by spatial and water engineers from a second Italian partner organisation brought into the project for this purpose. The designated water partner was the mayor of the municipality in which the pilot was sited. The pilot aimed to raise local awareness of the importance of sewage in the integrated water cycle by organising exchanges between municipalities, technicians (including the water distribution management company), scientists and local inhabitants.	The Dutch scientific partner (physicist, STS) led and implemented the pilot in cooperation with the Dutch technicians (a biologist and a technical engineer) employed as senior policy advisors at the water board company. This pilot aimed to stimulate 'green thinking' in the general company strategy via internal workshops and presentations built on research by the Dutch scientists and their students. The pilot involved company staff, management and directors and focused on how sustainability appeared in the current company strategy with a view towards future developments.

Note: STS – science, technology and society.

Challenges to knowing and learning

My task, as an interpretive researcher observing (inter)action, was to pick up on moments and manifestations of the enactment of knowledge. I had to combine intuition, a sensitivity to the project's idiosyncrasies and observation of a variety of dynamics that I perceived to be enabling or impeding the knowing and learning process. I watched: how partners spoke across different frames (scientists versus technicians; Bulgarian male versus Dutch female); how they formed alliances (the Italians, the Dutch, the Bulgarians, the leaders of the group, the general project partners, the communication group, the scientists, the water partners, the WP leaders); and who said what, when, where, how and why about the project's progress, its leadership, its successes and its failures. People entered into the collaboration with particular identities, vocabularies, practices and perceptions, each of which was unremarkable in any given scientific, technical or epistemic community. In the EU project, however, these elements required explanation, negotiation and reconciliation to make space for the multiple understandings inherent in a group of people from different countries, disciplines and sectors. Space had to be made to allow for the generation of *collective* knowing and learning. In practice, however, my notion that the creation of such space would be key to the project's learning was much too simple.

To illustrate my misconception, I take the example of the Dutch technicians – *water partners* – who, unlike the water partners from the other partner countries, were water sanitation professionals who participated directly and throughout the project. Contrary to what one might expect by reading the original project description, the Dutch water partners did not end up having technical sparring partners in the EU project – with the exception of conversations assisted by local translators and held with local experts during the two field visits in Bulgaria and Italy. This was the result not of a lack of space or time for negotiation within the project, but of a combination of non-attendance at meetings, lack of English-language proficiency and lack of technical background on the part of the other technicians in the partnership. This led to a situation in which the Dutch water partners felt like they were alone in a project run by scientists (interview, 6 July 2009).

With the exception of the local pilot projects, attempts to share local understandings of water sanitation issues were limited and mostly based on what Dutch water partners contributed to steering committee meetings. The absence of specialised knowledge of water sanitation in the partnership was less significant to the leadership of the project than the ability of a scientific partner to meet the formal requirements of the EU project (cf Blackler, 1993). In practice, few people in the partnership – scientists, technicians or networkers – had expertise on sanitation issues. In contrast, the scientific partners leading the project's discursive practices did have expertise on knowledge brokerage. Knowledge brokerage outweighed sanitation as the substantive footing of the project, and sanitation ended up as no more than a setting used to research knowledge brokerage.

On the other hand, the local pilot projects did generate local knowledge based on the cooperation of scientists, technicians and other local stakeholders. These results, used to feed into the thinking at transnational level, were used to build an appreciation of knowledge brokerage. Whether or not the original project description intended to explore knowing and learning across professional sectors more equally, the enactment of comparison in this cross-national, cross-cultural, cross-sectoral and cross-disciplinary group still made sense in the context of knowing and learning because:

> in a constellation of interconnected practices, discourse among communities is a specific practice whose aim is not only to reach understanding and/or to produce collective action, but also to foster learning by comparison with the perspectives of all the co-participants in a practice. Nevertheless, comparing among different perspectives does not necessarily involve the merging of diversity into some sort of synthesis – harmonizing individual voices and instruments into consonance or unison – but rather contemplation of the harmonies *and* dissonance, consonance *and* cacophony, that may coexist with in the same performance. (Gherardi and Nicolini, 2002, p 420, emphasis in original)

The building blocks of collective knowing situated in the partners' shared activities offered moments for reflection, deliberation and creativity. In the way that generating documents together was an important vehicle for expressing project norms and practices, spending time together during meetings made it possible to enact available knowledge and to generate norms and practices because meetings were a forum for socialisation (Freeman, 2008). What partners did when they were together went beyond matters of EU project task division, reporting, deadline-setting and budget-reviewing. Partners left their homes for one to four days and spent entire days together. On the whole, they stayed at the same hotel, travelled together to and from the venue, sat together for full day meetings, ate together, and had after-hour drinks together. The meetings were intensive. They were a round-the-clock commitment: days and evenings were meticulously planned to make the most of the scarce face-to-face time available. Yet, time and time again, partners repeated: *we need a meeting*.

In time, I came to understand how meetings were the place to pick up on conversations and listen to each other's stories – face to face. It was then that partners explained, sorted out, compared, complained, questioned, presented, assessed, learned, grew and really listened to one another. This is what John Forester (1980, p 222) describes poetically as 'pay[ing] attention not to the sound of the person, but to the person of the sound' in order to nurture the sense of collective. The meetings provided the highest level of 'we' in the project, giving it form and unity. While it cannot be said that more meeting leads unequivocally to more knowing and learning, the social interaction that took place in these meetings was key to building trust and community among the project partners, and it was *this* that was indeed relevant for the construction of collective knowing (Bracken and Oughton, 2006):

> Meeting both presumes and finds common ground. It is a process of seeing, identifying and sorting similarity and difference. The meeting establishes an 'axis of recognition' which is bidirectional and both political and epistemological: we recognize others' right to be present and to (re)present what they do, just as they do to us. But as they speak, we recognize unimagined aspects of their situation and unthought of dimensions and implications of our own. (Freeman, 2008, p7)

How these EU partners worked together became visible only over time through the activities they shaped and gave substance to and for which they created a practice. By enacting collective knowledge, ideas that were originally only theoretically described on paper – the successful project application – were brought to life through ongoing discussions, procedures, events, structures and the crystallisation of leadership and role-taking in the group. The evolution of patterns and habits specifically enacted through face-to-face interaction developed project norms that, in time, allowed partners to enact their project; the practice itself was the manifestation of the collective construction of knowing that steered the entire European-level endeavour.

Whether or not the creativity and significance of face-to-face interaction would have faded over a longer period of time because of the very patterns and routines it produced and that enabled the partners to act together remains unknown. What can be said is that the project was the working out of the combination of 'knowledges' in the group and the way these developed anew to create the situated meanings that allowed it to carry out the research. It was a constant translation of expertise into something that could only make sense in *this* setting, at *this* time, to *these* people and in *these* circumstances. It was a process made possible through action and interaction, that is to say, through practices people constructed, negotiated and enacted collectively.

Part Three

Knowledge interests, knowledge conflict and knowledge work

EIGHT

Knowledge interests: promoting and resisting change in mental health in Hungary

Bori Fernezelyi and Gábor Eröss

Introduction

International policy transfer is an extensive global phenomenon, evident not least in Central and Eastern Europe. In the early 1990s, drawing lessons from international policy ideas was considered a means of the region 'catching up' with its Western counterparts – both politically and economically (Rose, 1993). Policy transfer appeared an appealing solution to the unversed policymaker, promising a quick fix to policy problems with no necessity to reinvent the wheel (Rose, 2005; Stead et al, 2010). New policymaking standards presented a challenge to politicians and civil servants who lacked skills and experience in policy formulation. Thus, it appeared easier to emulate or adapt foreign programmes than to start from scratch (Stead et al, 2010). Furthermore, European Union (EU) accession – or, at least, the goal of accession – required the harmonisation of many policy issues. Indeed, beyond accession, EU membership requires certain policy recommendations to be accounted for in national policymaking, many bearing little relation to a previous policy path.

This kind of policy transfer was evident in the process through which Hungary's first mental health policy programme was formulated. This development, introduced in Chapter Four, was prompted by the *Mental health declaration* and *Action plan* agreed at Helsinki. The symbolic enactment of the Declaration and Action Plan set off an indirect coercive transfer process (Dolowitz and Marsh, 1996), through the course of which the first Hungarian National Programme for Mental Health (NPMH) – a domestic re-inscription of the original content – was created. The story of the Hungarian mental health policy began with a ceremonial enactment – the signing of the World Health Organization (WHO) documents in Helsinki – followed by the appearance of inscribed knowledge forms – translation of the policy documents and the drafting of the NPMH. However, the extent to which the original ideas are embodied and internalised in the process remains questionable, as every transition of knowledge from one phase to the next opened up opportunities for local interests to influence and deflect it.

Knowledge is enacted at very different scales throughout the policy process. The ceremonial enactment introduced here stands as an extreme form, a large-scale event that involves a wide range of players in interaction with one another. Policymaking, however, involves micro-enactments, as every item of knowledge considered must be enacted: voiced, debated, written down, displayed. Nonetheless, this chapter focuses primarily on two highly institutionalised ceremonial enactments, given their special significance for international policy transfer.

The case examined here is drawn from a specific empirical setting in which an international agreement collided with local embodied knowledge. We contend that the way in which that agreement was interpreted was deeply influenced by the original structure of the policy field and its existing distribution of embodied and inscribed knowledge. This chapter thus examines the extent to which international knowledge infiltrated domestic epistemology, exploring the way in which theories of policy change and the forms or phases of knowledge can be integrated and arguing that real policy change occurs only when the embodied knowledge of policy actors is transformed. Creating symbolic knowledge enactments and inscriptions for new policy trends remains a far easier feat than changing the embodied knowledge of actors.

Psychiatry or mental health?

On 15 January 2005, Hungary, together with the other 52 member states of WHO Europe, signed the *Mental health declaration* and *Action plan* for Europe (WHO Europe, 2005a, 2005b; see also Chapter Four). WHO's agenda is to take mental health policy in Europe in a public health direction, the aim of the Helsinki event being for members to declare their cooperation in that goal (see Chapter Four). Simply put, this amounted to a shift from psychiatry to mental health in the policy approach of every signatory country. In some countries, this process was already under way or completed, while others had previously had very little experience with the issue. Hungary found itself among the latter.

Prior to the Helsinki *Declaration*, Hungary had never had a national programme for mental health, apart from a Parliamentary Resolution on the National Strategy for the Reduction of Drug Problems passed in 2000, and a National Alcohol Policy that was developed between 2004 and 2005 but never implemented. The National Public Health Programme approved by Parliament in 2003 named mental health as one of its priorities, but no mental health policy actions followed. Hungarian policymakers did not take an active part in the production of the Helsinki documents either, despite the fact that internationally recognised Hungarian professionals had been involved in WHO Europe's mental health activities previously. The only professional present during the preparatory phase, the Hungarian Mental Health Counterpart,[1] played a relatively passive role. Coming from a clinical psychiatry background, he did not readily identify with the main principles of the plan.

Moreover, Hungary, together with only two other European countries, failed to send either its Health Minister or a deputy to the Ministerial Conference. This left only the Counterpart – who was also serving as President of the Hungarian Psychiatric Association at the time – to represent the country. This omission became a common topic in professional discourse, referred to in terms of 'shame' and a signal of the disinterestedness of decision-makers. Indeed, as this chapter later outlines, this disregard can be further explained by the cognitive distance of policy actors from the content and the language of the key documents.

Nevertheless, the conference initiated a process through which WHO principles were transferred to Hungary. The symbolic enactment of signing the *Mental health declaration* and *Action plan* highlighted an issue previously neglected in the national policy agenda. Written documents served to insert WHO concepts into the Hungarian health policy framework: they include the official Hungarian translation of the WHO document and the current Biennial Collaborative Agreement (BCA).[2] In the course of the preparation of the BCA in general, the Hungarian Ministry of Health endeavoured to localise issues that were important for Hungary and, at the same time, fitted WHO's priorities. As a common consequence, issues that have been far down the national list of priorities move to the forefront of policy discussions. Additional documents written in response to the Helsinki *Declaration* were an agreement on the production of a national programme for mental health based on the priorities indicated in the WHO *Declaration* and, in turn, the successive drafts of that programme. The earlier documents functioned as instruments for the creation of the later one – a national document to be built upon the European antecedent.

The structure of the Hungarian mental health field is a peculiar one. Despite major political change, a restructuring of the health care financing system (Gaál, 2004) and significant health reforms, mental health policy and provision has resisted fundamental change. On the contrary, the structure of the field was reinforced by the economic influence of the pharmacological industry in the early 1990s. The mental health policy community remains highly centred upon institutional psychiatry, while professionals doing prevention and providing alternative types of care occupy a marginal position (Fernezelyi, 2007). The recently formed non-governmental organisations (NGOs) composed of mental health service users and/or their carers remain weak, still trying to find a voice. As a result, the psychiatrists who hold positions of authority in the field enjoy commanding lobbying capacity, with close formal and informal links with the ministry. They are thus in a position to represent Hungary in the international policy arena. As international organisations identify and recruit professionals through administrative channels, and as the ministry recognises a small number of leading hospital psychiatrists as most competent, their influence is thus reinforced. Consequently, their interests tower above the rest of the policy community, and it is their influence that is evident in the NPMH.

The National Programme for Mental Health

In Freeman and Sturdy's framework, phase transitions hold significant interest. These are moments in which knowledge alterations occur to create the multilayered knowledge base of a policy. In the case of international policy transfer, phase transitions take place not only in time, but also in space and across linguistic boundaries (Stone, 1999). This usually involves the translation of policy documents. In the formulation of the NPMH, one document or inscription (the Helsinki document) has been converted into another (the NPMH) – requiring enactments in writing, meetings, discussions and judgements informed by the embodied knowledge and interests of the actors involved.

According to the agreement with WHO, the Hungarian mental health programme was to adapt the internationally recognised knowledge of the Helsinki principles to Hungarian circumstances. A close reading of the NPMH, however, reveals the marginality of WHO within the document. In more than 100 pages of the NPMH, only eight direct references are made to WHO, just one of which is a reference to the

Helsinki documents. Six out of the remaining seven use the authority of WHO to bolster its arguments:

> According to the prediction of the WHO, the frequency and burden of the mental breakdowns will increase in the future.....According to the WHO, the social, environmental and economic factors of mental health are the following.... According to the prognosis of WHO the frequency and burden of mental disorders will grow in the future. (PCPHPA, 2007, pp 3, 37, 62)

On only one occasion do the authors draw upon an instrument developed by WHO, in referring to the WHO Welfare Index. Although it reviewed all the topics prioritised by the WHO document, NPMH placed far greater emphasis on the institutional development of psychiatric services (see Table 8.1).

Table 8.1: Appearances of key words in each document

	Mental health: facing the challenges, building solutions (WHO Europe, 2005c, 104 pp)	Hungarian National Programme for Mental Health (PCPHPA, 2007, 103 pp)
Community care	40	8
Prevention	142	2
Stigma	83	9
Psychiatric services	76	332

Comparing the content of the WHO document to that of the Hungarian documents, it emerges that the accents have been shifted. The keyword 'psychiatry', for example, is mentioned 332 times in the Hungarian documents, yet only 76 times in the WHO document. Issues that appear in the WHO *Declaration* and *Action plan*, though present in the Hungarian documents, are granted much less significance there. For instance, in the first version of the NPMH, the issue of *stigma* was clearly not a priority: while the keyword 'stigma' appeared 83 times in the WHO document, it was mentioned only nine times in the Hungarian documents. In the second version, this had shifted somewhat, with an explicit reference to the European Pact on Mental Health – an EU document that directly linked to the WHO *Declaration* and *Action plan*.[3] This second version of the NPMH included a short-term priority list identical to that of the Pact, which embraced stigma and social exclusion. Another issue accorded great significance in the WHO documents but understated in the NPMH is *prevention* (mentioned 142 times in the WHO document and only twice in the Hungarian documents). One of its authors explains the neglect of prevention as follows:

> "It is obvious that we are not talking about the same conditions in the case of, let's say, the Netherlands, or even Britain and Hungary. In some regions of Hungary, the psychiatric service is on the level of a third world country. I agree that it is not right to set prevention against medical intervention: I do not believe that mental health education, or the struggle against work-related stress, is not important, but one must see clearly that prevention is very expensive, like a Mercedes or another luxury car. Even in the USA these programmes were stopped, because they could not finance them. And these programmes have very poor efficiency; one cannot really measure their effects." (Interview with a leader of the Hungarian Psychiatric Association, 3 November 2008)

Furthermore, community care – one of the fundamental elements of WHO mental health initiatives – remains in its infancy in Hungary. The matter was mentioned a few times in the document, but only at a rhetorical level, without any plan for how this new paradigm might be realised.

To summarise, the Helsinki documents declared that mental health policies and services must address the needs of the population as a whole; they must be comprehensive and integrated, covering mental health promotion, early intervention, innovative community-based care and social inclusion (WHO Europe, 2005c). Nevertheless, in the Hungarian papers, the shift from psychiatry to mental health occurred only at the level of rhetoric. Although these documents embody certain WHO-inspired mental health policy issues, their frequency and significance are much lower. Indeed, they demonstrate the distance between the authors' embodied knowledge and the original inscription. This became particularly evident at an event that closed the policy process and introduced the NPMH – the 'Consensus Conference'.

The Consensus Conference

The Ministry of Health hosted a 'Consensus Conference of the NPMH' in March 2009, with the proclaimed goal of bringing together every member of the mental health policy community. This included assembling all of those who claimed a stake in the framing of Hungary's first mental health programme, to review the comments received by the ministry on the NPMH and to reach a consensus on the final version of the document. Although this suggests that the goal of the conference was to align distinct viewpoints and reach agreement, in fact, it can be better described as a legitimation mechanism, through which the ministry sought to convince the policy community of the necessity and appropriateness of its version of mental health. The 'final' document was not the outcome of, but the input to, the conference.

Before describing the event, we must introduce the participants. In consultations with the ministry, the profession is usually represented by leaders of organisations such as the Hungarian Psychiatric Association and the Professional College of Psychiatry. These positions are occupied by a small number of clinical psychiatrists, as there are overlapping functions between the two organisations. These figures are Heads of Departments in leading hospitals, while also holding national positions in psychiatric education. In this way, Hungarian institutions are dominated by biological psychiatry – biological in terms of both models of causation and in therapeutic practice.

A small number of representatives of a group who termed themselves 'reform psychiatrists' were also present. With professional perspectives and activities closer to WHO intentions than their colleagues, these constitute critical players. Indeed, many are involved in ongoing community psychiatry projects to enhance user involvement and fight stigma. Such professionals, who advocate alternative paths for psychiatry, are neglected and often discredited by leaders in the field. Furthermore, as our interviews illustrate, while many psychiatrists do not take sides, they do sympathise with the critics' views. The wider mental health policy field also includes psychologists, educators and health care and social workers, though their presence in the Hungarian context remains marginal.

In line with international expectations and the Helsinki documents' purposes, NGOs were also invited to attend the conference and comment on the NPMH. NGOs occupy a paradoxical position in Eastern Europe, as many have argued (Hemment, 1998). While the stimulation of civil society has been crucial to the democratisation of post-socialist states, these organisations – despite encouragement from international agencies – have been less likely to evolve from grassroots initiatives. In the mental health policy field, several 'insider NGOs' exist, founded by major professional groups in order to apply for certain projects and funds. User groups, on the other hand, barely feature and wield only marginal influence. Ironically, international NGOs enjoy greater influence in national policy processes:

> "This conference [referring to a conference in Budapest in 2005] on mental health issues was organised by a Brussels lobby group of users of psychiatry. They organised it, using EU funding, and their goal was to spread the word and educate the Hungarian professionals." (Interview with former Secretary of State for Health Policy and International Affairs, 30 January 2009)

Having reviewed the attendees of the Consensus Conference, we now turn to the event itself. It presented a significant opportunity to gain a sense of the actors' real understandings of mental health policy, whether publicly expressed before an audience or in private discussions before or after the event. The conference began with a speech by one of the authors of the NPMH, the former Mental Health Counterpart who had named the WHO *Declaration* and *Action plan* as the foundational document for Hungarian policy. In this talk, however, the departure from WHO's intentions was easily discernible. The following quotation provides a condensed example:

> WHO declared many times that there is no health without mental health. I absolutely agree with this statement and I do believe that it would be a huge step if Hungary got a mental health programme – however partial or small it would be – which pins down that, in Hungary, national health cannot exist without taking the problem of psychiatric services into account. (Conference transcript, 4 March 2009)

Immediately after the introduction of the WHO documents, a connection to EU mental health initiatives, including the Green Paper and the European Pact, was established. The speaker thus interpreted all of these documents as mere instruments to highlight mental illness as an epidemic. This interpretation implied that by signing the documents, Hungary was agreeing to treat mental illness as a priority, but sidestepped the fact that by doing so, it was also accepting the shift from psychiatry to a mental health approach. Moreover, the translation of the expression of 'mental health' into psychiatry was explicitly addressed:

> Although it is true that mental health is a broad term, it includes social aspects as well, but if we consider the term in the sense of 'mental health institutes', these are institutes dealing with mentally ill patients, or preventing psychiatric diseases in the realm of healthcare. (Conference transcript, 4 March 2009)

At this point, a selection of pictures of huge mental health institutions from the US, Germany and Poland was projected before the audience. As the talk continued, the former Counterpart – the very person in charge when the BCA with WHO was signed, which committed the country to the production of a national programme – referred to the BCA as an agreement to create a 'psychiatry strategy'.

Criticisms of the proposed mental health programme were expressed before the conference in writing, during the conference in the form of comments and in interviews we conducted with members of the mental health community. These arguments formed two broad strands. On the one hand, the translation from mental health to psychiatry was criticised, primarily by those members of the community whose interest was not limited to psychiatry, such as advocates of community-oriented psychiatric care, prevention-focused organisations, churches and others. Their objections were based on a conviction that a programme with mental health in its name should include prevention, education and other mental health issues not immediately focused on psychiatry.

On the other hand, the feasibility of any mental health programme in the current economic climate was contested. Participants questioned whether any extra money – without which any programme is destined to fail – would be invested in health care. Some, similarly, criticised the generality of the proposal and urged something more specific to help ensure implementation. The combination of these two critiques – the latter overriding the former – led to an approval of the proposed programme by the majority of those involved. As the President of the Hungarian Society for Mental Hygiene explained:

> In this present economic and political situation, following a serious demolition of the health care system [referring to the health reform process under the previous Health Minister, in the course of which health institutions were closed down, including the National Institute of Psychiatry

and Neurology], I welcome the plan of enhancing the state of psychiatry in Hungary as it seems to be a time of possibilities stemming from the Europe-wide mental health initiatives, but please do not call it the National Programme for Mental Health. Psychiatry is only one pillar of mental health. It is a very important pillar, but it is a very big mistake to confuse the pillar with the bridge. (Conference transcript, 4 March 2009)

Accordingly, most members of the mental health community reluctantly acknowledged that to attain any kind of mental health reform, they had to accept a programme confined to the institutional development of psychiatry. Many remained dissatisfied with the name of the programme, however, arguing that it was misleading. Indeed, in her closing remarks, the Secretary of State for Health Policy openly admitted on behalf of the ministry that the use of 'mental health' in the name of the programme was probably too ambitious, but – referring to the agreement with WHO – ruled out renaming it.

Transfer and translation

The three-phase framework of 'embodied', 'inscribed' and 'enacted' knowledge describes an iterative process in which knowledge moves continuously, in phases and from one form to another. The Hungarian reception of the Helsinki documents outlined earlier represents a particular case of this process being initiated outside the country. WHO's mental health documents were produced in a context where the structure of psychiatry and mental health policy is fundamentally different from that in Hungary, deriving its relevance from that context. Confronted with such different experiences and unfamiliar language, the relevant Hungarian actors could not fully take part in the procreation of the policy. Those actors committed to WHO's conception of mental health were few and far between, and were struggling for recognition. However, as a Europe-wide initiative, Hungary had little choice but to sign the document. In being transferred to a fundamentally different environment, the Helsinki documents had to be reinterpreted or translated. WHO knowledge and expertise entered Hungary in inscribed form through the official translation of the document and the BCA. It was enacted in signing the BCA with WHO, where it encountered the embodied knowledge and interests of the Hungarian mental health policy community.

As a consequence, WHO's mental health approach was translated into *psychiatry* in line with the interests and knowledge of the influential players. The translation process was conducted and controlled by clinical rather than community interests, as the hospital psychiatrists exploited the ministry's lack of interest and appropriated the WHO instrument. This group thus secured an advantageous position in which it could present its knowledge to the ministry as the only option – or, at least, the most relevant for Hungary. The influential members of the psychiatric lobby, who occupied leading positions and worked on the NPMH, managed to cast policy formulation as an either/or choice between developing the existing structure of psychiatry and doing nothing. In this way, the possibility of any fundamental reinterpretation of mental health services was ruled out:

> "The main problem is that the professional elite is composed of a number of hospital psychiatrists with an interest in biological psychiatry, influenced by the pharmaceutical industry…. The most important policy decisions are made not in the professional community, but among the members of this informal group…. This explains the shortcomings of NPMH: those reform psychiatrists who already had experiences in community psychiatry or other alternative practices were excluded from the formulation process." (Interview with reform psychiatrist, 26 February 2009)

As a result, WHO's precepts of shifting psychiatric care to a wider understanding of mental health were interpreted in a way that reinforced the clinical authority they were meant to challenge.

As it was drafted, the NPMH took account of every topic and theme covered by the *Declaration* and *Action plan*. In this sense, we might speak of a Europeanisation of mental health policy in Hungary. Europeanisation processes are always complemented by domestication processes, with domestic factors (including pre-existing structures, traditions, domestic interests and organisational capacities) exerting a significant effect on the outcome (Bugdahn, 2005). It has often been argued that transferring policy ideas across cultural, linguistic and national boundaries, far from being a mechanistic, top-down process, involves complex cultural, political and social practices. Instead, the process should be seen as one involving negotiations and translations arising from forces of simultaneous domination and resistance (Lendvai and Stubbs, 2007). Transferring policies from one context to another necessarily entails the translation of their content to meet new conditions: here, however, the most fundamental principles of the policy were altered.

The significant distance between the original policy goal and the knowledge, organisation and interests of local actors made the policy transfer troublesome, however. Among the most important factors affecting new policy processes are previous policies and existing structures. Policymakers use current standards and frameworks to determine policy goals and instruments and even to identify policy problems. They thus fit new policy initiatives into these existing structures, which are cognitive as much as organisational (Hall, 1993). The ways of thinking of the clinical psychiatrists who dominated the Hungarian mental health field and took part in the formulation of the NPMH were very different from those of WHO. Its approach to mental health challenged not only their established interests, but also their styles of thought.

This raises the question of why the policy transfer took place in the first place if its fundamentals were so unappealing to the recipients. Two conditions affected the process. On the one hand, it is evident that 'we learn from (and with) others with whom we identify in some way' (Freeman, 2006b, p 382), and the Hungarian policy actors clearly wanted to identify with a European mental health policy community simply because they wanted Hungary to be up to European standards. At the same time, however, one of the key assumptions underlying this initiative was that funds would be made available to address WHO priorities. It was anticipated that the issues on WHO's agenda would also be a priority for other international and supranational actors (such as the EU), which would in turn afford access to a variety of resources for Hungary.

In order to understand why the Hungarian mental health policy has run the course it has, one must consider the perspective of the Ministry of Health. When it comes to policy formation, the ministry is in a double-bind. On the one hand, it tries to conform to 'European expectations', while, on the other, existing structures, established operational mechanisms and economic constraints frustrate the reception of policies and the development of procedures. Therefore, while Hungary formally endeavoured to embrace the European policy, in reality, its civil servants and decision-makers were absorbed by the country's own problems. In other words, the ministry's main concern was to maintain 'face' in Europe, in Goffman's (1955) sense. As the Mental Health Counterpart observed of the data it supplied for a WHO report:

"For a long time, Hungary was deferring the data transmission, which made the relation strained; finally, they sent the data. After that, I let the ministry know that I was aware of the invalidity of some of it. I do not know the exact numbers, but, for example, I am aware that there are not 1,300 psychiatrists in Hungary, which was a figure they were talking about. I do not know where this figure came from, maybe the number of those who had taken a specialty exam in psychiatry in the past 40 years, but only around half of them work as psychiatrists in Hungary; 1,300 is certainly a false figure." (Interview, 11 March 2008)

Thus, the sudden concern with mental health policy in Hungary was not the consequence of an internal urge or recognition of the ineffectiveness of the present structure; rather, it was triggered by external factors. An international consensus can in itself be sufficient to constitute a push factor in policy change, as Dolowitz and Marsh (1996, p 349) point out:

When the international community defines a problem in a particular way, and even more when a common solution to that problem has been introduced in a number of nations, then nations not adopting this definition or solution will face increasing pressure to join the international 'community' by implementing similar programmes or policies.

From the ministry's perspective, Hungarian mental health policy had to satisfy three criteria: it had to have some connection to the WHO mental health initiatives; it had to be accepted in the Hungarian mental health community (dominated by hospital psychiatrists); and it had to be feasible under current economic conditions. The translation of mental health to psychiatry emerged as the solution.

Knowledge change and policy change

Policy transfers, so common in Central and Eastern Europe, are rarely undertaken voluntarily, but much more often as a result of overt or subtle pressure. The nature of these transfers indicates that it is an oversimplification to suggest a sharp distinction between voluntary policy learning and coercive policy transfer. While the slow and faltering character of much policy diffusion tends to be attributed to the resistance of established local interests, the perspective gained in this research suggests that it could be a function of the way knowledge operates.

Peter Hall (1993) defines a framework of policy ideas, concepts and solutions as a policy paradigm. For him, 'normal policymaking' is a process that adjusts policy without challenging the terms of a given paradigm: normal policy change takes place within existing frameworks, comprising adjustments to policy settings or the instruments by which it is regulated. A paradigm change occurs, however, when these structures and cognitive frameworks become insufficient and new ones come to replace them (Hall, 1993). In this sense, the aim of WHO's Helsinki *Declaration* was to attain a paradigm shift in mental health policy in Europe, in the belief that the old structures were no longer sufficient.

A paradigm shift happens either when the cognitive frames of the actors in power change or when new actors with distinct cognitive frames seize power. Either way, the cognitive frame of the entire policy community eventually shifts accordingly. In the case of a successful international policy transfer, new knowledge appears in the domestic policy field in all three phases of embodied, inscribed and enacted knowledge. In such a case, however, the chain of transition typically assumes a different order than it does when policy develops organically from within a particular policy community. In the latter case, development generally begins with the evolution of the actors' embodied knowledge, which only subsequently comes to be inscribed, enacted, confronted, selected and disseminated. In the case of an externally imposed policy transfer, by contrast, new inscribed knowledge often appears first, as it is in this form that knowledge is most readily transferable from one place to another. Such a transfer will not always induce change in the embodied knowledge of policy actors, however, since embodied knowledge cannot be forcibly changed, and inscriptions alone do not determine what knowledge will become embodied. Consequently, even if the language of policy changes, actors may continue to behave as they did previously. The old paradigm will therefore remain intact, while the policy actors do no more than pay lip service to the new language and concepts. In Hungary, the dominant policy actors were not convinced that the existing structure was to blame for the shortcomings of the mental health system; instead, most believed that insufficient resources lay at the root of the problems. The new knowledge of mental health inscribed in the WHO documents thus clashed with the established and embodied knowledge of the principal players in national mental health policy. The previously existing domestic distribution of knowledge and interest fundamentally determined the final outcome of the policy transfer process.

Interests and embodied knowledge are clearly interdependent: our interests are formed and informed by the knowledge we embody, while, at the same time, our embodied knowledge is deeply shaped by the way we comprehend the world according to our interests (Habermas, 1966). Our embodied knowledge, our beliefs and convictions, determine the way we want to see, structure and shape reality, and our interests frequently lie in maintaining that reality as long as possible. Small shifts are possible without radical external interference, but comprehensive restructuring only occurs when something upsets these cognitive foundations. This is true not only for individuals, but also for a policy community composed of individuals with separate but more or less harmonised embodied knowledge. If these individuals come from similar backgrounds, in which similar qualifications and experience are applied in similar political and institutional contexts, their embodied knowledge is likely to be similar and their interests similar, too (though they may be rival as well as shared).

The interests that inform our knowledge are often invisible to us. In many cases, those involved in policymaking may not be aware that they are pursuing interests; they believe that they are doing what is right, that they are acting according to the best of what they know. The connection between their knowledge and their interests may be very strong, but imperceptible. By applying the three-phase model in the way we have here, we can refine this understanding of the relationship between knowledge and interests. While knowledge may be inscribed into documents with particular interests in mind, those documents remain open to interpretation in the light of other interests. By contrast, embodied knowledge, and the interests with which it is associated, is often much harder to revise, particularly where it is embodied not just in individuals, but in a community of actors. It is this embodied knowledge that typically informs the way that inscribed knowledge is interpreted and enacted. As our case study shows, the degree of interpretive flexibility available to policy actors may be considerable, to the extent that the enactment of a policy document may be entirely at odds with the interests and intentions that informed the original inscribing of that document. This serves to clarify what we meant when we spoke, earlier in this chapter, about the 'symbolic enactment' of the knowledge inscribed in the WHO policy documents: although the new Hungarian mental health policy claimed to be inspired and informed by those documents, it is clear that the purpose of the enactment, and the interests that informed it, was quite different from the intentions and interests behind the original inscriptions.

Thus, as we have tried to show, the transfer of inscriptions from one setting to another does not necessarily lead to a paradigm shift as those inscriptions are enacted in the new setting. As our case study illustrates, even coercive efforts to effect policy transfer through new documents and agreements can result in enactments that do not require any change in the reservoir of embodied knowledge. Nevertheless, we might wonder whether such externally induced policy transfer will come to affect the embodied knowledge of policy actors in the long run. Our case does not offer any definite answer to this question: it demonstrates no more than that the way in which policy documents were interpreted and enacted at a key moment in the policy process did not correspond to the intentions of the authors of those documents. To fully understand the long-term effects of this transfer, a longitudinal study would be necessary. We can assume, however, that policy transfers set off some form of change, if not a paradigm shift. At the very least, in the case we studied here, new terms and concepts became a part of policy discussions, as forums were created where all members of the policy community could meet and voice their opinion on and in new terms.

This chapter has applied and explored the concept of phase transitions in knowledge to international policy transfer, arguing that it is crucial that transfer encompasses every phase. For profound change to occur, we contend, embodied knowledge must be transformed, for without it, policy transfer is likely to occur only superficially, in symbolic enactments. This tends to happen when external push factors trigger transfer against the embodied knowledge and interests of local actors. The structure and distribution of the local policy community's pre-existing knowledge fundamentally determines the interpretation and enactment of the transferred policy.

Notes

[1] The Counterparts are members of a network established by WHO's European office. They serve as the principal point of communication between the Regional Office and mental health services in WHO member countries.

[2] The BCA is a contract between WHO's Regional Office for Europe and the government of Hungary. The document includes priorities for cooperation, expected outcomes, a WHO budget and other sources of funds.

[3] In November 2005, the European Commission published a Green Paper, a mental health strategy for the EU, in response to the Helsinki documents. Following on from the Green Paper, an EU mental health conference on 13 June 2008 launched the European Pact for Mental Health and Well-Being.

NINE

Knowledge conflicts: embodiment, inscription and the education of children with learning disabilities in Germany

Alma Demszky

Introduction

The struggle of activist parents of disabled children for inclusion of their children in kindergarten and school has a long history in Europe that begins in the 1970s. In Bavaria, some parents have been fighting hard since the 1990s for the right of their children to an element of normality in their lives. In their view, these children are not ill, but as normal and healthy as other children, from whom they should not be separated in everyday life. Heralded by the parents as a great achievement, the Bavarian Education Act was reformed in 2003, permitting inclusion of disabled children in regular schools. Then, in 2009, Germany signed the United Nations (UN) Convention on the Rights of Persons with Disabilities,[1] rekindling discussion about the right to inclusion in Bavarian schools. To the great satisfaction of concerned parents, the new legislation of 2011 made inclusion not only possible, but compulsory, should parents wish it.

The history of inclusion in Bavaria can be read as a history of conflicts between different types of knowledge. The knowledge of the parents of disabled children is a striking example of embodied knowledge: inextricably bound to its holders, who are living human beings, and to their lived experience of the minds and bodies of their children. This kind of knowledge cannot be considered separately from the point of view of the person who holds it, and points to the narrow line between knowledge, feelings and beliefs. In the case we study here, this person-held, embodied knowledge conflicted with the inscription of the law, which is an impersonal form of knowledge. As we shall see, this conflict was partly dissolved and partly reproduced in the application or enactment of the law in the everyday life of the school.

Amendments to the Bavarian Education Act

Our case study analyses the history of integration of disabled children into regular schools in Bavaria. Due to the fact that Germany's constitution delegates legal authority over education to its 16 federal states, we cannot speak of a German national education system, only of the system of a particular state. Our arguments are therefore valid only for Bavaria, where this study was conducted. Since 1962, the majority party in Bavaria has been the Christlich-Soziale Union (CSU), a Catholic conservative party, which has given the Bavarian education system a rather conservative flavour. The history of integration is therefore, at the same time, a history of the reform of part of a long-established system.

The case study presented here was conducted by researchers of the Institute of Sociology of the University of Munich, mainly between 2007 and 2009, but complemented by further investigation of recent changes to the Education Act in 2011. The analysis was based on documents, expert interviews and focus groups. Thirty interviews of between one and three hours were conducted: in the Bavarian Ministry of Education, in the government and in the Bavarian Parliament; with state school advisors, parents' associations and teachers' associations; in both special needs and regular schools; and with several individual experts. The documentary analysis covered official protocols of meetings and hearings, press releases, and newspaper articles.

Our case study concerns what we call a 'knowledge conflict' regarding children with learning disabilities, and what this means for decisions about what is the right school for them. Is a child with Down's syndrome ill or not? Should he or she be separated from other children of the same age and from the same neighbourhood and made to attend a special school 50 miles from home? Does it matter if such children cannot make the same progress in educational terms as their classmates? Some parents of disabled children and some experts have been saying for decades that these children are not ill, but perfectly healthy, and do not need to be separated from others. They insist that their children have a right to normality just like other children. The law, however, has long expressed a very different view: disabled children have to be educated in special schools, which best meet their needs and where the teaching staff are specially trained for these pupils. A long professional tradition of special education theory and practice also supports this position.

Our interviewees pointed to a vigorous public debate in Germany around the issue of integrating disabled children into public schools, beginning in the 1970s. This debate began from parents' ideas and experiences regarding what they thought their child was capable of, and what would best benefit their child. While most teachers and school directors favoured the status quo and refused to integrate children with additional needs, some schools made exceptions. These schools and teachers were able to acquire experiential knowledge about the everyday praxis of integration. This public debate about integration gained momentum in the late 1990s as the media reported several cases of teachers and principals integrating disabled children, in contravention of the law in force at that time. With the issue of integration finally out in the open, and with the Bavarian Parliament basically supporting a softening of the strict separation of non-disabled and disabled children, a phase of active information-gathering and expert consultation began, culminating in December 2001 in the drafting of an amendment to the Bavarian Education Act by the Social Democratic Party (SPD) in the Bavarian Parliament.

At that time, the SPD was in opposition to the majority CSU, which made it both easy and expedient to demand far-reaching changes in provision for educational integration. The draft amendment was introduced into the parliamentary process and then referred to the relevant committees, where it was discussed and several changes were made, ranging from seemingly minor ones, such as changing the term 'disabled' to 'needing assistance', to more substantial issues, for instance, concerning the provisions for testing children against their parents' will. This process was mainly an intra-party one, during which issues of desirability and feasibility in the respective parties' positions were elaborated. All of our respondents said that in this period from 2001 to 2003, before the amendment was passed, there were numerous occasions when experts were invited to the Bavarian Parliament, committees, private meetings or hearings, and other symposia.

The first amendment to the legislation relating to integration was passed in 2003. Although modified in the light of extensive consultation over the previous years, it remained essentially intact in its purpose, imposing an obligation on public schools to educate children with all kinds of additional needs when it was possible to do so. However, the story of educational inclusion in Bavaria did not end there. The UN Convention on the Rights of Persons with Disabilities of 2008 was ratified by Germany in 2009, and the German federal government obliged all states to change their education laws accordingly. Bavaria was one of the first to open a public debate about the new situation, supported by the parents' organisations, which had maintained strong personal contacts with ministerial staff since they worked together on the amendment of 2003. Persuaded by the parents' activity and commitment, the Ministry of Education appeared ready for a rapid ratification of the UN Convention. The new amendment was passed in 2011, and the law now not only allows integration of children with additional needs into regular schools, but makes it compulsory when that is what parents want. This most recent amendment to the legislation shows the extent to which policymaking is intertwined with national and international endeavours. The parents' wish for integration led after several years of campaigning to the amendment of the law in 2003, but their demand for unrestricted integration could not be met at that time. In the end, it was an external authority, the UN Convention, which forced national policymakers to accede to the parents' wishes.

The rest of this chapter is concerned with the evolution of national policy thinking and practice, and so focuses primarily on the amendment of 2003. In particular, we observe how different forms of knowledge interacted and partly conflicted, and how what was known about children with disabilities changed. The amendments to the Bavarian Education Act concerning integration serve as an empirical example of the different ways in which different forms of knowledge may be mobilised, and the different purposes they can serve, in the negotiation and implementation of policy.

For and against integration

This chapter examines an intense conflict between two bodies of knowledge, which might be described as being for and against integration. We begin by identifying the main contours of the debate – though this inevitably means simplifying what were actually very complex and changing positions.

First, we need an overview of the various actors involved. These included individual parents, parents' organisations, teachers, school directors, teachers' organisations (both regular teachers and specialist teachers of disabled children), experts, scientists, media reporters, Members of Parliament (MPs) (both CSU and SPD) and members of the Bavarian government and the Ministry of Education. Key groupings included:

- The parents of disabled children, who wanted to achieve integration in regular schools. They put the issue on the agenda and kept it there. Later, some parents formed groups and organisations, such as 'Live together, learn together'.[2]

- Members of the Bavarian government and administration, especially from the Ministry of Education and the Education Committee of the Bavarian Parliament.
- Scientific experts from the University of Munich and other universities or research institutes.
- Teachers' organisations: here we have to differentiate between regular school teachers' organisations and those of specialist teachers of children with disabilities.

These four bigger groups of actors represented different viewpoints concerning integration: Figure 9.1 presents them graphically.

Figure 9.1: Relevant actors and their positions

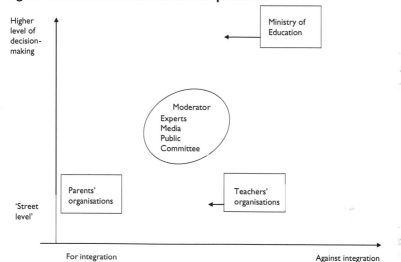

The axis 'for–against integration' is self-explanatory. The Ministry of Education and the teachers' organisations favoured the existing (segregated) situation, primarily for reasons of convenience. The second axis reflects the actors' proximity to or distance from the everyday world of the classroom and the daily life of children. On this axis, the ministry must take decisions at some remove, in contrast to the 'street-level' decision-making of teachers and parents; the state administration thus has to develop and dispose of a more abstract, universalistic kind of knowledge than the everyday decisions of a classroom teacher. Our interviews and documents confirmed that the workings of bureaucratic regulation presuppose a degree of abstraction from the particular case or the single individual. Regulations cannot specify what to do in every situation, but rather have to set case-independent frameworks within which solutions to particular problems can be formulated. Knowledge, experience and information flowing into the state administration thus have to go through a process of abstraction and depersonalisation, which ends sometimes, but not necessarily, in the inscription of a law. By contrast, the implementation of regulations in the everyday praxis of a classroom involves taking decisions in a particularistic, case-by-case fashion. The bureaucratic regulation has to be converted and translated into the circumstances of everyday life.

The second axis of Figure 9.1 thus points to the different kinds of knowledge and experiences that the different actors were able to call upon. Parents of disabled children have experiential knowledge about the minds and bodies of their children, and a special and individualised idea of how integration can work in the everyday. Over time, these parents succeeded in persuading some teachers to integrate children with special needs into regular schools. These teachers and principals thus also acquired experiential knowledge about the possibilities and constraints of integration in the life of a classroom. Both the parents' and the teachers' knowledge is largely embodied, because it is based on personal experience of children's needs and of the everyday praxis of integration, and it is largely individualised, based on knowledge of single cases. As time went on, however, educational experts and even international actors also got involved in the Bavarian debate. In consequence, a different form of knowledge began to be formulated – moving from knowledge of individual cases to the articulation of a general principle that integration was a real alternative to separation. This more abstract and case-independent knowledge was inscribed in research publications and media reports.

The clash between the different standpoints for and against integration thus led to changes in the content and form of knowledge on all sides. The biggest apparent change of attitude occurred on the side of the government, which became increasingly favourable towards integration. Some decision-makers and experts changed their position from defending the status quo towards change and reform. An ex-teacher and government member of the parliamentary education committee explained his own position as follows:

> "I was asked to move over to the education committee, because this whole discussion about integration was very lively back then, and it was considered that it could be cushioned better that way, so one wouldn't have to get in this integration movement, and – I'm speaking very openly,

you see – and there they probably set the fox to keep the geese." (Interview, 3 May 2008)

As a former head of a special school, he was expected to defend segregation, but he himself felt that this was not the right solution for the future. As our interviewees explained, the question of education involves multiple emotions and ideas. It cannot be treated as an ethically neutral question or a technical decision. Education, especially education of children that some people consider to be sick, is a highly loaded question in ethical terms. Given that expert opinion is divided for and against, whether one prefers integrated or segregated education depends mainly on one's personal experiences, beliefs and knowledge. Changes in standpoint, especially towards integration and reform, happened often not only on the basis of expert knowledge, but through personal contacts and persuasion. The insistence of parents and their efforts to maintain nearly daily contact with decision-makers in the ministry was crucial for the changes in the Education Act. Dry, expert arguments were given life through the lived experience and knowledge of the parents and experts involved. The following excerpt from an interview with an MP who was active in the debate highlights this aspect of knowledge very well, describing it in terms of a 'personal story', a 'personal issue' and an 'impression':

> "We are having lots of talks with the teachers' associations; we are in constant contact with the association of special needs teachers, also in constant contact with the parents. The third level is that of personal experience: when you know someone from your circle of acquaintances or your district, then, of course, this is a personal experience that is not at all insignificant, because it is a very personal story, when you have somebody in your family with a disabled child, then it is a very personal issue. That leaves an impression on you, when you see that not everything is going the way it should." (Interview, 25 April 2009)

The kind of knowledge our respondent is talking about here is gained through personal experience and impression, and cannot be substituted by other sources, such as reading an article or seeking expert advice. In the parents' and teachers' case, such knowledge is inseparably bound to bodily praxis, emotions and beliefs. In the MP's case, too, it was bound up with personal interactions and relationships, and so likewise involved a strong emotional charge. The way that this kind of embodied knowledge came eventually to be written into law, and then the way that law was implemented, was far from straightforward, and involved a process of transformation or translation as much as transcription; in effect, it involved changes of content as well as form. The following section spells this out in more detail.

First steps towards integration

The motivating factor in changing not only Bavarian education law, but also public attitudes towards the schooling of disabled children, was the embodied knowledge of parents. Some made individual attempts to get their children into regular schools even before the law was changed – like the Wild family, who went through all available legal procedures, in vain, to get their child into a public school, and who then emigrated to Austria:

> "That went through the whole inter-regional press, the newspaper *Bild* reported it, this issue was really being pursued there, this story of the Wilds. They had filed a petition for the schooling of their child in a public school in Berchingen, which, of course, had been declined, so they took legal action.... They went to the Administrative Court in Munich and lost, they lost in the Higher Administrative Court of Bavaria, and their lawsuit wasn't even accepted in the Federal Constitutional Court, and so they emigrated to Reuthe, Austria. And, of course, this went through the press, and the pressure exerted by the parents was incredibly high.... Then, reacting to this pressure, in 1998, a decision by the Bavarian Parliament ... initiated by some CSU politicians, saying that in cases of children suffering from Down's syndrome, it should first of all be established whether they could possibly be educated at a public school. And that was actually going against the law in force at that time, which proclaimed the equality of learning goals for all children educated at the same school ... and, at that moment, it became evident that in the CSU, in the government, a change of mentality had taken place."
> (Interview, 22 October 2008)

The momentum gained by this story exemplifies how inscriptions, in this case, the published story of the Wild family, can circulate, and how they can help to mobilise other knowledge sources and actors. In this instance, it marked a turning point in the government's position, whose insistence on the equality of learning goals was partly reconsidered in favour of inclusion.

After the revision of 1998, the media began to report cases of legal 'misconduct' by parents or school directors who allowed other disabled children, and not just those suffering from Down's syndrome, to be integrated into regular schools, contrary to the legal regulations. The reaction of the administration, which moved to stop these kinds of experiments in spite of their apparently satisfactory results, led to great indignation in the media. As one of our interviewees recalled:

> "[A] child, a mentally disabled child, had been taken out of the [regular] school, the state's supervisory authority did this, and put the child in a school for disabled children, although all the people involved had said that what was happening there was great. The parents had been satisfied, the school had been happy, the teachers were content, so everybody agreed with what had been done there, and, just because of the law, the child was taken out of there and put into a school for children with learning disabilities. There was a decision, taken in 1998 by the Higher Administrative Court of Bavaria, that this action is legal." (Interview, 22 October 2008)

The publicity given to such removals placed mounting pressure on the government. Meanwhile, the views of parents and teachers about disabled children benefiting from attending regular schools were increasingly backed up by international experts:

> "Well, I have found in the last two decades in my research and my practical work that we can basically educate and assist all children with disabilities, no matter how severe, at general schools, right? This doesn't depend on the children, but on the conditions we create. So, good personnel and certain educational models have to be realised, there has to be someone with special training in reference to the particular needs of the individual children, right? But then it works, and it works in a qualitatively good way from kindergarten through school to other social contexts, and this is actually not controversial any more in scientific opinion." (Interview, 10 May 2008)

Largely as a result of this accumulation of experience and research knowledge, and the publicity it received in the press, attitudes within the Bavarian Parliament also began to change increasingly.

Changing the Education Act

Change in the knowledge and understanding of members of the administration was ultimately indispensable for the eventual amendment of the Bavarian Education Act. They told us about the gradual change in their thinking:

> "We realised that, firstly, in these special institutions, these children do not get better support and, secondly, that they are even more excluded in this fashion, and that this actually exacerbates the effect of their disability. That means that the positive effect we wanted to achieve reverted to its opposite, the exclusion is made worse by these special institutions. And since this became clear, which was actually at the beginning of the 20th century, there have been counter-movements, at first only sporadic, and then in Germany massively since the 1970s." (Interview, 10 May 2008)

The case we described earlier, in which a child was allowed to attend a regular school in contravention of the legal regulations but was subsequently removed to a special school, was reported by one member of the administration as a particularly important moment in the movement towards the legalisation of integration:

> "The principal of the school in Trostberg was praised for doing things here that weren't even possible in law, yet. So he accepted the child in his school before the amendment of the law, but with the agreement of the petitions committee of the Bavarian Parliament. We in the administration, we couldn't authorise that to begin with, the petitions committee was needed because the legal frame didn't yet exist. And then the voices multiplied, arguing specifically for integration. There were demonstrations in the Ministry of Education. So, for us in the special needs sector and the schools inspector, this was overdue back then and we knew that it was coming. And we actually welcomed that. Because we were caught in the middle, one has to say, with the parents on the one hand coming to us with reasonable

arguments, and on the other hand a school system not yet able to meet the wishes of the parents, you know. So, here, a social development was taking place, which eventually found its anchorage in the law." (Interview, 8 January 2009)

As a mark of how attitudes changed, it is interesting to compare this account of the school director's misconduct with the reports in the press. At the time, the papers reported how an illegal but sensible decision by the headmaster was penalised by an insensitive administrative apparatus. In contrast, our respondent appeared to recast the episode, with the benefit of hindsight, as a strategic move in a largely consensual progress towards legal reform. Earlier events are reported as if they prefigured later changes, while the rigid position on the governmental side is legitimised as a necessary step towards those changes. The headmaster's 'misconduct' in turn becomes almost heroic, with the head now being praised for "doing things here that weren't even possible in law".

The spread of pro-integration opinion within the Bavarian Parliament was also conditioned by political expediency. Initial steps towards legalising integration had happened piecemeal, with an acceptance, first, that children with Down's syndrome could be educated in normal schools, and that exception subsequently being extended to other disabilities. The parents of disabled children entered the political arena with more radical demands: they wanted inclusion with no exceptions. For them, their children are just as normal as others, because there is no such thing as 'normality': each child is a special, individual and unique subject. In the Bavarian Parliament, the parents' organisations found support from the opposition parties: the SPD and the Greens. Not only did these parties back them during the consultation phase, but the SPD also took the initiative of drafting the first version of the Amendment to the Education Act in 2001. One expert involved, when asked how the integration issue came to be such a fervent political topic in Bavaria, explained simply that the position of the SPD in the Bavarian Parliament was the reason:

"Well, the SPD is open, is willing. They are not in that situation of having to preserve what they built, you see ... even if you are convinced that it's maybe not the right way anymore. And for the opposition, it's different, of course, that's exactly what they want, to put the government under pressure, the legislator, the majority party." (Interview, 22 October 2008)

The opposition has much greater freedom to adopt new positions than the governing party. It is less hampered by institutional and processual constraints, funding structures, vested interests, or the need to save face. The opposition parties can thus present themselves as willing reformers. In this instance, they were at liberty to mobilise those aspects of the parents' knowledge and experience, backed up by expert insights, which could be aligned with their own profile as liberal reformers.

That MPs were very selective in the way in which they made use of different kinds of knowledge in the debates around integration is made clear by the following quotation:

> "We want to make policy; we don't want to comment on scientific publications, right? This is a very basic question, and if we want to make policy, then we do it according to our programme.... And we have to make policy actively, which means we have to try to realise these points. We don't wait until some university has written something and then start to make policy, but, rather, we have our central issues and around these issues we search, if it makes sense, for some professional support." (Interview, 6 December 2008)

Both the government and opposition used expert advice selectively. However, the opposition had a lot more freedom and space to experiment with projects and arguments, while the governing party was bound by the prevailing legal and institutional framework and by its own previous decisions. The opposition could thus present different expert views and try to bring them into the public debate, as in this press release from the Greens:

> Ina Stein [special adviser for disabled people's interests in the Bavarian Parliament] justly demands the right for parents with disabled children to enrol them in a general school, and therefore calls for improvement in the conditions at the general schools.[3]

The efforts of the opposition parties were ultimately successful in achieving a fundamental reorientation of educational assumptions and expectations, as represented in the relevant legal instruments. Thus, the amendment of 2003 declared in Article 2 that special needs education is 'within the limits of feasibility, a responsibility of all kinds of regular schools' (BayEUG 2003, art 2).[4] This amendment also removed the highly restrictive principle of equality of learning goals, replacing the requirement for 'successful' participation as a condition for admission into a school with a requirement that the child only be capable of 'active participation' (BayEUG 2003, art 41). At the same time, the final responsibility for decisions about the right schools for children with additional needs was devolved to the school authority. The amendment of 2011 would go even further. Here, the qualifying phrase that regular schools were responsible for educating disabled children 'within the limits of feasibility' was deleted, and replaced with a declaration that 'inclusive education is the responsibility of all schools' (BayEUG 2011, art 2). This version also authorised the parents of disabled children to decide what sort of school their child should attend (BayEUG 2011, art 41). In this version of the law, any option for the schools or other authorities to refuse to admit children with additional needs on grounds of feasibility was eliminated.

In summary, this phase of the reform of the Bavarian education system was achieved through mobilisation of the embodied knowledge of parents and school teachers, backed up by the embodied and inscribed views of education experts, leading to a corresponding change in the knowledge and views of members of the Bavarian Parliament, particularly those least invested in the status quo. Finally, through the action of those MPs, significant changes were inscribed into Bavarian education law, which, in part, reflected the parents' knowledge of what their children were capable of, and what kind of education would be most beneficial for them.

Knowledge dynamics

It is important to recognise, however, that the amendment of 2003 was not simply a verbatim transcription of parents' views about how their children should be educated. On the contrary, significant changes occurred in the language and aims of educational reform as the initiative passed from parents to legislators and eventually onto the statute books. Most notably, where parents had argued for 'inclusion' of disabled children in mainstream education, members of the administration, and especially of the governing conservative CSU, were more inclined to talk of 'integration'. There is a big difference between the two concepts. 'Inclusion', as the parents understood it, signifies that there is one world in which all are included, without distinction between 'normal' and 'not normal'. 'Integration', in contrast, maintains the idea of difference, and keeps open the possibility that there might be different ways of integrating disabled children into regular schools. The politicians' preference for the language of 'integration' over 'inclusion' is indicative of their inclination to leave schools with considerable leeway to decide just how they should accommodate and teach the disabled children that they were now increasingly expected to admit. This carried over into the way that the 2003 amendment to the Education Act was worded. For all its radical insistence that children were required only to participate rather than to meet prescribed standards of achievement, the amendment was nonetheless distinctly non-prescriptive about just how regular schools should integrate children with additional needs alongside others.

This appears to have been quite deliberate. Although many changes of individual and institutional standpoint had taken place along the road to the 2003 amendment, the practices of segregation have their own logic and resistances, and institutions cannot be changed from one day to the next. As one expert put it:

> "The problem is that there are institutions with long traditions, a long history, which, of course, have developed an excellence, often educate very well, but which also have developed their singularities, sometimes financial needs, interests – this is a problem. For example, an institution with a day-care centre, if they suddenly lose all their day-care children because they don't spend the afternoons in the institution anymore, then this might imply their financial ruin." (Interview, 28 May 2010)

For reasons such as this, maintaining prevailing structures seemed appropriate to the governing CSU because the structures that would have had to be substantially modified were those that the government itself is responsible for. Another expert described this as follows: "Because that's very hard to account for, why you're suddenly changing the way you have been managing for 30 years, why this is suddenly no good anymore. That's somewhat difficult to communicate [laughter]" (interview, 22 October 2008).

In this way, our respondents often noted that integration cannot be realised by decree, but only by the active collaboration and commitment of teachers, principals and parents. The Ministry of Education official responsible for integration put it like this:

> "You cannot prescribe integration. I can write in the Act wonderfully 'Integration is compulsory' – but how should this work? Law is law and reality is something different. And so we formulated the Act very openly, and

we placed much of the responsibility on the implementing partners. As a result, many creative solutions evolved in its implementation." (Interview, 10 September 2010)

For the Ministry of Education, caught between the reformist claims of parents and non-governmental organisations (NGOs) and existing and entrenched institutional arrangements, the most practicable solution seemed to be not to try to prescribe all actions to be taken at the local level, but, rather, to leave a degree of interpretive freedom to those charged with implementation. The amendment of 2003 was accordingly drafted as a piece of permissive legislation, both in the way it allowed schools to judge for themselves the 'feasibility' of admitting children with additional needs, and in the way it held back from specifying what form integration should take. Thus, a press release issued by the CSU in 2003 claimed that the 'question of general vs. special needs schooling is not merely a question of "either/or", but "as well as"'.[5] A Ministry of Education official understood the compromise between ideal aspirations and practical feasibility as follows:

> "I can assure you that, for example, in the category of 'mental development', the clear position of the scientific community – that integration is indivisible and that integration is possible – has given the discussion a tremendous momentum. And then the Bavarian Parliament hasn't wholly endorsed these ideal and optimal demands by enforcing total integration ... but, rather, one has tried to find a solution that is viable, which is 'as much of a class together as possible'." (Interview, 13 November 2008)

As a result, the implementation of the new law in practice took many different forms in different schools. Between exclusion, as previously practised, at one extreme and the kind of totally non-discriminatory 'inclusion' favoured by parents at the other lies a range of intermediate possibilities and compromises, according to which children with learning disabilities may be admitted to mainstream schools without being treated exactly the same as other children. As implemented in Bavaria, such compromises include 'cooperation classes' – where separate classes of disabled children are educated within regular schools under the supervision of the regular school principal and following the normal curriculum – and so-called 'outward classes' – where integration is reduced to co-location, with separate classes of disabled children being educated in the same building as the regular school but following the curriculum for special schools and under the supervision of a separate Director. In the latter, integration amounts simply to the opportunity for disabled school children and others to meet during breaks or for collaborative projects in gymnastics or art.

Such compromises arose through negotiations between parents, teachers and the education authorities over how to interpret and implement the law in different local settings. Implementation – or, as we might express it now, the enactment of the knowledge inscribed in the law – inevitably depends upon local actors, who interpret that law in the light of their own knowledge, beliefs and interests. Respondents in the Ministry of Education cast this in a positive light, as a creative and beneficial response to weak legislation:

> "The Act doesn't read that well, in fact, but you wonder every time how many great arrangements come out of it. But, here and there, an individual teacher or principal takes some initiative to make the best of it." (Interview, 4 May 2010)

However, for many of the pro-inclusion activists, the measures that actually came to be implemented in schools were something of a disappointment, experienced as a loss of 'what they really knew'. The former Bavarian government spokesman for the disabled summed up the feelings of various NGOs at the outcome of what had been a long process of consultation and engagement: "We had made our proposals and, of course, they had not all been adopted by the ministry. And when it was finished, then we said, 'Yes, we are quite disappointed'" (interview, 10 September 2010).

This feeling of disappointment at the lack of concordance between the embodied knowledge of parents and activists, on the one hand, and the knowledge inscribed in legal statute and enacted in its implementation, on the other, was often articulated by our interviewees.

Discussion

One of the most interesting aspects of the 'embodied, inscribed, enacted' framework is the suggestion that the content of knowledge may change each time it passes from one form or phase to another. Since embodied knowledge generally involves far more than can be expressed in words, it cannot be inscribed verbatim into texts; neither can any form of inscribed knowledge be enacted, for instance, through reading, without adding layers of interpretation. Our case study provides striking examples of such transformations in the reform and implementation of the Bavarian Education Act.

The amendments of 2003 and 2011 were a direct consequence of the mobilisation of the embodied knowledge of parents, teachers and experts through personal networks, direct communication and even the movement of individuals with relevant experience into government. This knowledge was bound to the bodily realities of the persons involved, much of which could not easily be expressed in words, or even through actions. It was mixed with impressions and sentiments: feelings, fears, likes and dislikes, presuppositions, and prejudices are just as much part of embodiment as experiences and skills. As we have seen, the affective aspects of this knowledge were a significant factor in mobilising opinion for change within the Bavarian Parliament. However, the amendments themselves inscribed very little of that knowledge into statute, saying very little about just what kind of education children with learning disabilities should receive, and even less about the emotional reasons for such education.

Conversely, while the law as inscribed in the amendments was minimally prescriptive, it could be interpreted and enacted in a wide range of ways. As Freeman and Sturdy emphasise in Chapter One (p 13): 'Enactment always allows room for interpretation and judgement. Even rules and laws – forms of knowledge that are expressly intended as a means of directing action – do not entirely determine such action'. Inscribed knowledge is interpreted and enacted in light of the embodied knowledge of actors, and in this process, new knowledge evolves. The compromises worked out in the implementation of the amendments show how the inscription of the law has to be translated back into practice. This translation process involves interpretation and negotiation: theoretical frameworks and ideals have to be fitted to the real circumstances, possibilities and limitations of everyday life; established institutions have to change their attitudes and modes of operation; and institutional and organisational learning and change is needed. These long-lasting processes generate, through various compromises and interpretations of the inscriptions of the law, new embodied and inscribed knowledges.

All of this is to stress the essential dynamism of what we call knowledge. Knowledge can never be 'held' – it is never static or singular, existing only in flux and multiplicity. Even during the individual enactment of individual embodied knowledge, the content and meaning of that knowledge is transformed and changed. In the case of the collective enactment of the inscribed knowledge of a law, the same transformation process takes place: enactment, in this case, the implementation of a law, passes through the filter of the embodied knowledge of all the actors involved. Therefore, as their embodied knowledge changes, the implementation of the law inevitably changes with it – no law will be executed in exactly the way originally intended either by its advocates or by the legislator. Our case study illustrates this by showing how the reform of Bavarian education policy involved not just different forms of knowledge, but also transformations in the content of that knowledge as it was enacted, inscribed and re-enacted in educational practice.

The idea that knowledge creates the world we live in is not new in sociology (Berger and Luckmann, 1966). However, the schema of embodied, inscribed and enacted knowledge helps to clarify how this process of creating the world through knowledge proceeds. The schema not only states that knowledge of any given object may exist in more than one form or phase, but also points to the dynamics of transformation of the content of that knowledge when it passes from one phase to another. Social life emerges out of the endless individual and institutional enactments of knowledge. It is the task of institutions to perpetuate the mode of enactment of certain kinds of knowledge in certain ways. However, individuals' knowledge changes faster and more easily than institutions and legal regulations. Knowledge change on the part of individuals provokes changes on the institutional level; however, during this prolonged process, the content of that knowledge also changes through multiple translation processes of the kind described here. Their outcome is characterised by indeterminacy and open-endedness, precisely because the behaviour of 'intermediate actors' is never wholly predictable (Pellizzoni, 2003). The concept of enactment can help us to identify and to understand this uncertainty.

Conclusion

Who knows best? Our case study of the legal regulation of schools for children with learning disabilities in Germany pits the embodied knowledge and expertise of parents and teachers against the inscribed wisdom of the law. The parents of disabled children have a very special knowledge of the bodies and minds of their children, which sometimes conflicts with the knowledge of teachers or policymakers. This conflict is managed and settled in practical decision-making in the moment of enactment. The law is interpreted and enacted in the everyday decision-making of the school, and this need for enactment makes for the possibility of accommodation or translation between embodied and inscribed forms of knowledge.

The legal regulation of schools for disabled children in Bavaria has culminated in the latest amendment of the Bavarian Education Act, which sets no limits to parents' entitlement to have their children taught in regular schools. The process began in the 1970s, as some parents began to object to their children's segregation, bringing about a change in the law in 2003. However, this still left discretion about whether or not to admit disabled children with the school rather than with parents. It was an international initiative, the UN Convention, which gave parents the final decision over the schooling of their children. Our story is one of multiple actors, including parents and their children, public officials, politicians, teachers, and researchers; it is one of legal and administrative regulations, research findings, and guidelines, and it is one of different individuals and agencies, in different ways, trying to do the right thing. The social world we live in is created by the knowledge in our minds, in our documents and artefacts, and in our actions. This is what the conceptual framework of embodied, inscribed and enacted knowledges is designed to show.

Each time it crosses boundaries, as much as when changing phase as when entering new situations or crossing international borders, the content of knowledge is prone to change. The embodied knowledge we hold in our minds has to be translated into words, which have to be written down – this is the process of inscription. As in the case of translation between different languages, this process of translation inevitably involves transformation. The words we speak are never identical with the pictures and feelings in our heads; the text we write is never the same as living speech. This is true not only at the level of individuals, but also at the level of the social inscription or enactment of knowledge. The inscription of a law can never be entirely identical with the embodied knowledge of social actors. This translation process is often experienced as a loss: parents and experts are disappointed by a new law because they feel that their knowledge has not been considered properly. Likewise, the execution or implementation of a law, the enactment of the inscribed knowledge, happens through the filter of the embodied knowledge of the actors involved and can therefore never be identical with the original intentions of lawmakers. However, the translation process should not be conceived only as loss, it is enrichment as well. Actors translating inscribed knowledge also necessarily mobilise their own embodied knowledge, and through this amalgam, new knowledge and new practice arise.

So, what do we gain by viewing this process through the framework of embodied, inscribed and enacted knowledge? In this case study, it helps to throw light on the relationship between changes in general educational principles, as inscribed in legislation, and changes in educational practice, as enacted in schools and classrooms. It makes clear that that relationship is not necessarily a straightforward one: in this case, change in legal principle can be seen as a rationalisation and endorsement of changes in practice that are already being explored, while, at the same time, there remains room for negotiation over just what kind of practice might count as enactment of that principle. This does not mean that politics are unimportant. Clearly, the fact that the SPD were in opposition in the early 2000s, giving them much more room for manoeuvre than the ruling party, was an important factor in their decision to back reform of the Education Act; in addition, the declaration of the UN Convention in 2008, and the growth of national and international disability rights social movements more generally, were instrumental in the consolidation of that reform in 2011. Neither does this deny the importance of institutional and organisational factors, which both constrain and make possible different kinds of action. However, it does make clear the extent to which policy depends not just on the articulation and inscription of generalised principles that are intended to prescribe good practice, but also, and inevitably, upon changes in the embodied knowledge of actors on the ground, and in the way that they enact that knowledge.

Notes

[1] See: http://www.un.org/disabilities/convention/conventionfull.shtml

[2] '*Gemeinsam leben, gemeinsam lernen*'.

[3] Green Party press release, 1 August 2003.

[4] Bayerisches Gesetz über das Erziehungs- und Unterrichtswesen (BayEUG), amendments of 2003 and 2011. Available at: http://www.gesetze-bayern. de/jportal/portal/page/bsbayprod.psml?showdoccase=1&doc.id=jlr-EUGBY2000rahmen&doc.part=X (accessed 15 October 2013).

[5] CSU press release, 30 July 2003.

TEN

Knowledge work: organising mental health care networks in Belgium

Sophie Thunus, Gaëtan Cerfontaine and Frédéric Schoenaers

Introduction

This chapter analyses the production of knowledge in mental health care networks during a policy process that took place in Belgium between 2007 and 2010. This process intended to test 'The model of mental health care circuits and networks' (NACH, 1997, 2007) developed by the National Advisory Council for Hospital Services (NACH), with the aim of reforming a mental health system that still depended on a model of hospital care. The development opened with an initiative called 'Therapeutic Projects and Horizontal Consultation', which comprised a set of pilot projects designed to test new forms of local service delivery in mental health care and to inscribe the resulting knowledge in documentary forms. These pilots were both *local*, designed to develop 'therapeutic consultation', and *horizontal*, designed to articulate the outcomes of local pilots in cross-project discussions.

By drawing on a case study of the horizontal pilot 'Adults: General Psychiatry' (AGP) – the discussion of different local pilots in adult general psychiatry – this chapter sets out to investigate empirically: how practitioners embodied knowledge of the new practices; how they came to enact that knowledge in the course of cross-project discussions; and how they coped with its inscription in a proposal for structural reform. At the same time, by also drawing on Actor-Network Theory (ANT) and the sociology of translation (Callon, 1999; Latour, 2007; Freeman, 2009), the discussion shows how ANT and the phenomenology of embodied, inscribed and enacted knowledge complement each other.

This chapter is composed of four main parts. The first briefly explains the background to the initiative; the second describes its design, emphasising that it is a very complex policy instrument, involving a number of different kinds of actors and different kinds of knowledge. The third part focuses on the case study of the AGP pilot. It starts from an assumption that the way a policy initiative is implemented impacts upon its meaning, as the meaning of inscribed knowledge is likely to change while being enacted. Rather than adopting a 'static and compartmentalised' model of knowledge, we therefore consider knowing as 'something that people do' (Blackler, 1995, pp 1021–3). In keeping with this approach to seeing knowledge in process, our case study relates the translation of the experience of mental health practitioners into knowledge inscribed in proposals for the structural reform of mental health services more generally.

The discussion developed in the final part of the chapter summarises how ANT accounts for the enactment of knowledge and its inscription in documents as a process of translation. It also argues that this focus on the process through which particular actors or translators reach agreement on a common way of viewing the world (or 'problematisation') should not lead us to underestimate the influence of social context. This includes, for example, the impact of power struggles between different kinds of actors representing different interests and claiming different kinds of knowledge. Consequently, the discussion comes to stress how insights from the 'embodied, inscribed and enacted' framework can add to our analysis of the collective processing of policy-relevant knowledge.

Background to the initiative

Despite repeated attempts since the 1970s to deinstitutionalise psychiatry and promote community-based mental health care, the Belgian mental health system remains fundamentally hospital-centred. While a number of initiatives have resulted in the creation of alternative mental health services, including community mental health services (1975), sheltered housing (1989) and psychiatric nursing homes (1989), powerful professional and institutional interests have been effective in resisting reform of psychiatry itself. Consequently, while alternative services have been added to the system, successive initiatives have failed to reform its underlying logic, which remains residential and medical.

Recognising that previous attempts to reform psychiatry had not achieved the desired transformation of mental health services, policymakers and scientific experts marked the new millennium by renewed efforts to do so. At the end of the 1990s, the NACH was asked to think about new ways of reorganising mental health care provision, and duly issued a number of advisory notes outlining a new model of care that it called 'The model of mental health care circuits and networks' (NACH, 1997, 2007).[1] In 2002, the Interministerial Conference of Public Health (2002) decided to pursue the sought-for reorganisation through a Therapeutic Projects and Horizontal Consultation initiative. Explicitly referring to international calls to implement community psychiatry, especially World Health Organization documents, this aimed to establish new ways of working, including collaborative working and community-based treatment, as well as empowering new actors such as service users and scientific experts. Two years later, the Federal Minister of Public Health and Social Affairs issued a policy statement formally launching the initiative (Demotte, 2005).

The design of the initiative

The aim of the Therapeutic Projects and Horizontal Consultation initiative was to produce policy-relevant knowledge of the effectiveness of new forms of community mental health care, with a view to rolling out a general reform of the Belgian mental health system. As the NACH put it, the initiative aimed 'to identify ways of organising mental health care networks in their content and form, based on the trials conducted in local pilot projects, in order to generate a structural proposal for organizing such care networks and circuits' (NACH, 2007, p 40). In addition, however, it was anticipated that participation in the pilots should enable professionals and public authorities 'to acquire useful expertise before the concepts can be disseminated as organizational models for future mental healthcare' (NACH, 1997, p 8). Thus, it was assumed that knowledge derived from the initiative would be both *inscribed* in policy documents and *embodied* by the participants.

The initiative also included two layers of knowledge production. The first of these was the local pilots or Therapeutic Projects, in which new forms of community mental health practice were actually tried out. A total of 63 local projects across Belgium started in 2007. Crucially, the pilots were financed by additional funding allocated to psychiatric hospitals by the federal government. Each pilot therefore had to be sponsored by a local psychiatric hospital, which was also responsible for and employed the local coordinator charged with managing the project. Residential psychiatric institutions were thus in a position to exert considerable influence on the local pilots, preventing them from questioning too directly the hospital-based character of the Belgian mental health system.

The work of the local coordinators included organising therapeutic consultations, involving interdisciplinary professional work aimed at defining and regularly assessing an individual care plan for each patient involved in each of the 63 pilots. Each pilot was devoted to a particular target group of patients, and was required to provide care for at least 30 patients, whose care plan was to be assessed and adjusted three times a year. These administrative requirements were the principal means whereby the federal authorities sought to regulate and monitor the compliance of local pilots with the policy programme. As we shall see, however, in practice, these requirements gave rise to very specific developments, which led to therapeutic consultations being implemented in quite situated ways depending upon the particularities of the local context. These included material resources and constraints, but also human resources, including the attitudes of professionals and service providers towards community psychiatry.

The second layer of knowledge production was the Horizontal Consultation. This comprised three elements. For the purpose of this chapter, the most important was the cross-project discussions, where the practical knowledge generated in the local pilots was to be brought together, collated and inscribed in proposals for further reform of mental health services. These discussions were organised around the same target groups as the local pilots, and brought together the various actors – especially the local coordinators – who embodied the relevant knowledge: for instance, the cross-project discussions devoted to 'Adults: General Psychiatry' brought together the coordinators who managed the local pilots for this target group. The discussions were, in turn, managed by a convener employed by a Mental Health Care Consultation Platform, and entrusted by policymakers with implementing the whole process of cross-project discussion. These Platforms are associations representing the inpatient and outpatient mental health services for a given area, whose main functions are to ensure coherent local provision and to take an active part in programmes run by the public authority. Local actors were thus central to this element of the Horizontal Consultation, not just through the intermediaries of the local coordinators and discussion conveners who took part in the cross-project discussions, but also in representing mental health care providers through the Platforms.

The two other elements of the Horizontal Consultation – the Scientific Evaluation and the Participation Project – significantly impacted upon the development of the cross-project discussions. The Scientific Evaluation 'aimed to identify effective and efficient ways to organize and deliver high-quality care adapted to the care needs of (particular) patients (groups) and to understand the processes facilitating or impeding the functioning of the services' (Leys et al, 2009, p 12), and its findings were expected to feed into the cross-project discussions. The Scientific Evaluation was entrusted to the Belgian Health Care Knowledge Centre (KCE), a federal agency created in 2002 to produce study reports and evidence to help policymakers better allocate available funds to health care service providers. It was to incorporate: a literature review; a quantitative analysis based on measurement scales intended to assess the impact of the local pilots on patients' improvement; and a qualitative analysis, focused on organisational learning and based on semi-structured interviews with project coordinators. This also had implications for the conduct of the local pilots: in order to support the quantitative analysis, for instance, local coordinators were required to implement the measurement scales developed by the scientific experts.

By contrast, the main aspect of the Participation Project was to train and support service users and relatives to play an active role in the initiative. Service user groups were responsible for training 'experts by experience', who regularly took part both in the local pilots, in order to observe the innovations in therapeutic consultation, and in the cross-project discussions, where they were expected to share their opinions about user participation in therapeutic consultation with the local coordinators.

The Therapeutic Project and Horizontal Consultation were thus complex policy instruments, involving a number of different kinds of actors and different kinds of knowledge. These included the mental health practitioners involved in the local pilots, as well as the local pilot coordinators, scientific experts and service users who took part in the Horizontal Consultation. Ultimately, policymakers intended the cross-project discussions as sites where the different forms of knowledge and experience embodied by the participants would be discussed, negotiated, agreed upon and re-inscribed in policy-relevant reports and recommendations to provide comprehensive knowledge on mental health care circuits and networks. As we shall see, this proved to be a rather naive idea of how policy-relevant knowledge can be produced, particularly in a context where powerful groups have been impeding efforts to reorganise the mental health system around community psychiatry for several decades.

Case study: the Adults: General Psychiatry cross-project discussion

The case study of the AGP cross-project discussion involved documentary analysis, participant observation, semi-structured interviews and focus groups. First, every cross-project meeting (13 between December 2007 and March 2010) was attended. Second, the resulting observations were analysed in parallel with the minutes of those discussions. Third, the key actors engaged in the discussion were interviewed, including the discussion convener, the service user representatives, the local coordinators and the practitioners who participated in the local projects. Finally, in focus groups and feedback sessions, the researchers' hypotheses and analyses were presented for discussion and comment by the relevant actors.

Here, in this chapter, we analyse the process through which knowledge generated in the local pilots was enacted in the cross-project discussions. This knowledge included inscriptions such as the patient care plans produced in the course of the interdisciplinary therapeutic consultations, as well as the embodied knowledge that the local coordinators and patient 'experts by experience' brought to the discussions. We tell this story in some detail in order to highlight the many factors that influenced the way it unfolded.

We frame our narrative specifically in terms of what Michel Callon (1999) calls the sociology of translation. Adopting this framework serves to highlight the fundamental contingency of the outcome of the cross-project discussions. 'Translation is a process before it is a result', Callon (1999, p 81) tells us, and the notion of translation serves to emphasise the unpredictable and transformative character of that process. Moreover, using the sociology of translation to explicate the enactment process helps to focus observation on what actually happened: recognising that enacted knowledge is not only unforeseeable, but also definite, transient and collective (see Freeman and Sturdy, Chapter One), the concepts of the sociology of translation provide an opportunity to seize the moment when knowledge is enacted – to observe what happens and how it happens. Insofar as translation denotes the creation of meaning by transformation of meaning, the sociology of translation invites the researcher to identify what has been transformed and what new meaning has been created.

Callon defines four successive moments in the translation process, during which the meanings of things – including the identities of actors and the relationships between them – are negotiated and (re) defined in often unexpected ways. These he calls 'problematisation', 'interessement', 'enrolment' and 'mobilisation'. In what follows, we show how the development of the AGP cross-project discussions can be understood as a partial and problematic unfolding of these four stages of translation. Thereafter, we go on to discuss some of the limitations as well as the merits of using the sociology of translation to investigate this kind of policy development, and we reflect on how some of those limitations can be addressed by incorporating perspectives drawn from the three-part schema of embodied, inscribed and enacted knowledge.

Contested problematisation

Callon identifies the first moment in the translation process as one of 'problematisation'. According to Callon, this is the point at which the various actors in the translation process endeavour to define 'their identities in such a way as to establish themselves an obligatory passage point in the network of relationships they are building' (Callon, 1999, p 69). In effect, a successful problematisation is achieved when actors reach agreement on who they are, what roles they play and the nature of the relationships they expect to have with others.

We can clearly see this process occurring in the AGP cross-project discussions. These brought together the coordinators of 12 local projects (hereafter, 'local coordinators'), who were working either on mood disorders or psychoses, and were organised into two subgroups accordingly, managed by two discussion conveners: 'The purpose of this form of organization was for each convener to act as a more personal relay for specific local coordinators' (minutes of discussion, 31 March 2008). Thirteen such discussions took place during the course of the initiative. At the first of these, the convener began by presenting the local coordinators with what was, in effect, a prior problematisation put forward at the start of the initiative by policymakers: the cross-project discussion aimed to generate proposals for structural reorganisation of the mental health services, taking account of the sector's local specificities; the local coordinators were to share the knowledge drawn from their projects; service user 'experts by experience' were to share their knowledge of the user experience of the therapeutic consultations; and the discussion convener was to manage the sharing of knowledge and to play the role of intermediary between local actors and policymakers (minutes of discussion, 11 December 2007). In Callon's terms, this problematisation served to define who the actors were and what their roles should be. In doing so, it sought to establish the cross-project discussions as an 'obligatory passage point' for any local actors who wished to be involved in shaping the future of mental health care in Belgium. Having laid out this problematisation, the convener then suggested that the participants begin the discussion by sharing their appraisals of the local pilot projects.

What happened next was quite unexpected. Rather than proceed to an appraisal of the local pilots as directed, the local coordinators instead insisted on first discussing more general difficulties they were experiencing in implementing those pilots. In effect, the cross-project discussion came to focus on challenging the organisation and conduct of the policy initiative itself, and hence the problematisation initially put forward by the policymakers. These discussions, which kept the participants occupied for a whole year, can be summarised by three controversies.

The first controversy involved what the coordinators saw as an incompatibility between the administrative regulations imposed by the National Health Insurance Administration (NIHDI) and the flexibility needed if therapeutic consultations were to be effective. In order to facilitate comparison between the local pilots, and thus determine which pilots warranted continuing financial support, the NIHDI demanded that local pilots should all follow certain predefined rules. The local coordinators strongly objected to these rules. First, NIHDI insisted that each service user should be given a diagnosis according to the classifications of the Diagnostic and Statistical Manual (DSM) before he or she could be admitted into a project. Coordinators considered this problematic in many respects: professionals need time to make a reliable diagnosis; the DSM classifications cannot account for the complexity of every given situation; and social workers do not agree with such medico-psychiatric 'labelling' of service users. Second, NIHDI imposed 'caseload constraints' requiring each pilot to take on at least 30 patients a year. Coordinators objected that this was difficult for some of the most focused and innovative projects, while leading others to admit patients for whom the services provided were inappropriate. Third, NIHDI imposed a 'frequency constraint', compelling the projects to organise three therapeutic consultations a year for each user. Coordinators observed that this did not match users' clinical needs, either forcing participants to schedule pointless consultations or preventing them from being scheduled at times when they would be most beneficial.

A second controversy involved tensions between professional expertise and the experience of service users. The initial problematisation put forward by the policymakers envisaged that 'experts by experience' representing service user associations (SUAs) would take part in the cross-project discussion. However, the local coordinators disagreed. While accepting that the SUAs were key actors in mental health care, and thus should be involved in the initiative, they argued that such involvement should be on a different footing from that of professionals. In particular, since SUAs were not involved in sharing confidential medical information, they should only participate in the discussions when invited to by the coordinators. The SUAs disagreed, in turn:

aware that the Participation Project, in particular, gave them 'a unique opportunity to experience new models of user participation and for their participation to become institutionalized' (Participation Project, 2007, p 33), they continued to insist on attending the meetings.

In a third controversy, the Scientific Evaluation being undertaken by the KCE was strongly criticised on a number of grounds. For one thing, the coordinators professed themselves uncertain about whether the evaluation focused on the practice of the therapeutic consultations or on how much service users benefitted from the new forms of treatment and care being piloted. For another, the coordinators objected that they were expected to confront patients with questions that they felt constituted an intrusion into their private lives, and which were bound to have a detrimental impact on the doctor–patient relationship. But, most of all, the coordinators feared that the data collected by the KCE would be covertly used to measure the respective efficiency of the projects rather than their benefit to service users.

These controversies represented a major challenge to the policymakers' problematisation. In effect, the local coordinators refused to accept the identities and roles that policymakers had assigned to them and to the other actors involved in the pilot projects and the cross-project discussions. They did so, moreover, by arguing that the ways of knowing practised by those actors were incompatible with the kind of knowledge that would be required to pursue effective reform of the mental health system. First, they condemned the universalism of the administrative knowledge imposed by the NIHDI, which they argued was incompatible with the case-based particularism necessary for good mental health practice (cf Freidson, 1988). Second, in an attempt to exclude the SUAs, they argued that service users faced a conflict of interest with the need for medical confidentiality, as well as being unfamiliar with the technical language used by professionals (Hughes, 1997). Third, local coordinators objected to the insensitivity to the needs of service users exhibited by the Scientific Evaluation, and to what they saw as the efforts of the KCE to formalise professional practices that they believed should remain ad hoc. By thus endeavouring to disqualify all the other forms of knowledge and expertise at play in the initiative, the local pilot coordinators sought to establish their own identity as the only legitimate source of knowledge regarding the pilots, and hence as the obligatory passage point for further reform of the mental health system.

A new problematisation

Implicit in the local coordinators' objections to the original problematisation of the Therapeutic Project and Horizontal Consultation was a new problematisation, in which the coordinators themselves would play the lead role in the projected reforms, while other actors would remain distinctly subservient to them. However, the success or failure of that problematisation would depend on how successfully the coordinators were able to progress through the succeeding stages of the translation process. Following the methodology of the sociology of translation, the following paragraphs focus specifically on how the coordinators attempted to achieve that progression through 'interessement' to enrolment and, eventually, to mobilisation.

According to Callon, 'interessement' is the moment when one actor attempts to persuade or force others to accept the roles specified for them within a proposed problematisation. 'Enrolment' follows when interessement results in the creation of an alliance – in other words, when different actors come to accept the roles prescribed for them. Finally, mobilisation takes place when the various actors start to act in accordance with those prescribed roles, in pursuit of the goals specified in the proposed problematisation. In the case of the cross-project discussions, the local coordinators initially enjoyed some success in their efforts to interest, enrol and mobilise other actors, but subsequently encountered resistance that ultimately proved fatal to their attempted translation.

The work of the discussion conveners and local coordinators participating in the AGP cross-project discussions to interest, enrol and mobilise other actors began when they drafted a consensus note:

> In order to relay local project concerns ... we set out in this note some essential reflections taken from the horizontal process [cross-project discussions].... The projects are on-going trials.... In this respect, it is important to remember that experimentation necessarily comes before the formalization of any care network.... Our purpose is not to analyse or assess different professional practices separately, but rather the different ways of sharing them in these unique-in-time-and-place experimental configurations [the local projects].... The implementation of the initiative has revealed however that this humble position is hard to maintain.... Indeed, the system promoted by [the federal

administration] provides local actors with little opportunity
to adjust their practices to the new work methods....The
projects are now uncertain about the scientific value and
the relevance of the users' data registration for the KCE.
(De Coninck et al, 2009, pp 2–7)

This note was 'approved and signed by all the 21 [therapeutic] projects
in the French-speaking part of the country' and supported by 'the
Walloon platforms, the Brussels platform and the German-speaking
platform' (De Coninck et al, 2009, p 8). The coordinators were thus
successful in their attempted interessement and mobilisation of the
local actors, to the extent that the latter not only endorsed their
representation of the problem at hand, but also assented to their self-
designation as responsible for representing local concerns in the cross-
project discussions.

Reinforced by this mandate, the local coordinators next set out
to present their own understanding of the local pilot projects at the
cross-project discussions, with a view to inscribing that knowledge in
policy documents and recommendations that they hoped would be
accepted as representing the opinion of the Horizontal Consultation as
a whole. Their aim was thus to persuade the other actors – including the
scientific experts, service users and, ultimately, the policymakers – that
they possessed unique, and uniquely important, knowledge of how the
local pilot projects had fared, and of how reform of the mental health
system could ultimately be rolled out. If successful, they would thereby
interest, enrol and mobilise the other actors around the coordinators'
own role as an obligatory passage point for mental health reform.

At the invitation of the discussion conveners, the local coordinators
first presented their knowledge in the form of stories that they told
about the local pilot projects and the work of therapeutic consultation.
As specified by the conveners, these stories were expected to address a
range of issues that the discussion convener had defined. For instance,
each coordinator was to talk about: his or her own coordinating
function (including how to define this function); the therapeutic
consultation (how it was developing, how practitioners participated
in it and how service users experienced it); and continuity of care and
the coordination of local service delivery (ie what tools they were
using to ensure continuity of care). In the event, the stories that the
coordinators told often failed to distinguish between these different
topics. Rather than documenting the successes and challenges of
the cross-disciplinary professional work involved in the therapeutic

consultations, they typically returned over and over again to the strategic work of organising and managing a pilot. For instance:

> Project X reports difficulties in adhering to the requirement that at least three kinds of partners should attend each therapeutic consultation. As the coordinator is not always able to gather the requisite number of partners, he does not mention these therapeutic consultations when he reports the working of his project to the NIHDI, therefore threatening the continuation of its project.... Some other projects report all their consultations to the NIHDI, even those that are not attended by the required partners. To this end, they ask the partners to sign the document attesting to their attendance whether they actually attend the consultations or not. (Minutes of cross-project discussion, 18 November 2008)

Moreover, in their initial presentations, the local coordinators tended to focus on the peculiarities of the particular projects for which they were responsible. Each project appeared as a local and very particular experience managed by coordinators experiencing the initiative in a particular way, and developing specific strategies: '[E]ach project is born in a particular context, with particular partners, different routines and work cultures. Consequently, we observe a great diversity between them' (minutes of cross-project discussion, 30 April 2010).

It is notable that the discussion convener was inclined to admit the coordinators' emphasis on recounting the peculiarities rather than the generalities revealed by the local pilots, and to support the methodology of telling stories as the best way of conveying the necessary information. He recognised that this would require more work to summarise and report the findings of the cross-project discussions, but he was prepared to undertake that work if it would add to the richness of the findings: 'I preferred a qualitative discussion because I thought that we can obtain much more information this way, even if it subsequently takes more work to select and summarise what is relevant' (interview with a discussion convener, 21 June 2010).

In fact, such stories proved very resistant to the coordinators' and conveners' attempts to produce more formal generalisations and comparisons between the local projects. Consequently, with the exception of certain aspects of the pilots, such as the task of coordination that they were themselves undertaking, the participants in the cross-project discussions took perhaps too much time to draw general lessons regarding the organisational and therapeutic effectiveness of the local pilot projects. Inscribed in the local actors' proposals at the very end of the three-year horizontal process, these general lessons did not achieve any impact on policy.

Regarding the coordination function, the discussion conveners and local coordinators succeeded in producing more general knowledge of a kind that they anticipated would be useful in rolling out the reform of mental health services more widely. As Callon might express it, they sought first to mobilise the local pilot projects by displacing them 'from their home to a conference room' (Callon, 1999, p 78) in the form of stories about coordination, and then inscribing them in documents that other actors would be able to use in other places, at other times and possibly for other purposes. Knowledge of the coordinating function was thereby progressively displaced and abstracted from the context in which each project was born, and recast as the kind of proposal that the coordinators hoped would be of use to policymakers.

Thus, the initial stories that the coordinators told about the local pilots related how particular coordinators coped with the coordination of particular projects:

> In project A, the coordination function is jointly supported by X and Y … and that collaboration appears to be relevant and efficient with regard to their timetable…. Furthermore, users can request help from both of them. In project B, the coordinator fulfils the administrative requirement … but he is also the primary contact for users. (Field note, cross-project discussion, 19 February 2008)

From there, the intermediate proposals issued by the discussion convener moved towards a more abstract analysis of coordination, for instance, attempting to distinguish between organisational models in different projects:

> The organisational models of coordination were not modified in 2008: the projects had either one coordinator who was responsible for both the administrative and clinical coordination, or two coordinators, each of them managing one of those tasks. (MHCCP Bruxelles Charleroi, 2008, p 38)

Ultimately, in the final proposals, the discussion convener sought to define the coordination function in very general terms, without reference to any particular project. Thus, rather than distinguishing between the projects, the proposals distinguished between different aspects of coordination in an abstract way:

> Coordination is the core function of the projects. A primary learning outcome is that the projects have given different substantive content to the function. We can distinguish between three aspects: a process function which is made of all tasks related to the project support and control ... a clinical function related to the specific input the coordinator brings to the care plan established by the practitioners during the therapeutic consultations; an administrative function concerned with the invoicing of the therapeutic consultations and all other administrative requirements. (MHCCP Bruxelles Charleroi, 2010)

These final proposals thus offered a general definition of coordination that touched upon all aspects of mental health reorganisation and reform – processual, clinical and administrative – and thereby identified local coordinators as potential key actors in that process.

This representation of the coordination function, as well as other general lessons drawn from the therapeutic projects, came too late to enrol and mobilise the various scientific experts, service users and policymakers involved in the initiative as a whole. In effect, the first inscriptions of such general lessons and conclusions were produced only at the very end of the three-year horizontal process: the translation of mental health policy that the local coordinators sought to achieve through their preferred problematisation, and through the interessement, enrolment and mobilisation of the relevant actors in the course of this process, proved to be a failure. In particular, the scientific experts and service users refused to accept the roles defined for them by the local coordinators. Instead, they opposed the coordinators by reasserting their intention to perform the functions specified for them in the original design of the initiative. To understand the reasons for that failure, we need to understand the social and political context in which they sought to achieve that translation.

The politics of a failed translation

Typically, the methodology favoured by advocates of the sociology of translation recommends following the activities of a single actor or group of actors as they attempt to enrol and mobilise others with whom they contend, and to disregard the social context within which that translation occurs. As Friedberg (1997) has suggested, by inviting researchers to follow the translator(s) through the course of events, the sociology of translation enables researchers to share in the translator's experience of the uncertainties, the strategies and the gambles on the future that the work of translation entails. However, at the same time, it leads us to follow the thought of the translator(s) exclusively, rather than taking account of the position of other actors or the system of relations binding them (Friedberg, 1997, pp 212–17). In effect, by focusing solely on one group of actors, the sociology of translation fails to recognise the role that power, authority and politics may play in more contested instances of translation.

In the case study described in this chapter, it is clear that the outcome of the local coordinators' attempt to establish themselves as an obligatory point of passage in any future programme of mental health depended upon the political support that they and the other actors in the Therapeutic Projects and Horizontal Consultation initiatives were able to rally. This is evident, for instance, in the local coordinators' successful campaign to minimise the extent to which the scientific experts were able to claim authority over the local pilots. As we have seen, the coordinators objected that the metrics imposed by the KCE to enable quantitative assessment of the pilots were fundamentally flawed, because they embodied a way of knowing about mental health that was at odds with good clinical knowledge and practice. The scientific experts appealed to the policymakers in charge of the initiative, who sided with the scientific experts, holding information sessions to explain the metrics to local actors and insisting that local coordinators should implement the metrics required for the scientific quantitative evaluation.

However, the coordinators were able to mobilise rather stronger support than the scientists and policymakers, particularly at the local level. Indeed, the local coordinators were themselves local actors, appointed and employed by the psychiatric hospitals to oversee the local pilots. In consequence, they quickly secured the backing not just of local actors, but of medical professionals more generally, especially the general practitioner federations, which objected on ethical grounds to the methods proposed for the scientific evaluation. This resistance was further reinforced by opposition among the local actors to previously unannounced plans to expand the collection of data about individuals passing through the pilots. In the end, this resistance was strong enough to bring about the demise of the quantitative evaluation and to frustrate the scientific experts' efforts to develop quantitative evidence-based mental health policies:

> The content of the patient monitoring was developed but never implemented, owing to a decision by the [Federal Civil Service] motivated by technical problems and time delays in the implementation.... But [this] decision was also inspired by the resistance in the sector to the mere fact of implementing a registration system which was not announced in the call for projects. As a consequence we cannot provide information on case mix of patients or evolution of the condition of the patients over time. (Leys et al, 2010, p 8)

As a result, the scientific experts were ultimately unable to establish themselves as an obligatory passage point in Belgian mental health policymaking. Although they conducted a number of qualitative assessments of the local pilots, and used these as the basis for recommendations about how mental health services might best be restructured, these recommendations made little impact on policymakers, and the scientific experts were given no explicit role in the ensuing structural reforms, which began in the spring of 2010.

The local coordinators were less successful in their efforts to become the sole authoritative speakers in the cross-project discussions. Thus, when the coordinators argued that service users should be excluded from the cross-project discussions except when they were specifically invited to discuss topics on which the coordinators judged that they had appropriate knowledge and expertise, the service users, like the scientific experts, appealed to the policymakers, reminding them that the original design of the Therapeutic Project and Horizontal Consultation had cast service users as equal partners in all the cross-project discussions. The policymakers, in turn, gave their backing to the service users, insisting that their original mandate should be honoured. In this instance, the policymakers prevailed, as discussion conveners agreed to allow 'experts by experience' to attend the cross-project discussion meetings. The result was a stand-off: the two groups did not collaborate in any way while writing their proposals, to the extent that at the end of the process, local coordinators and service users remained unaware of what each other was drafting.

The coordinators thus found space within the cross-project discussions to issue their own reports and proposals as key outputs. However, those documents proved not to be of a sort that interested the policymakers. This was largely due to the difficulties the coordinators encountered in turning their experience of the local pilots into more general proposals for reform. As one of the discussion conveners put it:

> "we have not gone beyond the local projects level; we wondered what the rules were, how we would move forward…. But there was insufficient perspective: no real project that would result in real proposals for structural reorganisation." (Interview, 21 June 2010)

Meanwhile, the policymakers had run out of patience. Tired of the many controversies provoked by the Horizontal Consultation, they decided to end the horizontal process even before the local pilots had ended. In response to representations from the discussion conveners, they agreed to grant no more than a short extension in case the conveners should feel able to propose a different methodology. The conveners accordingly suggested rewriting some much more focused proposals, based on interviews but no further discussions with local coordinators. While the policymakers agreed that this work should go ahead, they did not wait for its outcome before launching new reforms.

In this way, the policymakers explicitly rejected the local coordinators' problematisation and attempted translation of mental health policy. In effect, the coordinators failed to achieve the various interessements and enrolments that would have established them as the obligatory passage point through which all discussion of mental health reform would have to pass. In contrast, service users gained considerably from their role in the Therapeutic Project and Horizontal Consultation. Other than insisting on their right to participate in the cross-project discussions, the 'experts by experience' remained largely aloof from other power struggles within the initiative. Thus, while they regularly voiced their views on what they thought was going wrong in the horizontal process, they refused to enter any coalitions, declining to support local actors in their struggle against the scientific evaluation for instance. Nonetheless, they managed to interest several different audiences in what they knew, including, most importantly, the policymakers.

Having drawn up their own proposals independently of the local coordinators and scientific experts, they delivered these proposals at a conference well attended by different kinds of actor. The conference ended with a speech by a spokesperson for the federal authorities, who stated that service user groups, and especially the 'experts by experience' trained in the course of the pilots, would be central to the coming reforms. In effect, it was the service users, more than any other group, who successfully enrolled the policymakers and thereby established themselves as an obligatory passage point in the mental health reform process.

Discussion

So far, our analysis of the Therapeutic Project and Horizontal Consultation initiatives, and especially of the Horizontal Consultation, has served to illustrate some of the benefits of using the sociology of translation to examine the role of knowledge in policy processes, but also some of the limitations. Thus, we have shown how using it as a lens through which to view the cross-project discussions serves to highlight how the local coordinators sought to define the purpose of those discussions, and the steps they took to represent their own knowledge of the local projects in ways that would make them central to future mental health reforms. We have also shown that the sociology of translation helps to emphasise the uncertain and experimental nature of such action, and the unpredictable and contingent character of the outcome. Finally, we have shown that in order to understand why particular outcomes occurred and not others, we need to appreciate the specific social and political context in which the cross-project discussions took place – something that is often neglected by advocates of the sociology of translation.

So what, if anything, can we add to this analysis by incorporating insights from the schema of embodied, inscribed and enacted knowledge? What might we gain by viewing the cross-project discussions as an arena in which different actors sought, first, to enact their embodied knowledge and then to inscribe it in reports and other documents that they hoped would inform policy?

For one thing, understanding the embodied nature of the coordinators' knowledge of the local pilots can add to our appreciation of the problems they encountered when they attempted to enact and inscribe that knowledge in ways that would appeal to policymakers. Enactment and inscription of embodied knowledge is not simply a matter of transcribing knowledge unchanged from one format to another. On the contrary, enactment and inscription themselves involve translation and transformation, particularly when they occur in settings that are different from the original context of embodiment. Thus, the local coordinators acquired their knowledge of the local pilots chiefly through their engagement with the practitioners who conducted them, and who insisted that the kinds of knowledge required for good psychiatric practice cannot be reduced to the kinds of standardised observations that permit scientific comparisons; hence the difficulties that the coordinators experienced when they sought to enact and inscribe such knowledge in terms of general recommendations for mental health care reform.

Second, the failure of the coordinators to enrol policymakers in their preferred problematisation highlights the extent to which policy is a collective achievement that depends upon the coordinated action of many actors. From the perspective of the sociology of translation, the key thing that determines success or failure in policymaking is whether or not one actor can succeed in enrolling and mobilising other actors around a preferred problematisation. However, thinking about this in terms of embodied, inscribed and enacted knowledge adds to our understanding of what that might entail. Effective policy is ultimately a matter of the coordinated enactment of knowledge. This may involve the circulation of inscriptions that help to describe and direct local action, but it also involves the distribution of agreed roles among the various actors – and this, in turn, necessitates the distribution of embodied knowledge of who occupies those roles and what sort of action they entail. In the case of the policy initiative examined in this chapter, the coordinators failed to achieve such a distribution of knowledge, either by creating inscriptions that policymakers were prepared to use as the basis for reorienting local action, or by persuading other actors to accept and learn the roles that the coordinators envisaged for them.

Third, by paying closer attention to the role of embodied knowledge in this setting, we can deepen our understanding not just of how the various actors acted, but also of why. It is clear from our case study that the local coordinators' embodied knowledge of the local pilots, and the way that they enacted that knowledge in the cross-project discussions, was profoundly shaped by aims and interests that derived from their professional and institutional affiliations. Indeed, the new problematisation of mental health policy that they sought to instantiate reflected not just the local coordinators' own embodied way of knowing the mental health system and its practices, but also the professional and institutional interests that informed that knowledge. By the same token, the refusal of other actors to endorse and align themselves with that problematisation was a consequence of their professional and other interests, as manifested in their own preferred ways of knowing and acting.

Finally, this case study makes clear that the making and implementation of policy knowledge is necessarily a matter of 'inter-enactment', in the sense that it involves the collective enactment of policy knowledge achieved through interaction between multiple actors. Crucially, this case study shows that in order to understand how such enactment is achieved or why it fails, we need to understand how the knowledge and interests of all the relevant actors are informed and constrained by their location within social networks of power and politics. Typically, the sociology of translation, and the larger framework of ANT of which it is a part, tends to minimise the explanatory importance of such structures, arguing that they are simply the consequence of ongoing translation processes. However, recognising that social structure is fluid and emergent is not to deny that it shapes the actions and interests of those caught up within it. Seeing policy in terms of embodied, inscribed and enacted knowledge helps us to understand that social structure is itself a matter of how knowledge, and the interests with which it is associated, is distributed through society, and that the inter-enactment of knowledge between differently situated actors serves both to reproduce and transform that knowledge and the structure it underpins.

In consequence, what the case studied in this chapter demonstrates – beyond the very uncertain and iterative process of producing knowledge – is the deep embeddedness of knowledge within social and power relations. In its embodied phase, the knowledge held by the coordinators was informed by their need to deal with administrative rules, the interests of fellow professionals and the strategies of partner organisations. In its enacted phase, it was realised in a collective setting that was highly constrained by the coordinators' awareness of the other actors and the way they sought to enact their own knowledge in pursuit of their own competing interests. When it eventually came to be inscribed into documents, the coordinators' knowledge was reformulated expressly in order to increase its mobility, in the sense of its ability to inform the reorganisation of mental health services in locations other than where that knowledge had first originated.

Overall, this process took place in a context characterised by the policymakers' long-standing commitment to reorganise the mental health system on the one hand, and the equally long-standing efforts of powerful local institutions to hinder any important change in that system on the other. The strong link between local coordinators and mental health service providers, including psychiatric hospitals, immediately gave a particular meaning to their attempted problematisation of mental health policy, which certainly did not help them to interest policymakers in their knowledge. By the same token, the failure of the scientific experts to enact their own ideas about evidence-based policy cannot be understood outside this specific context. By contrast, the ability of the service users to produce unproblematic inscriptions – that is, to write down clear proposals without precipitating many power struggles – secured their relevance to mental health policymaking. In effect, they managed to present themselves and their recommendations as apparently dis-embedded from social relations, or at least from the power struggle between local coordinators, the scientific experts and the federal administrations. Understanding the relevant social and political context thus enables us to see how the competing problematisations favoured by different actors made sense both in their own right and in relation to each other. It also enables us to understand which problematisation turned out to be most successful, and why.

This case study thus shows how the phenomenology of embodied, inscribed and enacted knowledge and the sociology of translation can complement one another – the latter providing a means of following and construing the very enactment of knowledge, and the former reminding the observer that enacted knowledge is, above all, situated knowledge. Together, these two perspectives reveal the many complexities that lie in the way of policy enactment, which entails not just displacing entities and meanings from one place to another, but also achieving such displacements in a social context that is highly constrained and ordered simply in consequence of its collective nature (Freeman and Sturdy, Chapter One).

Note
[1] Extracts from documents, policy statements and interviews quoted in this chapter have been translated by the authors for this purpose.

ELEVEN

Knowledge and policy in research and practice

Richard Freeman and Steve Sturdy

Introduction

Knowledge is at the heart of our lives as social beings. It is how we order our society, and it is how we order our personal lives within that society. We embody knowledge as we learn to navigate our way through the world. We inscribe it in the instruments with which we structure our world, and we enact it as we create and recreate our collective reality. This is nowhere more true than in the sphere of policy, which is a form of action that is fundamentally, intentionally concerned with the ordering of society. Understanding how knowledge works in policy is thus crucial for understanding how knowledge is used to organise the world we live in. However, in order to understand how knowledge works, we need the means to think about what knowledge is, and how we may observe it.

This volume offers a first step towards providing such means. We must again make clear what we mean by this. We have *not* set out to articulate an epistemological account of how knowledge may be distinguished from other states of belief, for instance, by attending to the methods and circumstances of its making. Rather, recognising the range and variety of epistemologies that policy analysts may bring to their work, we have endeavoured instead to develop a phenomenology of knowledge that will be compatible with any and all epistemologies. The embodied, inscribed and enacted framework is thus not an explanation, but a means of seeing what is to be explained. It might best be thought of as an exercise in what others have described as 'epistemography' (Drouhard, 2010). The empirical chapters that make up the bulk of this volume show what may be gained by seeing knowledge in this way.

We should also recall why we embarked upon this project. In common with many others in policy studies and related fields, all the contributors to this volume have become interested in the extent to which the work of policy consists in the production and mobilisation of knowledge. This interest in knowledge in policy is in part a function or effect of the move from government to governance. In a world of networks and partnerships of quasi-autonomous actors, what matters is what those actors think and know in relation to each other. We do not wish here to exaggerate the discontinuities between government and governance: the activity of governing has always been intrinsically bound up with the production and circulation of knowledge, from the census of Caesar Augustus to the current mass production of data on the lives and activities of individuals and populations. However, interest in the networked and decentralised character of governance has served to rekindle scholarly interest in the role of knowledge, and to problematise earlier assumptions about how categorical forms of social-scientific knowledge, in particular, serve the needs of centralised bureaucracies. The result has been a proliferation of research that seeks to characterise the role of knowledge in policy. However, such efforts have led, in turn, to a proliferation of ideas about how knowledge is to be defined, observed and explained that has resulted more in confusion and fragmentation of interest than in any coherent understanding of the way that knowledge works in the world of policy.

Our aim, therefore, was simply to provide a common language and a common set of ideas that might help to reunify this fragmenting field of endeavour – a common language and a common set of ideas that did not presume any particular epistemology or theory of knowledge, but that would at least enable scholars from disparate traditions of philosophy and social science to agree on where they should look to see knowledge in policy. The value of our contribution will ultimately be judged by how useful other scholars find it for conducting their own research. The present collection brings together a small number of researchers who have, indeed, found it useful, and whose chapters indicate some of the specific ways in which they have been able to put it to use.

Knowledge embodied, inscribed and enacted

Without seeking to repeat all the novel conclusions evinced by the contributors to this volume, it is worth rehearsing a few key insights that emerge from their adoption of the scheme of embodied, inscribed and enacted knowledge. To begin with embodied knowledge: while it is difficult to think of knowledge without some concept of mind, one consequence of the work collected here has been to emphasise the physical incorporation of minds, and the necessary association of the mind with the body. As Dorothy Smith explains in *Institutional ethnography*:

> Body ... [is] the site of consciousness, mind, thought, subjectivity, and agency as particular people's local doings. By pulling mind back into body, phenomena of mind and discourse – ideology, beliefs, concepts, theory, ideas and so on – are recognized as themselves the doings of actual people situated in particular local sites at particular times. They are no longer treated as if they were essentially inside people's heads. They become observable insofar as they are produced in the language as talk and/or text. (Smith, 2005, p 25)

Smith's formulation reminds us that in order to observe embodied knowledge – whether tacit, in the form of incommunicable skill, or explicit, in the sense that it may be expressed in words – we must inevitably look at and infer how that knowledge is enacted. However, it also reminds us that if we wish to see the knowledge that people hold in their minds, we must necessarily observe what they do with their bodies.

One immediate implication of this is to alert us to the fact that expertise, of all kinds, is necessarily embodied. It is easy to suppose, if we adopt a purely intellectualist understanding of expertise, that embodied knowledge is only important in the kinds of 'experience' that often form the basis of lay actors' claims to have a say in policy – claims of the kind that we have seen asserted by the users of health services and their carers (see Smith-Merry, Chapter Two) and by parents and other 'ordinary people' (see Demszky, Chapter Nine). However, as Jo Maybin (Chapter Five) and several other contributors show so compellingly here, and as Wendy Larner and Nina Laurie (2010) demonstrate in their account of the embodied knowledge of international technocrats, embodiment is a key facet even of the most rarified forms of expertise, too. Of course, part of our argument is that civil servants, politicians and other policymakers are themselves ordinary people, and use what they know from their everyday lives, as well as their special knowledge and skills, in policymaking. However, Maybin's account of civil servants reveals something more than that, namely, that expertise is ineluctably embodied in people, and that it is people, in the guise of experts, who are commonly seen to hold the most immediate, substantial and sought-after kinds of knowledge for policy.

Moreover, the very fact of its embodiment means that embodied knowledge, however intellectualised it might be, can never be entirely dissociated from other aspects of human existence. It is inevitably coloured and animated by the emotional and affective circumstances in which it is acquired and communicated, as Alma Demszky (Chapter Nine) shows, not just in the case of parents' knowledge of their disabled children, but also in the case of the experts and policymakers who concerned themselves with the plight of those children. This, in turn, means that embodied knowledge is inevitably partial, situated and interested – informed by the particular experiences of the individuals who hold it, including their social experiences of participating in groups and collectivities that are themselves shaped by the possession of shared knowledge and experience. We cannot understand the workings of policy knowledge – or, indeed, of any other kind of knowledge – without appreciating the particular social circumstances and experiences of those who hold and make use of that knowledge.

So, what happens to such knowledge when it becomes disembodied as a consequence of being inscribed into documents and other artefacts? Inscriptions, like bodies, appear constantly in the case studies described in the chapters of this volume; but inscriptions are not bodies, and documents are not people. Consequently, as our contributors repeatedly observe, the work of inscribing embodied knowledge into documents must be regarded not as transcription, but as translation: the content and meaning of knowledge is inevitably transformed as it is transferred from bodies into documents.

As with all translation, something is inevitably lost in the process of inscribing embodied knowledge. For one thing, documents, unlike bodies, have no feelings; consequently, those who draft policy documents can never do more than attempt to represent the affective dimensions of their own or others' embodied knowledge in carefully chosen words – though more often, the stylistic conventions that govern the drafting of policy documents tend to favour unemotional language rather than the language of feelings and sentiment. For another thing, much embodied knowledge – particularly so-called tacit knowledge – resists our attempts to express it in words, and is consequently lost in the writing of policy documents. Often, emotional and tacit knowledge are closely linked, as Jennifer Smith-Merry shows in the case of mental health service users' knowledge of what works in mental healthcare (Chapter Two): for these service users, as for the parents of disabled children discussed by Alma Demszky (Chapter Nine), the progressive writing-out of their experience-based knowledge from policy documents was as much a matter of emotional loss and alienation as of political exclusion. However, it is not just lay experts who suffer such experiences. As Sophie Thunus and colleagues show in their study of a mental health policy pilot in Belgium (Chapter Ten), expert psychiatrists were also disheartened by their inability to convey in documents the full complexity of their own local, situated knowledge of what worked in practice; the embodied knowledge of professional experts as much as lay actors inevitably has an affective dimension, informed by their professional aspirations and affiliations, as well as by their more private experiences and interests.

While something is inevitably lost in the translation of embodied into inscribed knowledge, however, something is also gained. We have already spoken about the properties of stability, reproducibility and mobility that inhere in documents and other inscriptions, and the value this gives them as resources for coordinating policy action at a distance. This is well exemplified in the case of the World Health Organization's (WHO's) *Mental health declaration* and *Action plan for Europe*. It was the opportunity to make this statement that warranted the meeting described by Richard Freeman and Steve Sturdy in Chapter Four, and it was the same document that diffused across countries as a prompt to policy, as in Hungary (Chapter Eight) and Belgium (Chapter Ten), among others. However, inscribed knowledge has other properties that can make it valuable in policy. Notably, Sotiria Grek's study of school inspectors (Chapter Six) shows how they have participated in a Europe-wide reform of the entire inspection system, from one that revolved in large part around the embodied professional knowledge and judgement of individual inspectors, to one in which documents – including the self-assessment documents compiled by schools under the inspectors' tutelage and oversight – play a much larger part. As Grek shows, the value of these documents resides partly in their ability to travel, linking different national inspection systems into a network that secures legitimacy from the fact that it is seen to be endorsed by other countries besides one's own. Furthermore, it also has the advantage, for the inspectors, of 'black-boxing' the work of inspection, giving a sense of technical inevitability and irresistibility to the practice of school self-assessment, while obscuring the extent to which inspectors continue to exercise authority within the system as a whole, not least through their collective embodied knowledge of how that system works.

That said, documents themselves *do* nothing. It is what is done by people in setting knowledge down on paper, setting it in motion and then reading, responding and using it that matters in practice. Documents themselves have only the most limited power to constrain how the knowledge they contain will be understood, interpreted and used. What matters is how that knowledge is enacted, and the factors that constrain and inform that enactment. As Bori Fernezelyi and Gábor Eröss show in their study of the reception of the WHO *Declaration* and *Action plan* in Hungary (Chapter Eight), the embodied knowledge of the dominant policy actors was crucial here, in that it was this knowledge that enabled those actors to interpret the documents in ways that departed significantly from the intentions of the original authors. Moreover, as other contributors besides Fernezelyi and Eröss make clear, knowledge is generally enacted in interaction with others, in meetings and consultations, whether formal or informal. As such, that enactment is further informed by the politics and social relations that structure all such interaction. In the Hungarian setting Fernezelyi and Eröss describe, it was the dominance of psychiatric institutions within the emerging mental health policy community that determined how the WHO policy documents would be interpreted and enacted. In Belgium, by contrast, Thunus and her colleagues (Chapter Ten) show that the relevant politics were far more contested, and ultimately worked to the advantage of mental health service users, whose embodied knowledge of effective service delivery came to play a far more important role than it had hitherto been granted. The interactional and structural politics of enactment are thus crucial to the way that both embodied and inscribed knowledge is experienced, interpreted and, ultimately, enacted in policy.

This focus on enactment also draws our attention to the importance of meetings as key sites for the creation, circulation and transformation of policy knowledge. This holds as much for the casual encounter in a corridor as for the committee hearing or research interview: meetings are occasions for the expression, articulation and negotiation of knowledge in response to a question or prompt or the sharing of a concern. Meetings, both informal and formal, feature in many of the case studies collected in this volume, and their role in the making and implementation of policy cannot be underestimated. Meetings involve peculiarly labile configurations of actors, interests and knowledges, and, as such, are peculiarly susceptible to the vagaries of social interaction and the pressures of politics. As Maria José dos Santos Freitas shows in her study of a European policy research project (Chapter Seven), meetings may themselves be sites for the working out of politics, and hence of the meaning of the knowledge they produce: for all the knowledge and experience of the project partners, and for all their previous meetings, the meaning of the project in which they were involved had to be realised anew, enacted at each and every turn. The outcome of meetings is always uncertain and underdetermined, as

Thunus and colleagues emphasise in their analysis of the meetings and negotiations that constituted the Belgian mental health policy initiative (Chapter Ten). However, they also show how external politics may supervene to limit or dictate the kinds of interactions and enactments that are possible in meetings, and hence the character of the embodied and inscribed knowledge that emerges from them. Indeed, as Smith-Merry observes (Chapter Two), political and practical decisions about how meetings should be structured and organised can be crucial in influencing what kinds of knowledge, including *whose* knowledge, gets incorporated into policy.

Ultimately, however, the way that policy knowledge is enacted in the world beyond meetings depends upon the larger structures of relationships and practices through which implementation takes place. Here, too, the radical uncertainty of enactment both challenges and is shaped by the constraining and directing forces of politics. The outcome is inevitably contingent upon local circumstances, as is clearly shown by the contrasting accounts given of knowledge politics in Chapters Eight and Nine. In Chapter Eight, Fernezelyi and Eröss point to the enduring capacity of Hungarian psychiatry to control the conditions and circumstances of the enactment of WHO policy in their own country. In Chapter Nine, by contrast, Alma Demszky describes the gradual resolution of conflict between the parents of children with learning disabilities and Bavarian education officials through slow and cumulative iterations of enactment. In the former case, politics effectively determined the possibilities of enactment; in the latter, by contrast, enactment effectively brought about a realignment and redefinition of politics. In both cases, politics and social relations were constituted through the medium of knowledge, and it is in the emergent organisation and circulation of knowledge – embodied, inscribed and enacted – that policy ultimately resides.

This is made particularly clear in Natércio Afonso and Estela Costa's study of school evaluation in Portugal (Chapter Three), which gives a vivid sense of the complex choreography of people, documents and actions through which policy is implemented and realised. Taking school evaluation as an instance of participatory governance rather than top-down government, they show how the regulation of educational practice is achieved through the collective endeavour of producing and circulating inscriptions, which, in turn, is shaped by a shared understanding of a 'cognitive script' which 'leaves actors with the freedom to *act*, though it requires them to *think* in very specific ways' (Afonso and Costa, Chapter Three, p 59, emphasis in original). Documents are just one element of this script, which resides also in the embodied knowledge of the various actors, and in shared appreciation of what kinds of judgements, decisions and other enactments are right and appropriate to the work of school evaluation. In this instance, the enactment of regulatory policy is informed as much by implicit organisational and professional norms as by the explicit demands of policy documents and overt efforts to fulfil those demands. However, at the same time, those norms are recreated, reinvented and potentially redirected with each enactment of the embodied and inscribed knowledge that constitutes the cognitive script of policy.

We might capture what we have tried to say about the different forms of knowledge in policy by way of a metaphor. As Donald Schön remarked in his reflections on architectural practice:

> When we go about the spontaneous, intuitive performance of the actions of everyday life, we show ourselves to be knowledgeable in a special way. Often, we cannot say what it is that we know. When we try to describe it, we find ourselves at a loss, or produce descriptions that are obviously inappropriate. Our knowing is ordinarily tacit, implicit in our patterns of action and in our feel for the stuff with which we are dealing. It seems right to say that our knowing is *in* our action. (Schön, 1985, p 21, emphasis in original)

Policymakers' designs are social and political rather than architectural, which is perhaps only to say that they are architectural in a different sense: they are about building and forming social and organisational space. The studios of policymaking are sometimes parliaments and presidential offices, but more often ministerial and agency buildings, committee rooms, and corridors. Furthermore, like architectural practice, the work of policy extends outwards, as plans are implemented and adapted to the realities of the particular spaces in which they are enacted.

The (embodied) knowledge that policy actors bring to those spaces is always provisional and partial. In the course of their work, they write – they make inscriptions – for something like the reasons why architects draw: to give substance to ideas, to explain what they mean, to communicate and collaborate with others, and to show others again what to do. However, what is meant and understood and done in consequence is fundamentally uncertain. In practice, enactment is often highly constrained by rules and norms, regulations, and guidelines, but these exist precisely because of the essential contingency and uncertainty of enactment. This uncertainty is only exacerbated by the multiplicity of knowledge claims that might be made in any given context by any number of actors (Pellizzoni, 2003), but its roots are more fundamental, in the nature of knowledge itself. The knowledge we embody (however strong our conviction), like the knowledge inscribed in documents (however clearly they are drafted), is always radically indeterminate, in the sense that it is always open to interpretation, always presents multiple options for action. Only when knowledge is enacted does it become real and concrete – and, as we have seen, any enactment is inevitably an act of translation, in which interpretive flexibility is only limited by the norms and conventions that obtain at the time and place of enactment. It is this that both constitutes the challenge for understanding the role of knowledge in policy, and offers – we contend – the starting point from which to achieve such understanding.

Implications for research

So, what does this imply for the pursuit of policy research? Our own experience of developing and applying the framework of embodied, inscribed and enacted knowledge provides some suggestions. The framework was itself developed as an immediate and pragmatic solution to a research problem. Most of the contributors to this volume had shared in the design of a major project on the mobilisation of knowledge in policy in European countries, and were now collaborating partners in that project. We had reviewed literatures in policy and public administration, sociology, science and technology studies, and organisation studies. We had translated research questions into interview questions, reviewed policy documents and interviewed national, international and local actors. We thought we understood the distinctive development of a policy field, its dynamics and its tensions. We began to sift through notes and transcripts, but, still, what and where was knowledge? What exactly were we trying to describe and explain?

It seemed impossible to assess precisely what any given policy actor at any given moment actually 'knew'. Neither did they speak very much of what they knew, we realised, but rather of what they did. They read something, they met somebody, they had been at a conference, they had seen a draft. Their stories were of talking and reading, speaking and writing, meetings and documents. These were sometimes quite closely connected: the documents they referred to were the outcomes of meetings and prompts or resources for others. However, they were also remarkably heterogeneous, spanning a range from informal chats and scribbled notes at one end to ceremonial meetings and highly formalised documents at the other. For all that our respondents were plainly in the knowledge business, that knowledge was often practically invisible to themselves, implicit in the more immediate activities of talking and writing, listening and reading.

This is why we think of our framework as rooted in phenomenology. So long as we were concerned with understanding the role of knowledge in policy, the way we observed knowledge had to be made commensurate with what we were able to observe in the real work of policy. We could not take the nature or meaning of knowledge for granted. Rather, we had to start with our actors, observing what they did, in all its diversity and mundanity, in order to discern the different forms of knowledge that they drew on and generated in the course of their policy work. This is what we distilled into our concepts of embodied, inscribed and enacted knowledge. While our framework remains to be further tested and developed, the contributors to this volume have done enough to show that it is at least a productive way of interrogating the world of policy, and of generating insights into the different ways that knowledge can figure in policy. But what exactly does it imply for the practice of research into policy, including data collection and analysis? And, beyond this, what sort of research agenda does it seem to imply?

Drawing on our own experience, the adoption of a phenomenological approach to knowledge was instrumental in helping to resolve the early difficulties we encountered in deciding just how to observe knowledge in policy. As we have already said, we quickly realised that we could not simply ask respondents and participants what they knew, and even less what they knew at any given point in time – not least because their answers were usually framed in terms of an essentialist epistemology that tended to equate knowledge with certain kinds of highly formalised truth claims that often played a strikingly small part in the work of making and implementing policy. By contrast, they rarely reflected on the wealth of other kinds of knowledge that clearly informed that work – perhaps because it is often so basic and taken for granted. This was particularly true of what we were coming to see as embodied knowledge: as Jennifer Smith-Merry relates in Chapter Two, it was their own embodied knowledge that often seemed least accessible to her participants. To the extent that knowledge is 'what we think with' (Barnes, 1995, p 91), it is inherently difficult to generate a meta-level reflection on it – that is, to think about what we think with (cf Bateson, 1973).

We also began to note the way in which the technique of interviewing our respondents renders the body inert. In the absence of any doing or enactment, embodied knowledge often becomes impossibly interior and remote; hence our turn to a focus on action and activity. We guided our respondents to describe scenes and moments, to tell stories, and these were always of bodies in action, of somebody doing something. In this way, as Jo Maybin (Chapter Five) discovered by asking civil servants what they did in trying to find out about a policy problem, it was bodies and persons who served as their principal resource. Asking about action thus enabled us to bypass our respondents' hesitancy in talking about embodied knowledge, and to get around their assumption that we were only interested in relatively high-status forms of formally inscribed knowledge. By the same token, it enabled us to take a much clearer and more direct view of just how they actually used inscriptions in their policy work, by asking: which papers and reports seemed important? Do you remember when you read X? Who wrote X? Could I see the minutes of that meeting? Do you still have the slides of that presentation? Are these the terms you used in writing the job description?

More difficult questions remain to be asked about inscriptions themselves: about their material form and about their meaning in both commonsensical and more critical or discursive terms. Key questions have to do with the evolution and elaboration of meaning across documents and over time. Any specific document is no more (and no less) than a temporary stabilisation of policy knowledge for a particular purpose at a particular point in time. Furthermore, while the material form of the inscription may remain constant, both purposes and policies change. So, we need not be distracted or deceived by the apparently enduring quality of the document: the question is not what a text seems to say to us, now, in reconstructing a policy story, but what it meant to particular actors at particular points in time.

Our questions about enactment also enabled us to address the importance of what we came to think of as 'knowledge moments' – 'moment', here, indicating both a point in time and a relationship of forces. What happened at that meeting? Why was there a need for a consultation? What surprised you about the discussion? Why did it seem right to conclude that? At each moment, enactment was to be inferred in the translation of knowledge from one form to another, and in the back-and-forth work of sense-making, as well as in the sequences of meetings and the chains of documents through which that knowledge was reconstituted and fixed. Still, the precise dynamics of enactment must remain elusive, captured only by inference and calculation. This is not least because, like embodiment, enactment is frequently seen as merely normal and mundane: highly routinised, sometimes almost automatic and often taken for granted. In these circumstances, the most useful questions may often be counterfactual, aimed at discovering whether something might have happened or been done differently. Methodologically, the important injunction is the ethnomethodologists' 'it could have been otherwise'.

Taken together, we think these lines of observation and questioning provided a useful starting point for the kind of research into knowledge and knowledge work – into the production and distribution of knowledge in the particular social and political context of policymaking – that we were looking to accomplish. For the reasons we set out in Chapter One, we think the framework within which they are articulated is both more comprehensive and more focused than the alternative prescriptions for research into knowledge and policy that we surveyed in that chapter. The case studies collected in the rest of the volume certainly indicate that that framework can be effectively operationalised in real-world research.

However, if this is what we have learned about research practice, what clues might there be as to an emerging research agenda? Recall that our framework was initially conceived under the auspices of a cross-national, comparative project. If we can describe knowledge as we do here, according to the embodied, inscribed and enacted forms it takes, we might compare the patterns or configurations of knowledge in use in different contexts. This would be to reiterate a long-standing agenda in comparative social and public policy that has proved productive in other areas. Thus, just as comparative analysis of social security arrangements in different countries has helped us to understand the origins, nature and effects of such arrangements, so we might look at the particular arrangements of knowledge in different countries in order to understand differences in policy. As analysts of welfare talk of different 'welfare regimes', we might, for instance, use the concept of 'knowledge regimes' as the basis for cross-national investigation of policy and the 'knowledge society'. Analysis of the relative roles of consultation, for example, or legislation, or any other of the tools of governance, might enable us to identify different kinds of 'knowledge style', something like the concept 'policy style' prominent in the literature of the 1980s (Freeman, 1985; Scharpf, 1989; see also Halffman, 2005). Jennifer Smith-Merry's chapter on Scotland in this volume clearly shows the potential of studies of this kind.

However, to develop this train of thought in any rigorous way would require a more precise operationalisation of our concepts – and more standardisation of the use of them across research teams and topics – than we have wanted to undertake here, in what we have always conceived of as an exploratory study. Indeed, our experience of working together, first in our common research project, and then in preparing this volume, forced us to confront our own knowledge practices as professional researchers working in different countries and drawing on and contributing to different disciplines. Respecting each other's interests and traditions led us to work bottom-up, through case studies, rather than top-down according to a research protocol specified in the abstract and a priori. This was derived from a dialogic model of comparison not as controlled scientific experiment, but as an exploratory encounter with the other (Freeman and Mangez, 2013), which, in turn, grew from our realisation that a standard conception of comparison would lead us to essentially static descriptions. We faced a version of Heisenberg's uncertainty principle: the more closely we specified the position of our object, the less able we would be to capture its movement.

Furthermore, it is its intrinsic dynamism, its being both mobile and labile, that is fundamental to our conception of knowledge. Our three-part categorisation of knowledge forms provided a way for us to capture something of that dynamism. Thus, our account of the different forms or phases of knowledge draws attention to the element of translation involved as knowledge moves from one phase to the other, and to the change of meaning such translation always involves. Above all, it alerts us to the fact that knowledge is realised in its enactment, and that such enactment is at once underdetermined and uncertain, yet constrained and informed by the circumstances in which it takes place. Our typology of embodied, inscribed and enacted phases of knowledge gives us a way of observing and accounting for precisely these features of the role that knowledge plays in the making and implementation of policy.

Implications for practice

So much for how our framework can help us as researchers to approach our work of studying and understanding policy. However, can it do more than that? Might it be useful to those who actually practice or participate in government and policy, in whatever way? Our own discussions with policy actors suggest that it might – that they recognise in our three-part schema of embodied, inscribed and enacted knowledge something that at once reflects their own experience of policy and helps them to see more clearly just what policy involves. We can perhaps now tentatively identify a number of general insights or precepts that could be of particular value for policy actors.

The first precept is that the different forms or phases that knowledge may take – embodied, inscribed and enacted – are not ordered hierarchically or in any linear way: one does not precede another, neither is one superior to the others. Rather, each has different characteristics, which are sometimes complementary and sometimes competing. Neither are different forms of knowledge to be identified or associated with any given kind of actor; rather, different actors embody, inscribe and enact knowledge in different ways for different purposes and effects. In order to know what knowledge is in play in any particular policy initiative, and to what effect, one cannot make assumptions: one must look.

Our second precept is that knowledge moves; it moves from place to place, in the form of persons and inscriptions. However, it also moves from one form to another, crucially, through moments of enactment, and it is in enactment that knowledge is realised in policy. This is the crucial implication of our notion of enactment: knowledge must be set in motion in order to be realised.

Our third precept is that knowledge inevitably changes as it is enacted. Knowledge, in this respect, is essentially unstable – with the corollary that where it appears fixed, we should attend to the often elaborate arrangements that make it so, which hold it in place.

Taking these precepts in turn, what use might they be to policy actors themselves? Consider, first, our precept regarding the non-hierarchical relationship between the different phases of knowledge. Policymakers and practitioners themselves – not to mention many of those who seek to advise on how best to configure the policy process – often implicitly adopt a hierarchical view that privileges 'evidence' and other forms of explicit, formalised knowledge, particularly when inscribed in documents, over other forms. By contrast, our framework directs attention, first, to embodied knowledge. To recognise it as important is to validate what is often otherwise described as 'lay' knowledge, but also the experienced know-how of the practitioner – indeed, a working definition of practice might be as knowledgeable activity that resists or eludes being written down. Thus, while the practitioner appears to work in a world of relatively few inscriptions, they are the very stuff of the work of the policymaker – though here, too, our approach also foregrounds the significance of the everyday, equally embodied knowledge of the policymaker.

The immediate significance of our work is that *all* the different kinds of knowledge used by policy actors become newly visible, to the actors themselves as much as to us as analysts. We think it important that policy actors, like us, should see the knowledge embodied in the care worker, inscribed in the new guideline and enacted in the practice of delivering home support. The prompt implicit in this is to ask what embodied knowledge each actor brings with them, what inscriptions they devise and use, what occasions and routines for enactment they recognise. Certainly, the idea of embodied knowledge has proved fruitful in our engagements with policymakers and practitioners in the course of our studies: explaining and thinking about how and why knowledge is embodied has seemed to be valuable to them, both in validating what they know and in understanding and exploring the scope and limits of that knowledge. Our framework asserts and respects the embodied knowledge of the practitioner, while alerting both policymaker and practitioner to the multiple moments in the work of each when what they know passes from embodiment to inscription and enactment.

Second, consider our precept regarding the mobility of knowledge. While all kinds of knowledge are mobile, some are more mobile than others. Indeed, mobility is a defining characteristic of inscriptions, and it seems that many inscriptions acquire the status they do at least in part because they so quickly become ubiquitous. At the same time, we begin to understand why inscriptions should also often appear so alien – authoritative but somehow unsatisfactory, even to those who write them – for inscription is no more or less than a representation of knowledge, the result of enactment, a sorting and focusing according to circumstance. Inscription can never capture the subtlety of embodied knowledge, though it will acquire and develop different subtleties of its own, in use. This points, in turn, to a distinctive feature of policy texts, which is their collective production and mobilisation (Freeman and Maybin, 2011). Different parts of policy documents may be contributed by different authors, and the whole may be synthesised, redrafted and edited by yet others. They are read collectively, too, received and discussed, contested and debated by communities of professionals, practitioners and others. What is a collective representation of knowledge is also an occasion for collective interpretation.

This leads, in turn, to our third precept, namely, that knowledge inevitably changes as it is enacted. This suggests that we might think of the continual movement of knowledge as a process of perpetual translation. This may be between natural languages, between English and Spanish, for example, but will more often be between organisational settings, as strategy documents are translated into managerial guidance and new job descriptions. However, whatever the special dimensions of such movement, it will always inevitably entail translation between forms, between embodiment, inscription and enactment. Translation is an inescapable aspect of the distribution of knowledge, and is always imperfect. That is not to say that translation is merely destructive of knowledge, for it entails gains as well as losses; but it does mean that we should expect the transmission of knowledge to be uneven, hybrid and evolutionary or 'rhizomic' (Freeman, 2009; Freeman et al, 2012). Furthermore, while the work of translation is usually invisible (Venuti, 1995), the effect of our model is to expose or reveal it, and to highlight its significance. The transmission and translation of knowledge in public policy comprises ill-defined sets of practices, including the constitution of formal meetings and consultations, the recording of proceedings, the production of guidelines, the assessment of performance, the issuing of statements, the conduct of interviews, and the habits and routines of encounters in corridors, at conferences, in offices and elsewhere. Thinking of all this in terms of translation does not lead to any conclusions regarding what counts as good or best practice in the knowledge work of making or implementing policy, but it does allow us to insist on the status of translation as practice, achieved according to the norms and judgements of its practitioners. In our terms, the practice of translation expresses the contingency of enactment: knowledge moves by human agency, and however it does so, it might have been otherwise. The injunction to the policymaker or practitioner, therefore, is to wonder how – when meetings are called, evidence is heard and statements are made – things might be otherwise, and why they are as they are.

Knowledge/policy

Through all of this, we consider knowledge and policy to be mutually constitutive. Thinking in these terms is particularly timely. Commentators and theorists often speak of the emergence of a 'knowledge society', entailing a shift from government to governance, from bureaucracy to 'post-bureaucracy'. In part, this reflects the increased value placed on specialist knowledge – in areas of finance and management, science and technology, for example – in post-industrial economies. In part, it also reflects the increased ability of a range of actors to press diverse knowledge claims in advanced liberal democracies. However, our framework of embodied, inscribed and enacted knowledge enables us to think of this not as a new intrusion of knowledge into the world of policy, or as a change in the forms of knowledge that figure in policy, but rather as a change in the specific configurations of knowledge through which policy is constituted.

Thus, bureaucratic government operates typically by command and control, according to a specified hierarchy of authority. In doing so, it depends particularly on professional knowledge of administration, law, science and medicine. By contrast, post-bureaucratic government works through distributed networks of interaction and mutual surveillance, involving a multiplicity of actors, both professional and lay. Where bureaucratic regulation was conducted a priori, through the enforcement of centrally agreed standards and rules, post-bureaucratic regulation operates a posteriori, through the measurement and comparison of performance. Where bureaucratic knowledge is fragmented according to department or discipline, post-bureaucratic knowledge is fluid and flexible, transmitted not only vertically, but also horizontally, in ways that are oriented not just to the maintenance, but to the development, of policy and practice; it achieves its effects by being widely distributed and constantly circulated.

However, what is consistent between these modes of regulation is perhaps more significant than what is different. Government has always been a privileged site of knowledge, and knowledge instruments – however embodied, inscribed or enacted – are political instruments. This is not simply because different actors with different kinds of knowledge come into conflict, though sometimes they do. More usually, it is because any given knowledge instrument privileges one way of knowing the world – the specific world of a policy, problem or practice – to the exclusion of others. In turn, this makes the ways in which knowledge is mobilised in any given field intrinsic to its politics. If we are to understand the nature of policy, whether bureaucratic or post-bureaucratic, and whether taking the form of government or governance, we must grasp this fact: that knowledge is political, and that politics is pursued through the mobilisation of knowledge.

Above all, the problem of understanding the role of knowledge in policy may be reconceived as the problem of understanding how the local immediacy of practice is transformed into the generalising, standardising, abstracting function of government and policy knowledge, and then transformed back again into coordinated practice. All social life is a realm of knowledge, but the role of policy is specifically to formulate and distribute knowledge in a way that brings a common order to different practices in different times and places. We can readily imagine very different approaches to theorising this shift: they may be rationalist, institutionalist, constructionist or structuralist, for example; they may take from Bourdieu and attend to the social capital harboured in particular bodies; they may take from Foucault's views on the disciplining effect of particular inscriptions and practices; they may take from Barnes' understanding of the routines and negotiations involved in collective enactment; or, indeed, they may take from any among the myriad critical feminist and postcolonialist perspectives. However, whatever theory of knowledge and social life we might choose to adopt, our purpose here is to suggest and to show that thinking of it as variously embodied, inscribed and enacted can offer a valuable resource in working with knowledge, whether in research, policy or practice.

References

Allen, G.C. (1960) 'H.M. Inspector of Schools: a personal impression', *International Review of Education*, vol 6, no 2, pp 235–42.

Argyris, C. and Schön, D.A. (1978) *Organizational learning: a theory of action perspective*, Reading, MA: Addison-Wesley.

Barnes, B. (1995) *The elements of social theory*, London: UCL Press.

Barnett, M.N. and Finnemore, M. (1999) 'The politics, power, and pathologies of international organizations', *International Organization*, vol 53, no 4, pp 699–732.

Barroso, J. (2000) 'Autonomie et modes de régulation locale dans le système éducatif', *Revue Française de Pédagogie*, vol 130, pp 57–71.

Barroso, J. (2005) 'O Estado, a Educação e a Regulação das Políticas Públicas', *Educação, Sociedade, Campinas*, vol 26, no 92, pp 725–51.

Barroso, J., Carvalho, L.M., Fontoura, M., Afonso, N. and Costa, E. (2008) 'The social and cognitive mapping of policy: the education sector in Portugal', report to the European Commission Integrated Project 0288848-2 KNOWandPOL, Louvain-la-Neuve, Université Catholique de Louvain. Available at: http://www.knowandpol.eu/

Bateson, G. (1973) 'The logical categories of learning and communication', in G. Bateson (ed) *Steps to an ecology of mind*, London: Granada Publishing.

Berger, P.L. and Luckmann, T. (1966) *The social construction of reality*, New York, NY: Anchor Books.

Bergeron, H. and Kopp, P. (2002) 'Policy paradigms, ideas, and interests: the case of the French public health policy toward drug abuse', *Annals of the American Academy of Political and Social Science*, vol 582, pp 37–48.

Bernstein, B. (1971) *Class, codes and control*, London: Routledge and Kegan Paul.

Blackler, F. (1993) 'Knowledge and the theory of organizations: organizations as activity systems and the reframing of management', *Journal of Management Studies*, vol 30, no 6, pp 863–84.

Blackler, F. (1995) 'Knowledge, knowledge work and organizations: an overview and interpretation', *Organization Studies*, vol 16, no 6, pp 1021–46.

Bloor, D. (1997) *Wittgenstein, rules and institutions*, London: Routledge.

Bourdieu, P. (1991) *Language and social power* (ed J. Thompson), Boston, MA: Harvard University Press.

Bracken, L.J. and Oughton, E.A. (2006) 'What do you mean? The importance of language in developing interdisciplinary research', *Transactions of the Institute of British Geographers*, vol 31, no 3, pp 371–82.

Brown, J.S. and Duguid, P. (1991) 'Organizational learning and communities of practice: toward a unified view of working, learning and innovation', *Organization Science*, vol 2, no 1, pp 40–57.

Brown, J.S. and Duguid, P. (2001) 'Knowledge and organization: a social-practice perspective', *Organization Science*, vol 12, no 2, pp 198–213.

Bugdahn, S. (2005) 'Of Europeanization and domestication: the implementation of the Environmental Information Directive in Ireland, Great Britain and Germany', *Journal of European Public Policy*, vol 12, no 1, pp 177–99.

Cabinet Office (1999) *Modernising government*, London: The Stationery Office.

Cairney, P. (2008) 'Has devolution changed the British policy style?', *British Politics*, vol 3, no 3, pp 350–72.

Cairney, P. (2011) 'The new British policy style: from a British to a Scottish political tradition?', *Political Studies Review*, vol 9, no 2, pp 208–20.

Callon, M. (1999) 'Some elements of a sociology of translation: domestication of the scallops and the fishermen of the St. Brieuc Bay', in M. Biagioli (ed) *The science studies reader*, New York, NY: Routledge.

Campbell, J.L. (2002) 'Ideas, politics and public policy', *Annual Review of Sociology*, vol 28, pp 21–38.

Canary, H.E. (2010) 'Knowledge types in cross-system policy knowledge construction', in H.E. Canary and R.D. McPhee (eds) *Communication and organizational knowledge: contemporary issues for theory and practice*, New York, NY: Routledge.

Caplan, N. (1979) 'The two-communities theory and knowledge utilization', *American Behavioral Scientist*, vol 22, no 3, pp 459–70.

Clarke, J. (2008) 'Living with/in and without neo-liberalism', *Focaal*, vol 51, pp 135–47.

Clarke, J. (2011) 'Inspection spoken here? Governing schooling at several distances', paper for American Anthropological Association Annual Conference panel on 'Tracing Policy: Translation and Assemblage', Montreal, 16–20 November.

Coia, D. (2009) *Grampian autumn 2008 implementation review outcome letter*, Edinburgh: The Scottish Government. Available at: http://www.scotland.gov.uk/Resource/Doc/924/0077945.doc

Coia, D. and Glassborow, R. (2009) 'Mental health quality and outcome measurement and improvement in Scotland', *Current Opinions in Psychiatry*, vol 22, no 6, pp 643–7.

Colebatch, H. (2006) 'What work makes policy?', *Policy Sciences*, vol 39, no 4, pp 309–21.

Colebatch, H., Hoppe, R. and Noordegraaf, M. (eds) (2010) *Working for policy*, Amsterdam: Amsterdam University Press.

Collingridge, D. and Reeve, C. (1986) *Science speaks to power: the role of experts in policy making*, London: Frances Pinter.

Collins, H.M. (1993) 'The structure of knowledge', *Social Research*, vol 60, no 1, pp 95–116.

Collins, H.M. (2010) *Tacit and explicit knowledge*, Chicago, IL: Chicago University Press.

Cook, S. and Brown, J.S. (1999) 'Bridging epistemologies: the generative dance between organizational knowledge and organizational knowing', *Organization Science*, vol 10, no 4, pp 381–400.

Cook, S. and Yanow, D. (1993) 'Culture and organizational learning', *Journal of Management Inquiry*, vol 2, no 4, pp 373–90.

Cyert, R. and March, J. (1992) *Behavioral theory of the firm* (2nd edn), Oxford: Blackwell.

Davies, H.T.O., Nutley, S. and Smith, P.C. (2000) *What works? Evidence-based policy and practice in public services*, Bristol: The Policy Press.

De Coninck, F., De Bellefroid, B., Schul, L., De Vleeschouwer, D., Gustin, F., Rahier, S., Costa, J. and Caels, Y. (2009) 'Les projets thérapeutiques: expérimentation versus formalisation? Etat des lieux au 1er septembre 2009: Note de consensus'. Available at: http://knowandpol.eu/IMG/pdf/o22.belgiumhealth.fr.pdf

Demotte, R. (2005) 'Note politique relative à la santé mentale'. Available at: http://inami.fgov.be/care/fr/mental-health/therapeuticProjects/pdf/demotte.pdf

Department of Health (2010) 'Revision to the operating framework for the NHS in England 2010/11'. Available at: http://webarchive.nationalarchives.gov.uk/20130107105354/http://www.dh.gov.uk/en/Publicationsandstatistics/Publications/PublicationsPolicyAndGuidance/DH_110107

Dolowitz, D.P. and Marsh, D. (1996) 'Who learns what from whom: a review of the policy transfer literature', *Political Studies*, vol 44, no 2, pp 343–57.

Drouhard, J.-P. (2010) 'Epistemography and algebra', *Proceedings of CERME 6*, 28 January–1 February 2009, Lyon, France. Available at: www.inrp.fr/editions/cerme6

EC–SICI (European Commission: Standing International Conference of Inspectorates) (2001) 'Effective School Self-Evaluation (ESSE)'. Available at: http://www.edubcn.cat/rcs_gene/extra/05_pla_de_formacio/direccions/primaria/bloc1/1_avaluacio/plugin-essereport.pdf

ETI (Education and Training Inspectorate) (2001) *Together towards improvement – A Process for Self-Evaluation*, Department of Education, Northern Ireland. Available at: http://www.etini.gov.uk/together-towards-improvement.pdf

European Commission (2005) 'Green Paper. Improving the mental health of the population. Towards a strategy on mental health for the European Union', COM(2005) 484 final, Brussels, 14 October.

Fernezelyi, B. (2007) *Depression debate – a Hungarian case study about the dominance of depression's biological model*, Saarbrücken: Vdm Verlag.

Fernezelyi, B. and Eröss, G. (with Tamási, P.) (2009) 'Lost in translation: from WHO mental health policy to a non-reform of psychiatric institutions', Orientation 3: regulation case study, report to EC integrated project 0288848-2 KNOWandPOL.

Fischer, F. (2003) *Reframing public policy: discursive politics and deliberative practices*, Oxford: Oxford University Press.

Fischer, F. and Gottweis, H. (eds) (2012) *The argumentative turn revisited: public policy as communicative practice*, Durham, NC: Duke University Press.

Forester, J. (1980) 'Listening: the social policy of everyday life (critical theory and hermeneutics in practice)', *Social Praxis*, vol 7, nos 3/4, pp 219–32.

Forester, J. (1999) *The deliberative practitioner: encouraging participatory planning processes*, Cambridge, MA: MIT Press.

Freeman, G.P. (1985) 'National styles and policy sectors: explaining structured variation', *Journal of Public Policy*, vol 5, no 4, pp 467–96.

Freeman, R. (2006a) 'The work the document does: research, policy, and equity in health', *Journal of Health Politics, Policy and Law*, vol 31, no 1, pp 51–70.

Freeman, R. (2006b) 'Learning in public policy', in M. Rein, M. Moran and R.E. Goodin (eds) *Oxford handbook of public policy*, Oxford: Oxford University Press.

Freeman, R. (2007) 'Epistemological bricolage: how practitioners make sense of learning', *Administration and Society*, vol 39, no 4, pp 476–96.

Freeman, R. (2008) 'Learning by meeting', *Critical Policy Analysis*, vol 2, no 1, pp 1–24.

Freeman, R. (2009) 'What is translation?', *Evidence and Policy*, vol 5, no 4, pp 429–47.

Freeman, R. (2012) 'Reverb: policy making in wave form', *Environment and Planning A*, vol 44, pp 13–20.

Freeman, R. and Mangez, E. (2013) 'For a (self-)critical comparison', *Critical Policy Studies*, vol 7, no 2, pp 198–206.

Freeman, R. and Maybin, J. (2011) 'Documents, practices and policy', *Evidence and Policy*, vol 7, no 2, pp 155–70.

Freeman, R., Smith-Merry, J. and Sturdy, S. (2009) 'WHO, mental health, Europe', report to the European Commission Integrated Project 0288848-2 KNOWandPOL, Louvain-la-Neuve, Université Catholique de Louvain.

Freeman, R., Griggs, S. and Boaz, A. (2011) 'The practice of policy making', *Evidence and Policy*, vol 7, no 2, pp 127–36.

Freeman, R., Smith-Merry, J. and Sturdy, S. (2012) 'Rhizomic regulation: mobilising knowledge for mental health in Europe', in J. Barroso and L.M. Carvalho (eds) *Knowledge and regulatory processes in health and education policies*, Lisbon: EDUCA.

Freidson, E. (1988) *Profession of medicine. A study in the sociology of applied knowledge*, Chicago, IL: University of Chicago Press.

Frese, F., Knight, E. and Saks, E. (2009) 'Recovery from schizophrenia: with views of psychiatrists, psychologists, and others diagnosed with this disorder', *Schizophrenia Bulletin*, vol 35, no 2, pp 370–80.

Friedberg, E. (1997) *Local orders. Dynamics of organised action*, London: JAI Press Ltd.

Gaál, P. (2004) *Health care systems in transition: Hungary*, Copenhagen: WHO Regional Office for Europe on behalf of the European Observatory on Health Systems and Policies.

Garfinkel, H. (1967) *Studies in ethnomethodology*, Engelwood Cliffs, NJ: Prentice Hall.

Gherardi, S. and Nicolini, D. (2002) 'Learning in a constellation of interconnected practices: cannon or dissonance?', *Journal of Management Studies*, vol 39, no 4, pp 419–36.

Gherardi, S. and Nicolini, D. (2003) 'To transfer is to transform: the circulation of safety knowledge', in D. Nicolini, S. Gherardi and D. Yanow (eds) *Knowing in organizations. A practice-based approach*, New York, NY: M.E. Sharpe, pp 204–24.

Gherardi, S., Nicolini, D. and Odella, F. (1998) 'Toward a social understanding of how people learn in organizations', *Management Learning*, vol 29, no 3, pp 273–97.

Gibbons, M., Limoges, C., Nowotny, H., Schwartzman, S., Scott, P. and Trow, M. (1994) *The new production of knowledge: the dynamics of science and research in contemporary societies*, London: Sage.

Gilbert, N. (1977) 'Referencing as persuasion', *Social Studies of Science*, vol 7, no 1, pp 113–22.

Goffman, E. (1955) 'On face-work: an analysis of ritual elements of social interaction', *Psychiatry: Journal for the Study of Interpersonal Processes*, vol 18, no 3, pp 213–31.

Granovetter, M. (1973) 'The strength of weak ties', *American Journal of Sociology*, vol 78, no 6, pp 1360–80.

Granovetter, M. (1983) 'The strength of weak ties: a network theory revisited', *Sociological Theory*, vol 1, pp 201–33.

Grant, R.M. (1996) 'Toward a knowledge-based theory of the firm', *Strategic Management Journal*, vol 17, pp 109–22.

Grek, S., Lawn, M., Lingard, B., Segerholm, C., Simola, H. and Ozga, J. (2009) 'National policy brokering and the construction of the European Education Space in England, Sweden, Finland and Scotland', *Comparative Education*, vol 45, no 1, pp 5–21.

Haas, P. (2004) 'When does power listen to truth? A constructivist approach to the policy process', *Journal of European Public Policy*, vol 11, no 4, pp 569–92.

Habermas, J. (1966) 'Knowledge and interest', *Inquiry*, vol 9, no 4, pp 285–300.

Hajer, M. and Wagenaar, H. (eds) (2003) *Deliberative policy analysis: understanding governance in the network society*, Cambridge: Cambridge University Press.

Halffman, W. (2005) 'Science–policy boundaries: national styles?', *Science and Public Policy*, vol 32, no 6, pp 457–68.

Hall, P. (1993) 'Policy paradigms, social learning and the state: the case of economic policy-making in Britain', *Comparative Politics*, vol 25, no 3, pp 275–96.

Hanney, S.R., Gonzalez-Block, M.A., Buxton M.J. and Kogan, M. (2003) 'The utilisation of health research in policy-making: concepts, examples and methods of assessment', *Health Research Policy and Systems*, no 1, p 2.

Hemment, J. (1998) 'Colonization or liberation? The paradox of NGOs in postsocialist states', *The Anthropology of East Europe Review*, vol 16, no 1, pp 31–9.

Higgins, D. and Mirza, M. (2012) 'Considering practice: a contemporary theoretical position towards social learning in the small firm', *Irish Journal of Management*, vol 31, no 2, pp 1–17.

Hilgartner, S. (2000) *Science on stage: expert advice as public drama*, Stanford, CA: Stanford University Press.

HM Government (2010) 'The Coalition: our programme for government'. Available at: http://www.cabinetoffice.gov.uk/news/coalition-documents

HMIE (Her Majesty's Inspectorate of Education) (2007a) 'How good is our school?'. Available at: http://www.educationscotland.gov.uk/Images/HowgoodisourschoolJtEpart3_tcm4-684258.pdf (accessed 14 November 2013).

HMIE (2007b) '*How good are we now?*'. Available at: http://www. educationscotland.gov.uk/Images/hwdwpcamtn_tcm4-712893.pdf

Howells, J. (1996) 'Tacit knowledge', *Technology Analysis and Strategic Management*, vol 8, no 2, pp 91–106.

Huggins, G. (2009) *Highland autumn 2008 implementation review outcome letter*, Edinburgh: The Scottish Government. Available at: http://www. scotland.gov.uk/Resource/Doc/924/0077947.doc

Hughes, E.C. (1997) 'Le regard sociologique. Essais choisis', in J.-M. Chapoulie (ed) *Textes rassemblés et présentés*, Paris: Editions de l'EHESS.

IGE/ME (Inspectorate General for Education/Ministry of Education, Portugal) (2007) *Plano de Actividades 2007*, Lisbon: IGE.

IGE/ME (2009) 'Referents and work instruments'. Available at: www. ige.min-edu.pt

Innvaer, S., Vist, G., Trommald, M. and Oxman, A. (2002) 'Health policy-makers' perceptions of their use of evidence: a systematic review', *Journal of Health Services Research and Policy*, vol 7, no 4, pp 239–44.

Interministerial Conference of Public Health and Social Affairs (2002) 'Déclaration conjointe des ministres de la santé publiques et des affaires sociales sur la politique en matière de santé mentale', Bruxelles.

Jasanoff, S. (1987) 'Contested boundaries in policy-relevant science', *Social Studies of Science*, vol 17, no 2, pp 195–230.

Jasanoff, S. (ed) (2004) *States of knowledge*, London: Routledge.

Jones, K. and Alexiadou, N. (2001) 'Travelling policy: local spaces', paper presented at The Global and the National symposium, ECER, Lille, September.

Keating, M. (2010) *The government of Scotland: public policy making after devolution*, Edinburgh: Edinburgh University Press.

Kooiman, J. (2003) *Governing as governance*, London: Sage.

Lam, A. (2000) 'Tacit knowledge, organizational learning and societal institutions: an integrated framework', *Organization Studies*, vol 21, no 3, pp 487–513.

Lapsley, I. (2009) 'New Public Management: cruellest invention of the human spirit?', *Abacus*, vol 45, no 1, pp 1–21.

Larner, W. and Laurie, N. (2010) 'Travelling technocrats, embodied knowledges: globalising privatization in telecoms and water', *Geoforum*, vol 41, pp 218–26.

Lascoumes, P. and Le Gales P. (2007) 'Introduction: understanding public policy through its instruments – from the nature of instruments to the sociology of public policy instrumentation', *Governance*, vol 20, no 1, pp 1–21.

Latour, B. (1987) *Science in action: how to follow scientists and engineers through society*, Cambridge, MA: Harvard University Press.

Latour, B. (2007) *Changer la société, refaire de la sociologie*, Paris: La Découverte.

Latour, B. and Woolgar, S. (1979) *Laboratory life: the construction of scientific facts*, Beverly Hills, CA: Sage.

Lave, J. and Wenger, E. (1991) *Situated learning: legitimate peripheral participation*, Cambridge: Cambridge University Press.

Lawn, M. (2006) 'Soft governance and the learning spaces of Europe', *Comparative European Politics*, vol 2, no 4, pp 272–88.

Lawn, M. (2011) 'HM Inspectors in England: the first 150 years', working paper 3, Governing by Inspection research project. Available at: http://www.education.ox.ac.uk/governing-by-inspection/

Lawn, M. and Grek, S. (2012) *Europeanising education: governing a new policy space*, Oxford: Symposium Publishers.

Lendvai, N. and Stubbs, P. (2007) 'Policies as translation: situating transnational social policies', in S.M. Hodgson and Z. Irving (eds) *Policy reconsidered: meanings, politics and practices*, Bristol: The Policy Press, pp 173–91.

Leys, M., Antoine, C., De Jaegere, V. and Schmitz, O. (2010) *Réformes dans l'organisation des soins de santé mentale: étude d'évaluation des 'projets thérapeutiques'*, KCE Reports 146B, D/2010/10.273/86, Bruxelles: Centre fédéral d'expertise des soins de santé (KCE).

Lindblom, C.E. (1990) *Inquiry and change: the troubled attempt to understand and change society*, New Haven, CT: Yale University Press.

Lindblom, C.E. and Cohen, D.K. (1979) *Usable knowledge: social science and social problem solving*, New Haven, CT: Yale University Press.

Lissoni, F. (2001) 'Knowledge codification and the geography of innovation: the case of Brescia mechanical cluster', *Research Policy*, vol 30, pp 1479–500.

Maclure, S. (1998) 'Through the revolution and out the other side', *Oxford Review of Education*, vol 24, no 1, pp 5–24.

Majone, G. (1989) *Evidence, argument and persuasion in the policy process*, New Haven, CT: Yale University Press.

March, J. (1991) 'Exploration and exploitation in organizational learning', *Organization Science*, vol 2, no 1, pp 71–87.

Maroy, C. (2008) 'Vers une régulation post-bureaucratique des systèmes d'enseignement?', *Sociologie et Sociétés*, vol 40, no 1, pp 31–54.

Maroy, C. and Dupriez, V. (2000) 'La régulation dans les systèmes scolaires: proposition théorique et analyse du cadre structurel en Belgique francophone', *Revue Française de Pédagogie*, vol 130, pp 73–87.

Maybin, J. (2012) *Knowledge and knowing in policy work: a case study of civil servants in England's Department of Health*, Edinburgh: University of Edinburgh.

McGarvey, N. and Cairney, P. (2008) *Scottish politics*, Basingstoke: Palgrave.

ME (Ministry of Education, Portugal) (2006) *Final report of the activity of the School Evaluation Working Group*, Lisbon: Ministry of Education.

MHCCP (Mental Health Care Consultation Platforms) Bruxelles Charleroi (2008) *Rapport de concertation transversale du cluster 'Psychiatrie générale: Adultes'*. Available at: http://www.pfrcc.com/admin/wysiwyg/assets/RA-Concertation%20Transversale_2008.pdf

MHCCP Bruxelles Charleroi (2010) *Rapport de concertation transversale du cluster 'Psychiatrie générale: Adultes'*. Available at: http://www.pfrcc.com/admin/wysiwyg/assets/CT%20PCSM%20rapport%202010%20-%20Adultes%20G%C3%A9n%C3%A9ral.pdf

Miettinen, R., Samra-Fredericks, D. and Yanow, D. (2009) 'Re-turn to practice: an introductory essay', *Organization Studies*, vol 30, no 12, pp 1309–27.

Morgan, G. (2007) *Images of the organization*, Thousand Oaks, CA: Sage.

NACH (National Advisory Council for Hospital Services) (1997) 'Avis concernant l'organisation et le développement futurs des soins de santé mentale', CNEH/D/ 115-3, Bruxelles.

NACH (2007) 'Avis partiels 2 et 3 «concertation transversale»: vers la définition de nouvelles modalités d'organisation des soins de santé mentale', CNEH/D/PSY/285-2, Bruxelles.

Nicolini, D., Gherardi, S. and Yanow, D. (eds) (2003) *Knowing in organizations. A practice-based approach*, New York, NY: M.E. Sharpe.

Nonaka, I. (1994) 'A dynamic theory of organizational knowledge creation', *Organization Science*, vol 5, no 1, pp 14–37.

Nowotny, H., Scott, P. and Gibbons, M. (2001) *Rethinking science: knowledge in an age of uncertainty*, Cambridge: Polity.

Nutley, S.M., Walter, I. and Davies, H.T.O. (2007) *Using evidence: How research can inform public services*, Bristol: The Policy Press.

O'Hagan, M. (2004) 'Recovery in New Zealand: lessons for Australia?', *Advances in Mental Health*, vol 3, no 1. Available at: http://amh.e-contentmanagement.com/

Ozga, J. and Jones, K. (2006) 'Travelling and embedded policy: the case of knowledge transfer', *Journal of Education Policy*, vol 21, no 1, pp 1–17.

Ozga, J., Dahler-Larsen, P., Segerholm, C. and Simola, H. (eds) (2011) *Fabricating quality in education: data and governance in Europe*, London: Routledge.

Packwood, A. (2002) 'Evidence-based policy, rhetoric and reality', *Social Policy and Society*, vol 1, no 3, pp 267–72.

Page, E. and Jenkins, W. (2005) *Policy bureaucracy: government with a cast of thousands*, Oxford: Oxford University Press.

Participation Project (2007) *Participation des représentations des patients et de leurs familles aux Projets thérapeutiques et à la Concertation transversale*, annual report ordered by the Federal Agency for Public Health, Food Chain Safety and the Environment. Available at: http://www.health. fgov.be/internet2Prd/groups/public/@public/@dg1/@mentalcare/ documents/ie2divers/13984502_fr.pdf

Pawson, R., Boaz, A., Grayson, L., Long, A. and Barnes, C. (2003) *Types and quality of knowledge in social care*, London: Social Care Institute for Excellence.

PCPHP (Professional College of Psychiatry and Hungarian Psychiatric Association) (2007) *National programme for mental health [A Lelki Egészség Országos Programja]*, Hungarian Ministry of Health, available at http://193.225.50.35/opk/hirek/20100616/2010_06_10_ LEGOP10_1.pdf

Pellizzoni, L. (2003) 'Knowledge, uncertainty and the transformation of the public sphere', *European Journal of Social Theory*, vol 6, no 3, pp 327–55.

PEPT2000 (Programa de Educação para Todos) (1994) *Observatório da Qualidade da Escola – um ano de implementação*, Lisboa: Ministério da Educação.

Pierre, J. and Peters, G.B. (2005) *Governing complex societies*, Basingstoke: Palgrave Macmillan.

Polanyi, M. (1958) *Personal knowledge: towards a post-critical philosophy*, Chicago, IL: University of Chicago Press.

Porter, T. (1995) *Trust in numbers*, Princeton, NJ: Princeton University Press.

Radaelli, C. (1995) 'The role of knowledge in the policy process', *Journal of European Public Policy*, vol 2, no 2, pp 159–83.

Rogers, E. (2003) *The diffusion of innovations* (5th edn), New York, NY: Free Press.

Rose, N. (1999) *Powers of freedom: reframing political thought*, Cambridge: Cambridge University Press.

Rose, R. (1993) *Lesson-drawing in public policy: a guide to learning across time and space*, New Jersey, NJ: Chatham House.

Rose, R. (2005) *Learning from comparative public policy. A practical guide*, London: Routledge.

Ryle, G. (1949) *The concept of mind*, London: Hutchinson.

Sabatier, P. (1987) 'Knowledge, policy-oriented learning, and policy change: an advocacy coalition framework', *Knowledge: Creation, Diffusion, Innovation*, vol 8, pp 649–92.

Sabatier, P. (1988) 'An advocacy coalition model of policy change and the role of policy-oriented learning therein', *Policy Sciences*, vol 21, pp 129–68.

Sandelands, L. and Srivatsan, V. (1993) 'The problem of experience in the study of organizations', *Organization Studies*, vol 14, no 1, pp 1–22.

Sanderson, I. (2002) 'Evaluation, policy learning and evidence-based policy making', *Public Administration*, vol 80, no 1, pp 1–22.

Sanderson, I. (2003) 'Is it what works that matters? Evaluation and evidence-based policy making', *Journal of Research Papers in Education*, vol 18, no 4, pp 329–43.

Sanderson, I. (2004) 'Getting evidence into practice: perspectives on rationality', *Evaluation*, vol 10, no 3, pp 364–77.

Sassen, S. (2007) *A sociology of globalisation*, New York, NY: W.W. Norton.

Scharpf, F.W. (1989) 'Decision rules, decision styles and policy choices', *Journal of Theoretical Politics*, vol 1, no 2, pp 149–76.

Schatzki, T.R. (2006) 'On organizations as they happen', *Organization Studies*, vol 27, no 12, pp 1863–73.

Schön, D.A. (1983) *The reflective practitioner: how professionals think in action*, New York, NY: Basic Books.

Schön, D.A. (1985) *Design studio. An exploration of its traditions and potentials*, London: RIBA publications.

Schön, D.A. and Rein, M. (1994) *Frame reflection: toward the resolution of intractable policy controversies*, New York, NY: Basic Books.

Scottish Development Centre for Mental Health (2002) 'Would recovery work in Scotland?', report of a one-day workshop at the West Park Centre, Dundee, 13 November. Available at: http://www.scottishrecovery.net/Download-document/144-Would-Recovery-Work-in-Scotland.html

Scottish Executive (2006) 'Quality improvement framework for integrated services for children and young people'. Available at: http://www.scotland.gov.uk/Resource/Doc/1141/0038322.pdf (accessed 14 November 2013).

Scottish Government (2008) 'Mental health project final report'. Available at: http://www.scotland.gov.uk/Resource/Doc/209996/0055497.pdf

Scottish Government (2010) *Rights, relationships and recovery: refreshed. Action plan 2010–2011*. Edinburgh: Scottish Government. Available at: http://www.scotland.gov.uk/Resource/Doc/924/0097678.pdf

Scottish Government Curriculum Review Group (2004) *A Curriculum for Excellence*. Available at: http://www.scotland.gov.uk/Publications/2004/11/20178/45862, accessed 30 January 2014

Shapin, S. (1984) 'Pump and circumstance: Robert Boyle's literary technology', *Social Studies of Science*, vol 14, no 4, pp 481–520.

Simon, H.A. (1955) 'A behavioral model of rational choice', *Quarterly Journal of Economics*, vol 69, no 1, pp 99–118.

Smith, A. (2009) 'Studying the government of the EU: the promise of political sociology', Europa Institute Seminar Series, University of Edinburgh.

Smith, D.E. (2005) *Institutional ethnography: a sociology for people*, Lanham, MD: AltaMira Press.

Smith, K. (2008) *Health inequalities in Scotland and England: the translation of ideas between research and policy*, Edinburgh: University of Edinburgh.

Smith-Merry, J. (2008) 'Improving mental health and wellbeing in Scotland: a model policy approach', *Advances in Mental Health*, vol 7, no 3. Available at: http://amh.e-contentmanagement.com/

Smith-Merry, J. (2012) 'Experiential knowledge in action: consulting practitioners for policy change', *Policy and Society*, vol 31, no 2, pp 131–43.

Smith-Merry, J. and Sturdy, S. (2013) 'Recovery in Scotland: the rise and uncertain future of a mental health social movement', *Society and Mental Health*, vol 3, no 2, pp 114–32.

Smith-Merry, J., Freeman, R. and Sturdy, S. (2008) 'Organising mental health in Scotland', *Mental Health Review Journal*, vol 13, no 4, pp 16–26.

Smith-Merry, J., Freeman, R. and Sturdy, S. (2009) 'Towards a mentally flourishing Scotland: the consultation process as public action', report to the European Commission Integrated Project 0288848-2 KNOWandPOL, Louvain-la-Neuve, Université Catholique de Louvain.

Smith-Merry, J., Sturdy, S. and Freeman, R. (2010) 'Indicating mental health in Scotland', report to the European Commission Integrated Project 0288848-2 KNOWandPOL, Louvain-la-Neuve, Université Catholique de Louvain.

Smith-Merry, J., Freeman, R. and Sturdy, S. (2011) 'Implementing recovery: an analysis of the key technologies in Scotland', *International Journal of Mental Health Systems*, vol 5, no 1. Available at: http://www.ijmhs.com/content/5/1/11

Smith-Merry, J., Freeman, R. and Sturdy, S. (2013) 'Reciprocal instrumentalism: Scotland, WHO Europe and mental health', *International Journal of Public Policy*, vol 9, nos 4–6, pp 260–76.

Star, S.L. (1999) 'The ethnography of infrastructure', *American Behavioral Scientist*, vol 43, no 3, pp 377–91.

Star, S.L. and Ruhleder, K. (1996) 'Steps toward an ecology of infrastructure: design and access for large information spaces', *Information Systems Research*, vol 7, no 1, pp 111–34.

Stead, D., De Jong, M. and Reinholde, I. (2010) 'West–east policy transfer: the case of urban transport policy', in P. Healey and R. Upton (eds) *Crossing borders: international exchange and planning practices*, London: Routledge, pp 173–90.

Steiner-Khamsi, G. (2002) 'Re-territorializing educational import: explorations into the politics of educational borrowing', in A. Novoa and M. Lawn (eds) *Fabricating Europe: the formation of an education space*, Utrecht: Kluwer.

Stern, C. and Döbrich, P. (1999) *Wie gut ist unsere Schule? Selbstevaluation mit Hilfe von Qualitätsindikatoren*, Gütersloh: Bertelsmann Stiftung.

Stone, D. (1999) 'Learning lessons and transferring policy across time, space and disciplines', *Politics*, vol 19, no 1, pp 51–9.

Stone, D. (2008) 'Global public policy, transnational policy communities, and their networks', *Policy Studies Journal*, vol 36, no 1, pp 19–38.

Sturdy, S. (2008) 'Knowledge', note for KNOWandPOL, unpublished paper.

Sturdy, S., Smith-Merry, J. and Freeman, R. (2012) 'Stakeholder consultation as social mobilization: framing Scottish mental health policy', *Social Policy and Administration*, vol 46, no 7, pp 823–44.

Sturdy, S., Freeman, R. and Smith-Merry, J. (2013) 'Making knowledge for international policy: WHO Europe and mental health policy, 1970–2008', *Social History of Medicine*, vol 26, no 3, pp 532–54.

Tenbensel, T. (2006) 'Policy knowledge for policy work', in H.K. Colebatch (ed) *The work of policy. An international survey*, Lanham, MD: Lexington Books.

Venuti, L. (1995) *The translator's invisibility: a history of translation*, London: Routledge.

Wagenaar, H. (2004) '"Knowing" the rules: administrative work as practice', *Public Administration Review*, vol 64, no 6, pp 643–55.

Wagenaar, H. and Cook, S.N. (2003) 'Understanding policy practices: action, dialectic and deliberation in policy analysis', in M. Hajer and H. Wagenaar (eds) *Deliberative policy analysis: understanding governance in the network society*, Cambridge: Cambridge University Press, pp 139–71.

Weber, M. (1947 [1924]) *The theory of social and economic organization*, Glencoe, IL: Free Press.

Weick, K.E. (1969) *The social psychology of organizing*, Reading, MA: Addison-Wesley.

Weick, K.E. and Westley, F. (1996) 'Organizational learning: affirming an oxymoron', in S. Clegg, C. Hardy and W. Nord (eds) *Handbook of organization studies*, London: Sage.

Weick, K., Sutcliffe, K. and Obstfeld, D. (2005) 'Organizing and the process of sensemaking', *Organization Science*, vol 16, no 4, pp 409–21.

Weiss, C.H. (1979) 'The many meanings of research utilisation', *Public Administration Review*, vol 39, no 5, pp 426–31.

Wenger, E. (1997) *Communities of practice: learning, meaning and identity*, Cambridge: Cambridge University Press.

WHO (World Health Organization) (2001) *The World Health Report 2001 – Mental health: new understanding, new hope*, Geneva: World Health Organization.

WHO Europe (World Health Organization Europe) (2001) *Athens declaration on mental health and man-made disasters, stigma and community care*, WHO EUR/RC51/R5, Copenhagen: WHO Regional Office for Europe.

WHO Europe (World Health Organization Europe) (2005a) *Mental health declaration for Europe: facing the challenges, building solutions*, WHO EUR/04/5047810/6, Copenhagen: WHO Regional Office for Europe.

WHO Europe (2005b) *Mental health action plan for Europe: facing the challenges, building solutions*, WHO EUR/04/5047810/7, Copenhagen: WHO Regional Office for Europe.

WHO Europe (2005c) *Mental health: facing the challenges, building solutions*, Copenhagen: WHO Regional Office for Europe. Available at: http://www.euro.who.int/document/e87301.pdf

WHO Europe (2008) *Policies and practices for mental health in Europe – meeting the challenges*, Copenhagen: WHO Regional Office for Europe.

Wildavsky, A.B. (1979) *Speaking truth to power: the art and craft of policy analysis*, Boston, MA: Little, Brown.

Yanow, D. (2000) 'Seeing organizational learning: a "cultural" view', *Organization*, vol 7, no 2, pp 247–68.

Yanow, D. and Tsoukas, H. (2009) 'What is reflection-in-action? A phenomenological account', *Journal of Management Studies*, vol 46, no 8, pp 1339–64.

Index

Note: The following abbreviations have been used – f = figure; n = note; t = table.